Th
CHOSEN
PEOPLE

To Christopher and Hannah

The
CHOSEN
PEOPLE

WALES &
THE JEWS

◊

Edited by
Grahame Davies

seren

Seren is the book imprint of
Poetry Wales Press Ltd
Nolton Street, Bridgend, CF31 1EF, Wales
www.seren-books.com

Selection, editorial work, notes and introduction
© Grahame Davies, 2002

ISBN 1-85411-309-7

A CIP record for this title is available from
the British Library

Cover lettering: Jonah Jones

*The publisher works with the financial assistance of the
Arts Council of Wales*

Printed in Plantin by Bell & Bain, Glasgow

CONTENTS

ACKNOWLEDGEMENTS

In compiling this anthology I am heavily indebted to the kindness and scholarship of other people who have helped me find material. My particular thanks must go to Dr. E. Wyn James for so generously making available to me the fruits of his encyclopaedic knowledge of the literature of Welsh nonconformity; I must also thank Dannie Abse, who provided invaluable advice, most notably in drawing my attention to the work of his aunt, Lily Tobias. I am grateful to the Arts Council of Wales who provided the scholarship which made it possible for me to produce the book. I would also like to express my sincere thanks to Dr David Weitzman and Stella Levey who read the book in typescript, made some valuable suggestions, and went to the trouble of researching the biographies of some of the Jewish contributors. Dr William D. Rubinstein's constructive and helpful reading of the work was also of great assistance. I am grateful to Jean Evans of the Israel Information Centre and Gerald Rapport, formerly of Cardiff and now of Israel, for arranging my visit to the synagogue in Cardiff. My thanks go also to Gareth Miles, James Stewart, Rosalind Harris, Meic Stephens, Dalia Tracz at the Jewish Studies section of UCL Library, the staff of Cardiff City Library and the Library of the University of Wales College of Cardiff, to Malcolm Lowe, Prof Ariel Shisha-Halevy, J. Gwyn Griffiths, Hazel Davies, Teddy Millward, and Y Prifardd Ieuan Wyn. I would like to thank Mick Felton and the staff at Seren for their professional work on this book. For the historical introduction, I have drawn on Ursula Henriques 1993 book *The Jews of South Wales*, and on an article 'The Jews in Wales' by Hal Weitzman and David Weitzman, which they kindly loaned to me, and also on Ivor Wynne Jones's 1988 booklet *Wales and Israel*. For the biographical information about the authors contained here, I have relied heavily on Meic Stephens' invaluable and comprehensive *Cydymaith i Lenyddiaeth Cymru/A Companion to the Literature of Wales*. Many other people have helped either in person or through their published work. I alone, however, am responsible for any errors or omissions. Finally, I give my special thanks to my wife Sally for her love and support. In the words of the Hebrew proverb: 'As iron sharpens iron, so one person sharpens another'.

INTRODUCTION

In the hills of the Brecon Beacons, on the steep slope of Cefn Cilsanws mountain, there stands a small cemetery. Thousands of motorists pass it every day on the main A470 north-to-south-Wales road between Merthyr Tydfil and Brecon. If they notice it at all, most of those who pass by would surely think it looks like any other small half-forgotten Valley burial ground; survivor of some vanished noncomformist chapel, perhaps, left isolated by the ebb and flow of settlement and religious belief in industrial Wales.

But if you were to stop the car, and make your way to this little mountainside resting place, you would soon find that this is part of a Wales very different to the one most people know. The names – Rosenburg, Schwartz, Sherman, Lipman; the inscriptions in the unfamiliar outlines of Hebrew; the little stones placed on the head-stones by visitors as a mark of respect; and the dates – based on a calendar which counts from the time of a covenant older than the Celts. All these things tell of how the Jews, a people with a unique calling, played out part of the drama of their destiny in the land of another small people – the Welsh. Or perhaps, having regard to the relative age of the two peoples, it would be more correct to say the Welsh had played a part in the millennia-long drama of the Jews.

I wrote a poem based on these reflections, which was published in English translation in the Cardiff Jewish community's journal. The warm response to this, together with a growing awareness of Jewish issues arising out of some doctoral research on which I was engaged at the time, prompted me to seek for further similar material from other Welsh authors. Initially, I had intended a small anthology of poems about Jewish subjects by Welsh writers, thinking that, with the single and often-quoted example of Saunders Lewis, they would without exception be animated by the values on which the Welsh pride themselves: respect for cultural diversity; compassion towards the suffering; solidarity with the oppressed, and an instinctive feeling for the spiritual, through whatever tradition it may be expressed.

As the research for the book progressed, I found my expectations wrong on two counts. First, I inevitably found the categories of mate-rial expanding to encompass prose and drama as well as poetry, so that I finally settled on defining the collection as a literary anthology, taking in material from all genres, with the only criteria being that the writing is of a creative kind, using heightened expression for effect, and that it is not simple reportage, reminiscence or historiography. I have also expanded it to include Jewish literary responses to Wales, of which there are a surprising number. Secondly, and more importantly, I found that Welsh responses to the Jews were not anything like as uniform in character as I had expected. Certainly, I am glad to say that the broad mass of material is characterised by those qualities of empathy which I had expected to find. But by no means all of it is: there is also material ranging from the well-meaning but patronising, through the insensitive to the prejudiced and downright offensive.

Perhaps this is indeed the message of the book, if it has a message: that one should be cautious about generalising about any people or any individual, whether to censure or to praise; that true respect for others, and true understanding of them, involves recognising that the truth is usually more complex than either the critic, or the eulogist, would like.

The Jews and the Welsh

Before embarking on the selections of material, it might be as well to provide a brief summary of the history and the literature from which the material arises.

It is difficult to pinpoint when the Welsh first came into contact with the Jews. If one were to believe the quack-historiography of those such as the popular and influential eighteenth-century Welsh religious author Theophilus Evans, then the Welsh connection with the Jews was a very intimate one. He subscribed to the widespread (and completely mistaken) belief that the Welsh were descended from one of the grandsons of Noah, Gomer, and that the Welsh language was a direct descendant of Hebrew. This theory was seriously maintained during this period by many eminent scholars, both within Wales and elsewhere.

If one were to believe some more ancient legends, then the first contact would have been when Joseph of Arimathea sailed to Britain early in the first century A.D., bringing with him the Holy Grail of the Last Supper, later to be known by the name of the mansion in Ceredigion where it was kept until very recently – the Cup of Nanteos.[1] According to that legend, Joseph also brought with him a

10

new religion based on the life and ministry of another Jew, Jesus of Nazareth, a religion which was to take deep root in Wales and which centuries later – however it may have arrived here[2] – would certainly leave the land studded with placenames recalling the Palestine from which it sprang, such as Bethel, Carmel, Hebron and Salem. Further legends have it that Joseph took a Celtic wife and founded the family from whom Arthur and the twelve knights of the round table were descended.[3]

Turning to more reliable historical sources, we find a parallel with the Jews being invoked by a Welsh author almost as soon as the Welsh people are emerging into a separate identity. This was when the Germanic invaders were pushing westwards into what had been, under Roman rule, a relatively united Brythonic Celtic island of Britain. Driving westwards, the invaders forced the Brythonic tribes to coalesce into territories which still define the boundaries of Wales today. Seeing this gradual dispossession of his people, the sixth century monk Gildas castigated their leaders in his polemical, quasi-historical Latin work, *De Excidio Britanniae*, invoking direct and extended historical parallels between the fate of the Brythons and that of the Israelites of the Bible.

It is not the purpose of this book, however, to look at the influence of the Bible on Welsh thought or literature. That is a whole immense subject in itself and has recently been tackled by Derec Llwyd Morgan's study *Y Beibl a Llenyddiaeth Gymraeg*.[4] Rather, we are concerned with the Welsh encounter with the Jews outside the context of the Bible, with the Welsh concept of the Jews as contemporaries in any particular age, with the Welsh people's attitude to the post-Biblical Jews as real people – a far more telling and significant attitude than their response to them as an abstract 'People' only encountered in the Bible. There is inevitably overlap between the two categories, of course: for the majority of their history, most Welsh people's attitudes to the real Jews of their own day were profoundly influenced by the Bible. However, I have tried to confine myself to material which refers to the Jews of post-Biblical times and which consequently truly reflects an encounter – however conceptual – between two contemporary peoples, an encounter that is therefore the real material of a study in ethnic relations. I have therefore excluded vast quantities of imaginative religious prose and poetry, which was based purely on the Bible stories.

With this in mind, then, if we consider the references to contemporary Jews in Welsh poetry of the Middle Ages, we find the Welsh sadly participating in the almost universal prejudice of Christian nations against the Jewish people. Poets ranging from the greats such as Dafydd ap Gwilym and Lewis Glyn Cothi to the comparatively obscure such as Deio ab Ieuan Du, use the word '*Iddew*', 'Jew', in a routinely pejorative context to denote rapacity or callousness. However, despite the fact that many Welshman had been involved in the third Crusade to the Holy Land in the twelfth century, when they would be likely to have encountered Jewish communities, I can find no extended passages dealing with the Jews, so these passing references are not represented in this book, which, as an anthology, is a collection of extended literary treatments of the subject rather than a catalogue of occasional references *en passant*. I deal with some of the more significant passing references in this introduction and in the notes to the collected pieces.

In the field of political rhetoric, we find another passing reference, but a telling one, in 1282, as Llywelyn ap Gruffudd, Llywelyn the Last, makes a moving and eloquent plea to the Archbishop of Canterbury complaining of the way the Welsh were being oppressed by Edward I (who was later to banish the Jews from England in 1290). Writing from his court at Garth Celyn on October 11, two months before his death in battle, he cited the way the Welsh, both lay and clergy, were being murdered and mistreated by the English invaders: 'We have taken up arms because circumstances force us to do so. We have been oppressed so much, have been trampled underfoot, have been destroyed and brought into captivity by the officers of the king, almost in the same way as the Saracens and the Jews.' In the context of the Crusades, of course, in which Christians massacred Saracens and Jews indiscriminately, this complaint is not a plea for sympathy by invoking fellow-feeling with the Jews, but rather is a plea that a Christian nation should not be treated in a way reserved only for the infidel.[5]

Coming into the post-Reformation period, we start to see the more familiar mental territory of Protestant Wales emerging, with attitudes that form a more recognisable part of our own cultural inheritance today. It is from this period onwards that we find more extended engagement with Jewish subjects by Welsh authors, and it is consequently from this period that the first items collected in this anthology date.

The Puritan mystic Morgan Llwyd in the seventeenth century was expecting the Second Coming and the Millennium to begin at any moment in the wake of the English Civil War, but he believed this had to be preceded by the conversion of the Jews, and his poetry and prose has many references to this desire. Henry Vaughan and George Herbert likewise expressed a desire for the Jews to be converted to Christianity, and their poems to this effect are collected here. This was a very common theme running through Protestant thought in Wales, although it was rarely based on any real experience of the Jews as people. Jews had only been allowed back into Britain in the second half of the seventeenth century and although there may have been isolated Jewish individuals in Wales, mainly itinerant traders, there were no communities here until around the middle of the eighteenth century. Only in the occasional visits of Welsh Christians to London synagogues were real Jews encountered.

The conversionist attitude of certain Welsh Christians towards the Jews perhaps reached its most refined point in the strange nineteenth century episode – collected here – in which Welsh Calvinistic Methodists sponsored a long-term project to convert the Jews, both in London and Palestine. This anthology also contains other examples, coming right up to the present day, of conversionism, an attitude which usually combines varying degrees of admiration and sensitivity towards the Jewish people with a desire – wholly offensive to a Jewish sensibility – to change them into something different. Certainly the most sensational example of this attitude, the *cause célèbre*, was the Cardiff Jewess Abduction Case of 1867, given here in short story form.

In Christian thought, of course, the conversion of the Jews was bound up with their return from exile to the Holy Land, two events which were seen as the necessary precursors of the Second Coming of Jesus Christ. This evangelical attitude provided fertile ground for Christians to sympathise with, and to support – albeit for different reasons to those of the Jews – the Zionist aspirations that began to be expressed in the middle of the nineteenth century. The Welsh involvement with this is quite fascinating, and is of real significance, not merely curiosity value. For instance, there is the novelist George Eliot, born Mary Ann Evans, whose father delighted in his distant noble Welsh ancestry and who inspired his young daughter with a pride in this remote ethnic prestige. This identification with lost and recovered roots can be said to be dealt with, in a transmuted form, in Eliot's novel *Daniel Deronda* in which the protagonist, brought up a Gentile, discovers he is really a Jew and finds fulfillment in recovering his heritage via learning Hebrew and settlement in Palestine. This book profoundly inspired Eliezer Ben Yehuda to work for the revival of Hebrew, a miraculous achievement which the Welsh a century later sought to import back into Wales by employing the Israeli '*Ulpan*' method of tuition to Welsh language classes. Even more significantly, there is David Lloyd George, who shows in a passage collected here how the Biblical basis of his Welsh religious upbringing prepared him to sympathise with and endorse the Jewish aspirations for a national home in Palestine which he authorised in the 1917 Balfour Declaration. It was the capture of Jerusalem by British forces late in 1917 – with a prominent role played by Welsh troops – which made it possible for that Declaration to be enacted; some materials recorded here show the enthusiastic response in Wales to that triumph and its implications for Jewish hopes. Later material on Palestine shows Welsh writers responding to the troubles during the British Mandate and the later Arab-Israeli conflict, and drawing inspiration for Welsh national aspirations from the example of Israel.

It is round about the turn of the twentieth century that Wales and the Jews begin to interact more in the realm of community than concept. There had been small, largely mercantile, communities of east European Ashkenazim Jews in Swansea since the middle of the eighteenth Century and in Cardiff since 1813, and these grew gradually through the nineteenth Century, augmented by successive waves of refugees from persecution in Eastern Europe. The pogroms in the Russian Empire reached their peak in the 1880s, forcing large numbers of poverty-stricken Jewish refugees to seek refuge abroad. Some of these Yiddish-speaking Eastern Europeans found themselves in the ports of south Wales, and, in search of an economic niche in the expanding coalfield, made their way into the mining communities of the south Wales Valleys, where a few Jewish pioneers were already established. Merthyr Tydfil's first synagogue opened in 1848. The history of Jewish settlement in the region is chronicled in Ursula Henriques' study *The Jews of South Wales*,[6] which shows that although south Wales was never a major destination for Jewish emigrants, Jewish communities, numbering a maximum total of around 5,000 persons at the peak in 1914, were to be found not only in prosperous Cardiff (where there were around 2,000 Jews in 1914) and Swansea, but in places such as Merthyr Tydfil, Pontypridd, Brynmawr, and Tredegar.[7] It is these communities whose members are remembered in Jewish cemeteries such as the one I described in Merthyr Tydfil, and it was in the Valleys that the Jewish people found themselves in most intimate contact with Welsh life – many of them in the western Valleys picking up the Welsh language quite naturally. It was also in the Valleys that the Jews encountered what must be the most shameful episode in Wales's dealings with them, the anti-Jewish riots of the Gwent valleys in 1911, represented here by an excerpt from the script of the recent film on the subject, *Solomon and Gaenor*.

As the century advanced, the coal industry declined and the Valleys' population fell, and so did that of the Jews, who increasingly moved to Cardiff or London, leaving the synagogues to close one by one. The last, in Merthyr Tydfil, closed in the 1980s. But the Jewish role in the Valleys experience of hardship and community had left its literary legacy: some of the material in this anthology, notably the stories of the Jewish author Lily Tobias, records the response of the two peoples to one another in the Valleys context. As the Jewish communities in the Valleys declined, the Welsh coastal towns and cities, and Cardiff particularly, became the main remaining centres of Jewish life in Wales, as they remain to the present day. As I write, there are around 1,000 Jews in Cardiff, counting both Orthodox and Reform, and small communities in Swansea and Newport, although Newport's synagogue has recently closed. In common with Jewish populations elsewhere in Britain, the number of Jews in the Welsh communities has been in slow decline due to a falling birthrate and due to emigration to London, to other countries, and, particularly since 1948, emigration – *aliyah* – to Israel.[8] The experience of Cardiff Jews is represented in this anthology most notably by the work of two of the most outstanding writers Wales has produced, Dannie Abse and Bernice Rubens. Literary work by other less well-known Welsh Jews is also represented, all of it illustrating the complexity of identity which being Welsh and Jewish involves.[9]

No book on the Jews can avoid confronting the terrible issue of their persecution. Therefore, the growth of fascism and the horrors of the Second World War are given a separate chapter, 'Conflict and *Shoah*', in which Welsh writers are seen responding to refugees from Nazism and to the victims – and in some cases the perpetrators – of the Holocaust. It is in this context too that I have collected the few examples of genuine anti-semitic prejudice in Welsh literature, specifically the disparaging remarks about supposed exploitative rootless Jewish capitalists made between the wars by Welsh writers such as Saunders Lewis and Geraint Goodwin, remarks that appear in sinister perspective in the light of the later atrocities.

However, while necessarily recording how Wales has interpreted the sorrows, prejudice and injustice that the Jewish people have suffered over the centuries, I have also sought to celebrate the way in which the two peoples have enriched one another. While it is implicit throughout the book, the Welsh identification with the Jews is dealt with specifically in two chapters, the first; 'The Children of Gomer', showing how Welsh writers have often stressed the sympathy and similarities between the two nations, both personally, culturally and ideologically, and the second, 'Diaspora', showing how the Welsh have responded to Jewish experiences and individuals in many varied contexts.

The diaspora experience suggests another, as yet unchronicled, way in which Wales can learn from the experience of the Jews. Increasingly, as Welsh speakers leave the *shtetls* of the Welsh-speaking western areas and settle in Wales's urban centres, particularly in the growing Welsh middle-class in Cardiff, they are discovering and creating ways of retaining their cultural distinctiveness, not in a ghetto, but as a network maintained within a broader overarching Western culture. As they do this, the parallels with the experience of Jews in Western societies through the centuries, but particularly in the present day, become striking. The Jews are the oldest example of a people who have succeeded in maintaining their values and identity while participating in other societies. Western society, fragmented by population mobility and the breakdown of traditional geographic community patterns, is increasingly becoming a shifting network of self-identified communities – religious, ethnic, linguistic, professional and political – which provide through conscious choice the roots and the sense of belonging previously conferred unconsciously by accidents of locality. The overarching Anglo-American culture provides the common ground and the advantages of widespread communication, while the self-identified chosen communities confer value and self-image. As this process increases, members of these communities of choice can learn a great deal from the Chosen People.

Introduction

As Wales embarks on its own tentative exercise in nation-building and self-determination, there is certainly inspiration to be drawn from the tenacity of the Jewish people, from their retention of their heritage within the diaspora, and from their revival of their language. There are also lessons about the need for inclusivity and tolerance to be drawn from the less edifying episodes of Wales's dealings with the oldest minority which it has encountered. In an increasingly pluralistic society, there is also a great deal to be learned from the literary testimonies of Welsh Jews as to how there can be many different kinds of experience of Welshness – something which will become increasingly apparent as Wales develops a civic, as opposed to ethnically-based, identity. To conclude, I am, for the reasons I gave earlier, rather reluctant to generalise about the Welsh response to the Jewish people as it is revealed in the material collected here. Many of the Welsh attitudes to the Jews are merely Welsh examples of responses which could be found in many other nations among the Gentiles. However, I believe it is safe to say, and indeed, is pleasing to record, that there is certainly, in very many passages, a definite thread to be discerned of mutual identification between two small peoples which have faced oppression, disenfranchisement and scorn, but which have, despite everything, survived.

A Note to the Content

In defining this collection as a literary anthology, I have allowed myself to cast my net widely for material. There are extracts from genres such as poetry, the novel, historiography, religious works, political rhetoric, biography, autobiography, journalism, drama, and even a screenplay. I have, however, tried to ensure that all the pieces are of a literary nature, that is, that they are all pieces of creative writing using heightened expression for effect, as opposed to simply bald factual accounts. As for the quality of the pieces, in the interests of using this material to give a comprehensive overview of Welsh and Jewish encounters through the centuries, I have allowed the inclusion of a few pieces of inferior literary quality when they are representative of a particular attitude or period and where no other work on that subject of greater literary merit is available. However, examples of this kind are few, and carry a 'health warning' in their preceding notes.

A Note to the Translations

More than half the material in this book is from Welsh language sources. In translating it I have tried to retain the flavour of the original, so that, for instance, the translations of eighteenth and ninteenth century prose reflect the archaic style, punctuation and capitalisation of the original. Where there is rhyme and metre, I have reproduced these verse forms exactly in the English translation. However, with those Welsh poems written in *cynghanedd* strict metre, I have inevitably been unable to replicate the intricate consonantal harmony of the original, and have had to be content with reproducing the end-rhyme and stress pattern, and occasionally hinting at the *cynghanedd* by means of simple alliteration.

NOTES

1. It is now, rather prosaically, kept for safe keeping in a bank vault in Hereford.
2. It is possible that Jews may have settled in Britain during the Roman occupation. In the Dark Ages, the holy man St Brynach, who is associated with Breconshire and Fishguard, was described as 'a son of Israel', which has been interpreted as meaning that he was of Jewish origin. In addition, medieval hagiographers claimed that St David himself was descended through 20 generations from Ann of Bethesda, mother of the Virgin Mary (Ivor Wynne Jones, *Wales and Israel*, 1988.)
3. Ivor Wynne Jones, *Wales and Israel*, 1988.
4. Llandysul, Gomer, 1998.
5. It reminds one rather of the way the some of the hierarchy of the churches in Germany responded to the Nazi tyrrany when its machinery of oppression began to be turned on them: they complained that they were being mistreated like the Jews, but failed to complain of the mistreatment of the Jews.
6. Cardiff, University of Wales Press, 1993.
7. There were also small communities in north Wales coast towns like Bangor and Llandudno.
8. The last major Jewish immigration to Wales was in the 1930s when refugees from Nazi Germany were encouraged by the Home Office to set up factories on the Treforest Industrial Estate, where, by 1939, 49 of the factories were Jewish-owned. (Hal Weitzman and David Weitzman 'The Jews in Wales').
9. Prof. William D. Rubenstein and Dr Hilary L. Rubenstein, authors of the study *Philosemitism* kindly drew my attention to two special supplements on Wales in *The Jewish Chronicle* (20.9.63 and 19.3.65, which included articles by prominent Welsh Jews.

THE CHILDREN OF GOMER

If imitation is the sincerest form of flattery, then the Welsh have certainly flattered the Jews. As a small nation historically denied the right of freedom and the prestige of having its language and culture officially recognised, Wales naturally found an affinity with the Jewish people. Although examples can be found in early writers such as Sildas, the expression of this affinity really becomes widespread after the Reformation, when the Bible became available in many of the main vernacular tongues of Europe. It was published in Welsh in 1588, and as its influence spread through the population, one of its effects was to give the Welsh a ready source of imagery to articulate their state as a small nation living in the shadow of a more powerful culture. Scholars in post-Reformation Wales became increasingly aware that Welsh culture and the Welsh language lacked prestige and needed to be consciously promoted and nurtured in the face of the greater institutional power of English. This provided fertile ground for the notion that the Welsh language had descended from Hebrew. This was a very widespread belief during the eighteenth century, and was incorporated more or less uncritically into the work of many Welsh linguists and lexicographers for generations as a favourite among the various claims of ancient ancestry made for the ancient British tongue. It also received support from notable scholars in England and Europe. The subject has been dealt with comprehensively in Caryl Davies's authoritative book on the linguistic ideas of the eighteenth century *Adfeilion Babel* ('Ruins of Babel').[1] Although the claiming of illustrious ancestry for Welsh was not so much a political attitude as a cultural one, it found the Jews a useful role-model, and the Welsh made great play of their supposed descent from Gomer son of Japheth, son of Noah.

Nationalism in the political sense in which we understand it today grew in Wales in the wake of developments in European nations in the nineteenth century, but again, right up to the present day, it has made use of an appeal to the moral authority of an affinity with the Jews. It is a kind of trump card that oppressed groups of all kinds can play: Verdi, whose Italy was occupied by the Austrians, used the 'Chorus of the Hebrew Slaves' in *Nabucco* to covertly express the Italians' desire for national freedom; Rastafarianism uses a comparison with Old Testament Jewish history to endorse its own members' defiance of 'Babylon'. The Welsh are far from unique in making the comparison, but their use of it has certainly been a sustained one and has been deepened by the huge influence the Bible has had in Welsh society, right through into this century, due to the historic strength of Nonconformity. The examples in this chapter, coming right through to the present day, show how the self-styled 'Children of Gomer' claimed an affinity with the Jews. The breadth depth and context of the 'Wales-Israel' identification as a theological and political phenomenon has recently been dealt with in admirable fashion by Dorian Llewellyn in *Sacred Place, Chosen People* (Cardiff, University of Wales Press, 1999).

Borrowing the Jews' victim status, conferred by millennia of persecution, and their divine calling, endorsed by their miraculous history, is certainly something of a one-way transaction. However, although it is an impertinence, and although the claims for a common ancestry are spurious, I would like to think the Welsh have partly repaid their borrowings from the Jews with an affinity which goes beyond mere expedience and is often a genuine and sympathetic identification. I hope the following material, collected in chronological order, gives some sense of that empathy.

CHARLES EDWARDS (1628-91)

This passage is an early example of a Welsh writer borrowing prestige for his language and his nation by claiming Jewish ancestry for them. It is taken from the revised 1671 edition of *Y Ffydd Ddi Ffuant*, 'The Sincere Faith', originally written in 1667 by Charles Edwards from Llansilin in Denbighshire. Edwards was a Puritan whose career as an editor, author and preacher, particularly in his later life, was shadowed by misfortune. This book, his first, was an historical outline of Christianity, a summary of its history in Wales – in which he made use of an extended comparison between the Welsh and ancient Israel – and a discussion on sanctification by faith. The following passage shows his theory that the Welsh language was descended from Hebrew,[2] and indicates that Edwards must have visited synagogues, where his belief in the relationship between the Welsh and the Jews was bolstered by the similarity of some Jewish and Welsh sacred music.

from THE SINCERE FAITH

The learned suppose that Hebrew was the only dialect among men from the creation of the world until the confusion of Babel, which caused other languages to borrow its words so often, and that the customary words in the ancient world correspond consistently to their meaning in that language alone. The first man was called Adam, because he was made from the Adamah, which is the earth: and the first woman was called Chauah, because she was the mother of every Chai, which is life: and she called her first child Cain, for she said I have had a Canithi. *Gen.*2.7 and 3.30 and 4.1. And this respected language, which was spoken by the first men before sin, and in which were written so many of the Scriptures, is the mother of Welsh, and that the Chaldean is its sister can be understood as follows: for undoubtedly, as I studied them so much I wondered and rejoiced to find the words of my country in strange languages which were so ancient and so honourable. Greek, Latin and English words were hurled into the Welsh language at swordpoint, or were dropped into it in the wake of commerce or learning, while the composition of those languages is actually different. But Hebrew has totally the same aspect and appearance. Its letters are more natural to our language than those which we use at the moment. For its single letters report the same sound as our double ones. The course of its expressions is also of the same manner as ours, calling the part of the world that is towards the noonday sun the south, and saying the 'mouth of' the sword, and 'the hand of' the river, while we say the 'lip of' the one and 'at the hand of' the other. And by connecting the single figure to the multiple, as in 'forty-one' and 'a hundred-one'. In the table which follows there are quite a number of words of the same sound and meaning in both languages: and where there is some difference between them I have set the appropriate meaning of the Hebrew after it, and then the Welsh word which corresponds to it, so that can be seen the similarity which is between them.

[*There then follows a long list of Hebrew words and their supposed Welsh equivalents*].

There follows a clutch of Hebrew expressions which can be understood in Wales, mostly taken out of the Hebrew Bible, where there are often others of their kind. And from them your faith about the truth of the scriptures in relation to some of the oldest things in creation can be assured, such as that the world was at the beginning of the same dialect, paternity and family. For if our nation had not come from the regions of the east where Adam had produced his heirs in the beginning, and the tribe of Noah after the flood, then there would not be so much of the language of the ancient world amongst us at this time, when we have been cut off by the sea from most of the rest of the world for such a long time, and when we have faded in learning through the grievous wars of old.

[*There then follows a list of Hebrew words and their supposed Welsh equivalents*].

There is also considerable correspondence between the Jews and our nation in terms of music. I have heard them in their synagogue singing the Hebrew Psalms on the same tunes that we, it appeared to me, use in our country on the days of Christmas and the Calends of May.

Translation from *Y Ffydd Ddi-ffuant*, 1667

THEOPHILUS EVANS, (1693-1767)

Like Charles Edwards in the previous passage, Theophilus Evans, writing in his influential history of Wales, *Drych y Prif Oesoedd*, 'Mirror of the First Ages', in 1716, claims that Welsh is descended from Hebrew. He goes even further than Edwards, claiming the Welsh people themselves were descended from Gomer, grandson of Noah. This claim, based as it is on the supposed similarity of the words '*Gomero*' and '*Cymro*', could, perhaps, only have occurred to a Welshman attuned to the internal consonantal correspondence which is such a fundamental feature of Welsh strict-metre *cynghanedd* poetry. There is some irony that in this passage Evans makes his baseless claim after having dismissed other historical fables as being too far-fetched. Theophilus Evans, born near Newcastle Emlyn in Carmarthenshire, was an Anglican priest who served mainly in Breconshire. A prolific religious writer, he combined a deep commitment to Wales and its culture with loyalty to the Church of England. He was an opponent of Methodism, and, when William Williams Pantycelyn, the great hymn-writer, was his curate, he opposed his full ordination because of Williams's methodist beliefs. Williams, whose work is dealt with in the introduction to the next chapter, later left the Anglican church to become one of Welsh methodism's greatest leaders. This extract is from the opening pages of Evans's *Drych y Prif Oesoedd*.

The Children of Gomer

from MIRROR OF THE FIRST AGES

Part 1. Chapter 1. The root-nation of the Welsh, and their first coming to this island.

It is a great work, but a sallow and awkward work, to tell the tale of the Welsh, of their failure and their worldly tribulations in every age and land in which they have dwelt, since the languages were confused in the Tower of Babel. For is it not a mournful and tiresome thing to tell how ungrateful they were to God, how eager to rebel against him, and how ready to fall into the temptation of the world, the flesh and the devil, which caused them to be so unfortunate and unsuccessful? And because our forefathers had drunk untruth like water, the proverb was true: 'Destruction will come upon those who do evil' (*Prov.* xxi, 15). And so we (like many other nations, in the end) after our sins had ripened, 'were left a small people, where we had been like the stars of heaven in number; because we had not listened to the Lord our God'. (*Deut.* xxviii. 62)

There is not, in truth, any nation under the sun which has kept its land and its language from the old former times whole and uncorrupted; nor is there one which has retained its privileges unmixed and unimpaired. Long have the Jews complained: 'Behold, we are now slaves; and as for the land that our fathers gave us, to eat of its fruit and its goodness, behold we are slaves within it,' (*Neh*, ix, 36). Because the Turks have conquered that land of Judea and the Jews do not have so much as a foot's breadth of ownership of it. Then the Greeks, those who in the ancient times were the rulers of the world, have been scattered, like the Jews themselves, across the face of the nations, and their extensive lands and kingdoms are in the hands of the Turk. The Romans too – those, who from around the time of our Lord Jesus, were masters of most of the known world at that time – they now, I say, for many hundreds of years, have ceased to be, both they and their language, except what may be found in books; and their great former authority has been devoured, like a corpse by birds of prey. And yet we, the remnant of the ancient Britons, dwell in a corner of this great island, of every part of which which we were once the masters, and retain our original language, if not completely perfectly, yet more purely than any other nation in the world. 'Their language they shall keep, their land they shall lose,' Taliesin says.

The ancient people in former times were so ignorant of the beginnings of the first inhabitants of this land that they had no competence or conception about it. I remember one English author, whom the Welsh called Gwilym Bach, who said, 'there was found in a cave in England, in the time of King Stephen, a boy and girl of a strange green colour, unlike any other person who had ever been seen in this world; and that the general opinion was that they had found their way up from an ocean hole or from the bowels of the earth', as this author so wisely tells at such length.

Although such crazy old legends as this are so foolish, yet there were some (some who took themselves to be learned men too) among the Greeks and Romans who were not a scrap more discerning in their untidy misconceptions regarding the first inhabitants of this island; for the opinion of some of them was that they had grown out of the ground like toadstools.

It is indeed a complicated enough task to search out the beginnings of our nation correctly and without distortion, and to trace it from its estuaries to the fountainhead; but I shall attempt to clear away the mist from the path, so that our journey towards the truth shall be clear.

After Adam had trespassed against the command of God, and he and his progeny had become subject to sin, the evil of mankind multiplied so much that 'the Lord repented of making man'. And in the year 1655 since God had created the world, the Almighty sent a general deluge to drown both man and animal; but Noah the righteous (and, for his sake, his family) found favour in his sight, and were saved from the oppression of the deluge of water in a ship we call the Ark.

After Noah had been saved like this, and he had come to create another generation as though in another world, his descendants conspired together, after a long time (which was around a hundred years after the deluge) to build 'a tower towards heaven'. (*Gen.* xi 4). Some supposed that the cause which urged them to undertake such an enormous task was lest a deluge should overtake them again and completely destroy them from the face of the earth; and that it was for fear of this that they built the tower and a city to keep them safe from the flow of the waters. 'We shall make a name for ourselves,' they said, 'lest we be scattered across the face of the earth'. However, the opinion of others is this, that they were now on their journey to the Garden of Paradise, and because the land around was so beautiful, full of perfumes, and herbs, and fruits, and every other agreeable thing, that they desired to stay there, they and their descendants for ever, and to that end they built the tower and the city, lest they be scattered from there. But however that may be, the Lord did not permit them to bring their work to completion, for he confused their language, so that the one could not understand what the other said; if one said to a friend 'Give me a stone', he would be given a pick instead of a stone; if another said, 'Keep the rope tight', the other would let it go; like this, the language confused, and each as it were a foreigner to the other, they could never take the work forward.

There had previously been only one speech throughout the whole wide world, which was, rightly enough, the Hebrew. But the world, which before that time had been of only one idiom and speech, now heard its inhabitants speaking twelve and three score languages; for to that number do the ancient histories say the mother-tongue, Hebrew, was divided. And in that great riot, very glad would anyone be to meet with one who could understand him; and they went here and there until they found another, and so, one by one, they all came together, and stayed with one another in so many separate groups, according to which dialect they spoke: and who, do you suppose, spoke Welsh at that time, but Gomer, eldest son of Japheth, son of Noah, son of Lamech, son of Methuselah, son of Enoch, son of Jared, son of Malaleel, son of Cainan, son of Enos, son of Seth, son of Adam, son of God?

Behold the bloodline and the lineage of the old Welsh, as exalted as that to which any earthly nobility could ever possibly reach, if only we, their descendants, were to realise it. And it is genuinely undoubted by me that this is nothing but the pure shining truth; for, 1. The ancient histories of the old times declare this; and what additional authority could there be for anything that happened in former days but that the records or the chronicles of the ages testify to it? 2. All the learned people of Christendom, especially now, as though from one mouth maintain this. 3. The name by which we are generally called, which is, Cymro, is as a livery to show to whom a servant belongs, and it advertises clearly from where we have derived; for there is scarcely any difference between Cymro and Gomero, as any man, yes, with half an eye, could see at first glance.

Translation from *Drych y Prif Oesoedd*, 1716

JOSEPH HARRIS (1773-1825)

Such was the identification of Joseph Harris with the myth of Welsh descent from 'Gomer ap Japheth', that he took the name 'Gomer' as his nom de plume. Born in Pembrokeshire, he was a minister and religious writer who founded and edited the religious magazine *Seren Gomer*, 'The Star of Gomer'. The following passage is taken from the first page of the first edition of the magazine on 28.1.1818. The mention of an earlier Seren is a reference to an earlier version of the magazine, which had been started in 1814. *Seren Gomer*, later to become the journal of the Welsh Baptists, continued until 1985, when it was subsumed with other publications into the inter-denominational magazine *Cristion*. The influence of the Gomer myth can be seen not only in the name of this important journal, but in the name of Gomer Press, which still flourishes today, and in the use of Gomer as a personal name in Wales.

SEREN GOMER
To the Welsh

Dearly beloved Brothers and Fathers, descendants, like us, of the glorious tribe of Gomer! Our fathers were famous in their day, not only in feats of arms, in the extent of their territory, and in the numerousness of their nation, but also in their commitment to embracing learning, through which they were enabled to educate uncivilised and oppressive nations in many beneficial things, relating to both the worlds; and particularly in their unshakeable adherence to the language of their forefather (as a particular nation) Gomer, in the face of great difficulties, bloody laws, and all kinds of cruel hardships, from oppressive foreigners. If they have lost, through violence and treachery, the most extensive and fertile part of their territory, yet they have transmitted to us their comprehensive strong-worded, self-sufficient language, which is worthy of the succour of their descendants until the end of time; a language which derives its essence from the age of Gomer, or, for all that is known to the contrary, was the one in which Adam and Eve conversed about the ineffable power and immortal wisdom of their blessed Creator. Must this perish for lack of succour in this age, or in the one that follows? We know of nothing that could be much more detestable and unnatural, other than the behaviour of patricide or matricide, than that a man should ignore the language of his mother, his nation, and all his ancestors, and should wish its dissolution, or should behave as though he wished it did not exist, such a particularly glorious language as Welsh, which everyone who understands different languages says without exception far excels the recent patchwork-languages of Europe. The words of the very famous man R Hall of Leicester, formerly of Cambridge, should foster jealousy in the heart of every Brython for the persistence of his language; 'I do not want, (he says) for all the world for the Welsh language to cease to be; that would be a loss of great significance to learning – every man of conscience should sustain the language of his country; the nearest thing to religion is this, he should consider an awareness of God the first and foremost thing, and next to that the language of his nation', or words to that effect.

We are confident that many yet in our land are yearning to see their language purified more and more, and every necessary patronage given to it, so that it can in its old age renew its strength, and appear like a young woman in the flower of her days, even though foreigners have eaten up her strength, and white-headedness has spread across her, of which her many sons take no heed. – We had reason to believe that our recent Seren had done greater good than we had foreseen, through guiding hundreds to read and understand Welsh who knew no more about the composition of any languages than they knew about the idioms and customs of the inhabitants of the moon, as many attest, and as show the speeches of many public men; and no small numbers of our countrymen have been drawn to take delight in knowledge and learning, yes, of those of whom it could have been said that they scarcely knew anything previously, save only where their pickaxe was, and when they would want dinner, and things of that kind.

Although this Seren is not in every sense as glorious as the one which has set, we hope that a host of the amiable sons and daughters of Gomer will find through its light much diversion and edification which would not otherwise be available to them through any other medium, therefore we earnestly call upon them to exert themselves for its continuance, at least, until its better should arise above the horizon.

Translation from *Seren Gomer*, 28.1.1818

THE CHURCH IN WALES

The Anglican church in Wales was disestablished in 1920, becoming an independent province of the Anglican Church. A 'broad church' politically as well as theologically, it has retained within its ranks both passionate Welsh patriots and those indifferent or even hostile to the claims of Wales as a nation. However, as an organisation which has inherited all the most historic buildings of Welsh Christianity together with a tradition of worship traceable to the earliest days of the faith in Wales, it is institutionally bound to a genuine identification with the country. This, the longer of the two collect prayers for the people of Wales contained in the church's *Book of Common Prayer*, shows how the writers compiling the book found the comparison of Wales and Israel impossible to resist.

FOR THE PEOPLE OF WALES

Almighty God, the King of the Nations, who chose the children of Israel, though a small nation, for a high purpose, grant us in Wales both to develop the gifts of nature and of grace with which thou hast endowed us and to be ready to share them with others, while joyfully accepting what they have to share with us, through thy Son Jesus Christ our Lord, who died and rose again for the whole world and who lives and reigns with thee and the Holy Spirit world without end. Amen.

Collect 16, from *The Book of Common Prayer*, Church in Wales

LEWIS VALENTINE (1893-1986)

Lewis Valentine, a Baptist minister who had served in the First World War, was one of the three leading members of *Plaid Genedlaethol Cymru*, the Welsh Nationalist Party, who committed a symbolic act of arson by setting fire to building materials at a planned airforce bombing range at Penyberth on the Llyn peninsula in 1936. The 'Fire in Llyn' was the first time since the days of Owain Glyndwr that Welsh people had dared to break the law to challenge English power in the name of Welsh freedom. Several sites for the bombing school had been considered in England but had been ruled out due to local objections. The War Office then sited the scheme in Wales, on land with strong Welsh cultural and religious associations, despite strong local and national Welsh protests. Moved to act, Lewis Valentine joined with Saunders Lewis and D.J. Williams to commit the symbolic arson in protest. They surrendered themselves to the police immediately afterwards and were duly tried at Caernarfon, basing their defence on Wales's right to self-determination. The jury failed to reach a verdict, and the authorities, determined to secure a conviction, moved the trial to the Old Bailey in London where 'The Three', as they had become known, were found guilty without the jury leaving the court. They were sentenced to nine months in prison. The following extract from Valentine's prison memoir, shows his sympathetic interest in the Jewish prisoners he encountered in Wormwood Scrubs. We will have occasion, in the passage following this, to consider the rather more complex attitude of Valentine's co-defendant, Saunders Lewis, towards the Jews.

from GRAVES OF THE LIVING

The Jews formed a special class, and they were numerous. Because some foods were forbidden them, special tables were set aside for them...

In their midst there were some striking characters, and we had benefit from the company of one of them, a physician and philosopher and novelist from Germany. He had lived his life without knowing he was a Jew – it was persecution by Hitler that made him realise it. He was put in one of the camps and was mistreated. There were wounds on his body – the effects of that mistreatment.

He managed to escape from the camp to Switzerland, and from there to France, and he crossed over to this country. He wrote a number of novels dealing with life in Germany immediately after the war, and a number of them were translated into English. His health was very frail, and he spent a lot of time in the hospital. He was released about a fortnight before us, and I believe he is now on a lecture tour in America.

He took a special interest in the National Party, and he envied us because we had a cause to live for and suffer for. He was a Communist, but his grasp on Communism was very slack – he clung to it lest his life should be completely without an anchor.

During the festival of Passover, the Jews were allowed to eat unleavened bread instead of the normal bread, and to have wine from the land of Canaan to drink, and they were very generous in sharing the 'matsis', as the unleavened bread was called, with the Gentiles, and we had many a wafer of unleavened bread from them.

A Jew and a foreman (a prison foreman, remember) called Levi was the most popular in the prison. A technical offence of some kind had brought him there, but he was a blessing to many, and he stood like steel against the viciousness or unfairness of many an officer.

D.J. Williams worked with another Jew in the library, and D.J. asserted that he was the wittiest person he had ever encountered. The greatest humour I ever saw in him was his attempt to pronounce Welsh proverbs D.J. had taught him – one of them beginning like this, '*Rhaid i'r gwychaf* ....' He recited that to everyone on the prison, and he considered it the most effective and truest proverb he had ever heard.

A good number of Jews joined the gardening class, but I never saw such clumsiness with spade and hoe in anyone. It was obvious that the Jews were not men of the soil. A very droll man was the tall thin and lordly Jew who could not for the life of him do anything with a spade, but he would assert endlessly that the Britons were the ten lost tribes of Israel – this was the great faith of his life. He could speak several languages. He was born in Spain, and had lived in every country in Europe and in the countries of the Mediterranean.

There were 'Dic Siôn Dafyddion'[3] amongst them too, such as the man who tried to change his name when he came to the prison and who swore that he was a member of the Church of England. He scorned everything Jewish, but he failed to convince anyone that he was an Englishman, and he had to admit in the end that he was a son of Abraham.

In England, there is no more affection towards the Jew than towards the Welshman, and on the whole the Jews had a rough time of it from their fellow-prisoners, but, on the surface, they accepted every indignity and scorn quietly. It was hard to accept them over-stressing their loyalty to the king and the throne. Slavishness cannot go much further than writing on the walls of the Synagogue a special prayer for the king. There's the stuff of harsh persecution in the hatred that is amongst Englishmen for Jews, and I believe that the opinion of the Englishmen of the prison about them was a mirror of the general opinion of England.

Translation from *Y Ddraig Goch*, November 1937 to February 1939.
Collected in Ed. John Emyr, *Dyddiadur Milwr a Gweithiau Eraill gan Lewis Valentine*, 1988

SAUNDERS LEWIS (1893-1985)

No Welsh writer has generated greater controversy in his attitude towards the Jews than Saunders Lewis. He was born on Merseyside into a situation of cultural dichotomy: although the Welsh-speaking son of a Calvinistic Methodist minister, he was educated at an English public school and served as an officer in the First World War. In the war, the experience of the catastrophic destruction of European civilisation moved him to try to preserve at least something out of the wreckage by seeking to save the culture of Wales, a country from which his upbringing had until then partly estranged him.

An uncompromising and visionary politician, he became one of the founders of the Welsh Nationalist Party in 1925, and was the prime mover behind the Penyberth arson protest discussed in the previous section. That protest cost him his livelihood when the University of Wales sacked him from his job as a lecturer and then blacklisted him. On his release from jail in 1937, he worked tirelessly as a politician, journalist, editor, dramatist, literary critic and poet to promote the ideals of Welsh freedom. His arson protest had proved a catalyst for Welsh activism, a movement which he gave a further push in 1962 with his radio talk *Tynged yr Iaith*, 'The Fate of the Language'. In that lecture he prophesied the death of the Welsh language unless civil disobedience were used in order to secure rights for Welsh speakers; it sparked the setting up of *Cymdeithas yr Iaith Gymraeg*, the Welsh Language Society, whose protests have since proved so effective in promoting the language's status.

However, despite these achievements, there was a darker thread running through the life and work of this complex man. Feeling threatened by what he saw as the uniformity and inhumanity of the modern industrialised world, he tended to an instinctive political conservatism, and nurtured ideals of hierarchy, order and organic, rooted communities. He was a convert to Catholicism and found himself in sympathy with neo-Catholic anti-modern idealists of the period such as Hilaire Belloc, G.K. Chesterton and T.S. Eliot, who proposed these ideals – rooted in the Catholic church's modern social teaching – as alternatives to what they saw as the twin evils of rampant capitalism and unbending totalitarianism. However, in imbibing these ideals and adapting them for Welsh consumption, he also willingly carried over elements of the anti-semitism which polluted the counsels of those writers. They believed a conspiracy theory – most virulent at the time among the French Right with whom they had much in common, and later to find its terrible extreme expression in German Nazism – that Jewish financiers, conceived of as a supra-national elite owing allegiance to one another rather than to their host national communities, were controlling the affairs of the nations for their own ends.

Lewis expressed this belief on several occasions in the 1920s and 1930s in speeches, articles, and, most notoriously, in two poems. One of the poems concerned is collected later in this book in the chapter 'Conflict and *Shoah*', where there is some further discussion of his attitude towards the Jews.

Lewis's central position in the history of Welsh nationalism in this century has made the question of his attitude towards the Jews a hugely touchy subject.

Some commentators have sought to portray Lewis as a committed anti-semite on the basis of those remarks; this has often been done with the intention of dismissing Welsh nationalism *per se* by association. Nationalists, on the other hand, embarrassed by those remarks, have tried to play them down and explain them away, and in doing so have often been too generous in their assessment of Lewis's motives. The truth is somewhere in the middle, and I have attempted to balance the two positions in a separate study of this subject in *Taliesin*[4] To summarise, Lewis undoubtedly subscribed, probably until as late as 1940, to the groundless and irrational conspiracy-theory I mentioned above. While he always denied that his remarks were based on anti-semitism (so, always, did Belloc, Chesterton and Eliot) he, like they, quite failed to see that however objective they may have thought those remarks to be, they were actually based on, and contributed to, a very dangerous prejudice. This is a serious failing to set against the record of Lewis's life and work, and it does not diminish Lewis's personal culpability to record that, thankfully, his comments found no response from his colleagues in the nationalist movement or among the members.

One must balance the picture, however, by recording that in his later articles and letters, from around the late 1930s onwards, Lewis can be seen abandoning those ideas rooted in anti-semitic prejudice and moving, belatedly, to a position of sympathy. Two of his later plays, *Brad*, 'Betrayal', (1958), and *1938* (1978), have as their heroes the German officers who conspired to assassinate Hitler, and his play *Esther* (1960), is a version of the Biblical story given from a standpoint sympathetic to the Jews. I have included an extract from the play in this section because of the way it seeks to establish an affinity between the subject status of the Jews in exile in Persia and the status of the Welsh under English rule. The mention, in this extract, of drowning the land of the oppressed people under water is a reference to the controversy, which was increasing during the time the play was being written, surrounding the decision by Liverpool Corporation – backed by Parliament in the face of almost universal Welsh protests – to drown the village of Capel Celyn near Bala to create a reservoir. Despite major protests, the drowning of the valley and the displacement of its Welsh-speaking residents went ahead, but it had become a *cause célèbre* which greatly increased the Welsh desire for greater self-government. In the extract from *Esther* here, the Jews have been facing annihilation due to the scheming of the anti-semitic prime minister Haman. Esther, wife of the Persian king Ahasferus and a secret Jewess, has braved a law saying that any who enter the chamber of the king without invitation may be summarily executed, and has successfully pleaded for mercy for the Jews.

ESTHER

HAMAN: It was the first time in my experience, sir, for anyone to trespass within the chamber and live afterwards. My lady the Queen is the bravest of the citizens of Persia.

ESTHER: Not brave, but lucky, Haman. In my weakness I was granted mercy and the sceptre was extended to me. You are a politician, Haman; have you any room for mercy?

HAMAN: This was not a political problem, my lady.

ESTHER: No, I know. But in a political matter....?

HAMAN: I will tell you a story, a true story. Something which happened to a king in my family. He was conquered in a battle and taken prisoner. The following day he stood unarmed before the enemy ruler, and extended his hand in peace to greet him and to ask mercy. He was put to death on the spot.

ESTHER: Appaling!

HAMAN: No, Queen. In politics that was the right thing. In politics, only force counts. Start showing mercy to a rebellious nation, start saving the life of one leader, and then your government is finished. Mercy is the beginning of your downfall.

ESTHER: My lord King, I shall remember the lesson of the prime minister. When it becomes a matter of politics, nation striking nation, I shall not go on my knees like today to beg for mercy.

HAMAN: You know nothing of the experience, my lady. It is also clear to see that you are not from a conquered nation. All nations like that, they are cowardly to the marrow of their bones. They will go to their destruction like sheep. You can drown their land under water, and they will cry and accept charity.

AHASFERUS: Tonight, Esther, you must tell me your story, your nation, your lineage, your family. I must know my queen.

ESTHER: I shall, my lord King, very gladly. I shall tell you everything tonight. Today I have had mercy.

Translation from Esther, 1960

HARRI WEBB (1920-1994)

Swansea-born Harri Webb was the folk poet of the nationalist movement in Wales throughout the 1960s and 1970s, using his humour, biting satire and powerful convictions to articulate and inspire the struggle for Welsh independence. Working mainly as a librarian, he was one of the leading figures in English-language poetry during that period, and was also a prolific journalist, and later a scriptwriter. By his period, the establishment of the state of Israel had changed forever people's views about the Jewish people, and had provided Wales with a model and an inspiration for how a nation could revive its fortunes. In the chapter on Wales and Palestine, 'Promised Land', we will be able to see a more extended treatment of this subject by Harri Webb. However, the following poem is a good example of the way a fellow-feeling between Wales and the Jews defined itself in a new way following the establishment of Israel, the Welsh attitude moving from one of mutual sympathy to one of admiration and a desire to emulate.

ISRAEL

Listen, Wales. Here was a people
Whom even you could afford to despise,
Growing nothing, making nothing,
Belonging nowhere, a people
Whose sweat-glands had atrophied,
Who lived by their wits,

Who lived by playing the violin
(A lot better, incidentally,
Than you ever played the harp).
And because they were such a people
They went like lambs to the slaughter.

But some survived (yes, listen closer now),
And these are a different people,
They have switched off Mendelssohn

And tuned in to Maccabeus.
The mountains are red with their blood,
The deserts are green with their seed.
Listen, Wales.

From Ed. Meic Stephens *Harri Webb, Collected Poems*, 1995

ALEXANDER CORDELL (1914-1997)

Born as George Alexander Graber to an English military family in Ceylon, Alexander Cordell came to Wales in 1936 after serving as a soldier. He had some Welsh ancestry and quickly came to feel an affinity with the Welsh people, particularly as the victims of the giant social injustice which was capitalism in the south Wales Valleys. In his sequences of historical novels based in industrial south Wales, *Rape of the Fair Country, Song of the Earth, The Fire People, The Hosts of Rebecca, Land of My Fathers* and *This Sweet and Bitter Earth*, he celebrated and articulated the experiences of the Valleys people in a style owing much to Richard Llewellyn's in *How Green Was My Valley* and its sequels, but still having a cavalier panache all of its own and an uncanny knack of resurrecting the feeling of historical events. In the following passage from *Song of the Earth* (Cordell also had an enviable talent for choosing titles), the Evans family are embarking on a career as bargees, and Cordell gives an affectionate, and typically boisterous, portrait of Welsh and Jewish friendship.

from SONG OF THE EARTH

Abercynon!

Down to the basin with us, and we were off that dirty old Merthyr barge sharper than monkeys and trundling down to Eli's wharf with the furniture with Dewi under the dresser this time, Ifor being with bandages, and Nell and Jed loaded to the forelocks, and at the back was Gran between the wheelbarrow shafts. Ifor was humping the tin bath, me with the mangle and Dada and the girls coming after with the chest of drawers and linen, Gran making sure that this was well presented since it came from Carmarthen and was best quality. And there was Mr. Eli Cohen waiting outside his cottage door with his fifteen women shrieking and chattering hind legs off donkeys, a couple of the matrons getting the vapours when Dewi came from under the dresser, and please come in, Mrs Evan, for the tea is ready and the kettle will be crying directly

Invitations and introductions all round then, with Sharon and Gwen dropping their new English curtseys, and Ifor being dragged out for presentation – all fingers and fumbles at the sight of so many women, though I think it was more blood-pressure than shyness for those Welsh-Jew girls were beauties with their brown, haughty faces and glorious red hair.

And one, Rebecca, aged seventeen, came from the back, one hand on her hip and her lips bright red in her smile, and I saw in a flash that Ifor, my brother, was done over fifteen rounds. So we left him to his fate, and me, Dada and Dewi went down to the wharf, and there was that Cohen barge all shining black and stacked with the furniture for the voyage round to Baglan. Three years we had worked for this; you get out of the soil what you put into it, said Dada.

'Got a good prow on her,' cried Eli. 'She is an inch above the water-line with the household effects. The mast is spruce, the sail is best Mary Walters down in Neath Arches. Float her in an hour, and with luck you catch the high tide at Cardiff before the bore runs out.'

'God bless you, Eli,' said my father.

'And God bless you, too, Mostyn, for I am back to fourteen now that Rebecca and Ifor have met up again.'

'Ach, no!'

'Like a sis, he is,' I said. 'Eh, look at it.'

Very girlish was Ifor, turning up his boots under the apple tree and Rebecca Cohen coming the delilah on him, and holding hands like a fairy instead of a thick-eared pugilist.

'Come on!' roared Dewi, disgusted.

Astonishing how Dewi treated women: disdainful, his dark eyes smouldering fire, his lips uncaring, and yet they died for him in their ravishing glances.

Second cup of tea for Gran, and can I slip out the back, Mrs Cohen, and she was ready, and old Eli lined his women up on the dancing lawn in front of the cottage and snapped his fingers and down they all went in their folds and crinolines, heads bowed, elbows wide, skirts out, and I could have shouted at the beauty of it.

'Sail aboard!' shouted Eli, and we all trooped down to the wharf, with Ifor and Rebecca lagging behind arm in arm and staring into each other's faces.

'Beautiful women you got here, Mr Cohen,' said Gran. 'And best kept clear of this rabble of fists that I am landed with.'

'We will get together ma'am,' chortled Eli. 'With your lot and my lot we could build a Welsh Jerusalem down the Vale of Neath, you think?'

'Many a true word said in jest, mind,' said Gran. 'See if we can manage it, for I would like to see all my boys wedded and bedded to the right women before I go under,' and she looked at my father, her eyes bright with unshed tears.

'Away to go, we are,' said Dada. 'We will not early forget the Cohens of Abercynon, and there will always be a welcome in Resolven, remember, especially at Michaelmas Fair!' and he helped Gran aboard the Cohen barge.

'Ifor, we are off directly!' cried Gran, and he came running with Rebecca flushed and watery behind him: mind, this had been going on for a month or two to my certain knowledge, though supposed to be a secret.

I got Nell and Jed Donkey shifting, and we glided through the Cohen Lock, waving and shouting to the Cohen tribe clustered on the bank, and down they all went again in their curtsey. Beautiful, they looked, clustered about Eli.

'May your Jew-God possess you Eli Cohen!'

'His hands above your house, Mostyn Evan, I will miss your sons!'

'Dear me! Dammo, what lovely people,' sobbed Gran, wet and dabbing.

From *Song of the Earth*, 1969

LESLIE THOMAS (b. 1931)

In coming to Newport-born Leslie Thomas, this chapter has travelled some distance from the earnest divines with which it began. Thomas's successful career as a novelist, typified by books such as *Virgin Soldiers* (1966) has been based on his talent for combining comedy with a deft handling of risqué material and an ability to deal with more serious matters sensitively. In the following extract, the eccentric Welsh preacher John Properjohn, 'The Man with the Power' of the book's title, has been hired by a rich American benefactor to lead a preaching tour across the United States. The tour party is travelling in two buses named 'Jesus Lives' and 'Jesus Loves' with a motley crew of largely hired help, of whom the narrator is a member.

from THE MAN WITH THE POWER

'Jews!' explained Properjohn.

'Wrong,' said Winston. 'They're not Jews.'

It was a fine countryside. Windless fields quiet, idling towards winter, trees standing on elevated ground as though to get a better view of the landscape, their leather leaves split by the silver streaks of birches. The rain had travelled away and we were journeying under a blue good-humoured sky with frail autumn light collected on rivers, streams and farm ponds. The farms themselves, spread with rural orderliness, barns prettily coloured with hex signs, each like a decorated ark, silo towers splendid as lighthouses, chestnut horses shining in perfect fields. Even the pigs looked clean.

'Lancaster County, Pennsylvania,' Winston had announced. Herbie was driving 'Jesus Lives'. Winston and I were in the bucket seats and Properjohn behind the driver's hairy ear. Hattie was in 'Jesus Loves' with the ladies.

'Jews,' repeated Properjohn, looking out. 'Anybody can see they're Jews.'

'Amish,' corrected Winston patiently. 'Amish people. They're Dutch.'

'Dutch Jews,' insisted Properjohn triumphantly. 'A blind man can see they're Jews. Black hats and coats, long beards, long noses. Jews!'

Herbie, the Hebrew in him stirring, glanced around rudely from the wheel and observed: 'You got a black hat, a black coat and a long nose.' He was squinting violently sideways, trying to take in Winston and myself and to get a glimpse of Properjohn sitting behind and to his right.

'WHAT DO YOU MEAN?' howled Properjohn, as though struck by a hot spear.

'Well, man, you could be a Jew,' said Herbie, blinking at the bellow.

'A Jew? Me, a Jew!'

'He said you dress like one,' pointed out Winston in a conciliatory tone. Then apologetically but with determination. 'And then, of course, there's your nose.'

'My God,' cried Properjohn, his huge Semitic head abruptly collapsing into his hands. 'I've never been called a Jew before. Never. Never, never, never.' He slowly came up from his palms, as though he had realised something even more horrific. 'The Jews crucified

Christ,' he whispered, adding unnecessarily, 'on the Cross.'

'The Pope forgave them,' pointed out Winston coolly. 'Couple of years ago.'

'Nice,' muttered Herbie. 'That's real nice.'

'The Pope?' croaked Properjohn unbelievingly. 'The Pope? What's it got to do with the bloody Pope? He's a heathen. I'd listen to a druid before I'd listen to a heathen like that.'

'Okay, okay,' said Winston, his hands making a calming motion. 'No need to get incensed. So all we're saying is that people who maybe *look* like Jews don't have to be Jews. And some that don't look like Jews, are Jews.'

Properjohn was staring from the window at the strange people gathered in a fruit and vegetable market. The sides of the road in the small town were blotched with the men's black hats and dotted with the white gauze bonnets of the women and girls. It was very animated, people bargaining and spitting dramatically on their hands, greeting friends and making jokes. It was like a happy funeral. 'They look like Jews,' Properjohn grunted. 'And those horse buggies they're riding in. They look like Jewish buggies.'

'They're Amish,' repeated Winston. 'Jews ride in cadillacs. These are strict Christian farmers. They won't have anything modern. No cars, no television, no combine harvesters. They do it all like it was two hundred years ago.'

'And they look like Jews,' mumbled Properjohn.

'Okay, so they do. But they've been kidding that they're Christians and everybody in America believes them. It took you to find out they were cheats.'

Properjohn seemed defeated and looked sulky at the sarcasm.

'They have strong family alliances,' said Winston. 'The home and the farm. And they don't have any churches. They pray at home.'

'Ah,' said Properjohn knowingly. 'In secret, you see. That's when they bring out the little skull caps and the candlesticks.'

'And they are rumoured to bundle,' continued Winston doggedly.

There was a three-point silence at that. I was first to ask. 'What's that?' I said. 'Bundle'.

'Bundling?' shrugged Winston. 'Alleged to be done all over the world by various sects. It's just young people, teenagers, you know, getting bedded down together before marriage.'

We all waited for the predictable howl from Properjohn. But no sound came from him. When he turned slowly towards Winston we saw that the howl was trapped on his face. 'What did you say?' he said hoarsely.

'Winston smiled reassuringly. 'It's okay,' he said. 'It's merely the custom, so they say. They kind of get into bed together, but they've still got all their clothes on, if you get it?'

'Do they get it?' inquired Herbie beneath his breath.

'Heathen practices,' seethed Properjohn. 'The devil's work.'

'Now I come to think of it, I've heard it's done in Wales,' I said. Then, as his face began to expand, I added: 'In remote areas'.

'Never!' he shouted. 'Not never!' He exploded into an abominable shaking rage, spluttering to spitting out his words, shaking his fists and becoming an extraordinary aubergine hue about the cheeks and brow. He frightened me, he frightened Winston, and Herbie, looking fearfully over his shoulder, let 'Jesus Lives' take a corner too sharply and sent two Amish buggies careering onto the sidewalk, their horses crying out, their passengers astonished and stiff as an old photograph.

Properjohn was thrown sideways but this did not prevent him scrambling up like a rugby player from a scrum, flinging down the window and howling back at the aghast Amish men: 'Jews! Jews!'.

From *The Man with the Power*, 1973

ROLAND MATHIAS (1915-)

Breconshire-born Roland Mathias, an historian and schoolteacher by profession, whose career took him to various posts in England and Wales, is also a poet, editor and critic of distinction, whose work has been marked by the range of its sources and interests. In the following poem, a performance of Handel's oratorio 'Judas Maccabeus', popular in the Welsh choral tradition, is the occasion for a reflection on the aspirations of ancient Israel, typified by the successful freedom fighter Maccabeus, and the similar, although differently expressed, aspirations of Wales.

JUDAS MACCABEUS

The gallery of faces is a cloud
Hiding a thunderbolt. Below stairs feet are loud

In the aisle. The tired unbroken
Smile of the pillars urging the blotched brown
Building inward upon the blown mouth
Alters, tightens upon the sharper breath of youth.
The lines of pressure straighten, tautly the hole of air
Purses and shapes to utterance. Shortly is heard the roll
Of despair, of Israelitish women crying at the wall
Dragging their sorrow like hair
Out of the dropped scalp, and threatening, nearing,
The male tormented morrow and the Syrian yelp.
'How vain is man,' seed cries in Mattathias dead,
'How vain', but the grey temples all a-sweat
With effort and the loud planted feet
Of the steady bass fronting the enemy hill give lie
To the feeble tale, the sword hacked with earth shakes
In the furrow, driving the work
Deeper, till the morrow breaks.

'How vain is man,' sings the hireling,
Making of vanity a measured sweep,
Then a sword-pass, pricking the word in the middle-leap
Of his art. 'How vain is man'
Runs the part, 'who boasts in fight',
And Maccabeus, every ringlet plain
In place, leans on his sword
Complacent, letting his word-distended face
Swell with humility now that the part is over
Like wind bellying under a canvas cover
And slapping the paunch with pride. Is the rank
    posturer here,
The talking sail, the tongue of cloth, in the pit clapping
For both? Vanity applauding vanity, can one fail
To win? Is any victor over the measure of man?

But rise, rise. Anticipate. Always the present ready
And foretold, always the rodlike serpent raised.
The full throat of effort is not cold
Whether the heart be praised or no. Tear down the
    notes, be bold
Out of the sky so that the pit

Remember it and lie amazed
At the labouring months, at the meeting years of sweat.
These wear work at their temples, get them tears
Lamenting in time for Israel, weathered eyes
Watching them from time beaten to time victorious
Over the swung shoulder of the hidden march,
O are they not ordinary, glorious, hounded, down,
To a crown bidden yet compelled to bone?
Bolder the step now, bounded eyes of the dog
And conqueror range over the pit and rise
Again. The planted feet are familiar and strange. The listening
spine creeps to the brain.
Hair greying, cheek and temple a-sweat,
Israel is down and up, vain but not beaten yet:
Dumb eyes and speaking eyes, lips praying like kings
In exaltation, torment, wrongs past counting or care,
It is Wales, it is Israel, Israel upon the stair,
Grey in the gallery, heavy under rod,
Weary and impenitent, the wanderers of God
In the desert chosen, compost of spine and brain –
Against the pit the pillar and in the pillar sign.

From *Burning Brambles*, 1983

GRAHAME DAVIES (1964-)

I thought it worth including this poem as it was really the starting point for the whole book. I wrote it after listening to a series of radio programmes by my then BBC Wales colleague James Stewart on the history of the Jews in the Valleys, and then visiting Merthyr's Jewish cemetery. Its reception in translation by the Jewish community in Cardiff led me to seek similar material by other Welsh writers, a search which resulted in the collection of material in this book.

MERTHYR JEWISH CEMETERY

Even in death
you are set apart,
in your special fold of land
on the slope of Cefn Cilsanws.

The Children of Gomer

In the earth of the South, David's lineage;
the Hebrew script,
the unfamiliar dates
and the little stone cairns
turn a part of Wales into Canaan.

Refugees from the egypts of the continent
among the nations of the wilderness of coal;
the challenge of your apartness
was a judgement day to us,
who had the choice
to welcome or to crucify the stranger.

Here your generations scratched a living
before venturing, dying, departing,
and leaving, by today,
only your empty synagogue,
and your dead in the land.

Although it's years since you raised your tabernacles from our
                                                    midst,
I feel –
when I see the rocks of your pre-celtic covenant
on these hills –
that it is not you but us
who are short-lived, who are sojourners.

If only we had a tithe of your tenacity,
of your talent for overcoming evil;
if only we had a scrap of the pride
that carried the ark of your language and history
through every desert, to the land of your promise.

For bringing the fact of the chosen people
to our land of fake Bethels and Salems;
for the wealth of your wandering religion in our memory;
for drawing the glance of the God of Israel to this valley,
and setting its name on the landscape of your long pilgrimage;
for bringing the miracle of your survival to us,
in the earth below us, *shalom*.

Translation from Adennill Tir, 1997.

NOTES

1. Cardiff, 2000.

2. Griffith Jones (1683-1761), the vicar of Llanddowror in Carmarthenshire, was another contemporary proponent of this belief. Jones stood firm against the establishment's drive to force Welsh people to receive their education through English. He established thousands of circulating schools which succeeded in making literacy in Welsh very widespread. In promoting Welsh, the ability to claim its Biblical, indeed divine, origin was very useful. In his work *Welch Piety*, Jones explains the similarity of Welsh and Hebrew as follows: 'Let who pleases compare the Welsh and Hebrew Old Testament with this view, he will be surprised (sic) with the great number of words and expressions he will observe to have a near affinity in their pronunciation and meaning; which would be the more evident if the Welsh were written in the Hebrew characters: insomuch that the British language may be fairly supposed to be one of those which sprung out of the Hebrew at the tower of Babel; consequently may be said to have God himself for the immediate Author of it; and, as it began at the confusion of tongues, will, perhaps, be hardly utterly destroyed till the dissolution of the world, and the end of time.'

3. 'Dick John David', a derogatory term for Welsh speakers who turn their backs on their origins and language and who affect to be English.

4. '*Rhagfur a Rhagfarn: Agweddau tuag at yr Iddewon yng ngwaith T.S. Eliot, Saunders Lewis a Simone Weil*,' ('Buttress and Bigotry: Attitudes towards the Jews in the work of T.S. Eliot, Saunders Lewis and Simone Weil') *Taliesin*, Volume 100, Winter 1997, 61.

JERUSALEM DESTROYED

This chapter looks at Welsh religious attitudes to the Jewish people. Evangelical Protestantism was a strong force in Wales from the Methodist revival of the eighteenth century onwards. It was inspired by an instinctive impulse to 'save' whatever groups or individuals came to its attention – whether the natives of the Khasia Hills in India where Welsh missionaries conducted a long-term evangelistic project, or the English immigrants to industrial Wales in the nineteenth century, for whom the Calvinistic Methodists set up special English-language churches. The Jews were not exempted from this missionary activity, and many of the pieces in this chapter express a desire to convert them to Christianity; indeed, there was an extra motive for converting the Jews because, according to evangelical belief, the Second Coming would have to be preceded by the conversion of the Jews and their return to Palestine. The missionaries were only too happy to give the Almighty a helping hand to complete his purposes. An early example of this desire is found in the work of the Puritan mystic Morgan Llwyd (1619-59), who believed the Second Coming was imminent. In his English poem 'The Summer', he anticipates the ènd times:

> Harke what a sound the dead bones make
> The Jewes with Jesus rise
> O Tartar, East and Caspian Hills
> Deliver up your prise.
>
> Make way, Remove the blocks, stand by
> O wellcome Jewes by mee
> A shulamite in Jesus coach
> I long thy face to see.
>
> Thy face shall brighten all these lands
> Thy moone looks like the sun
> The sun like seven. The bridegroome now
> that famous race will run.
>
> Where shall we dwell when summer comes?
> with mother Salem sweet.
> A perfect state. A wondrous place
> Where God and we shall meet.

In the eighteenth century, the hymn-writer and Methodist leader William Williams Pantycelyn (who was mentioned in the previous chapter as the victim of his vicar Theophilus Evans's anti-Methodist prejudice), also gave typical expression to beliefs like those of Morgan Llwyd concerning the Jews. Dewi Arwel Hughes's study of the eighteenth century missionary movement in Wales, *Meddiannu Tir Immanuel*,[1] 'Possessing the Land of Emmanuel,' quotes Williams saying that the Gospel shall find its way: '...once again to old Jerusalem...and to the Jews who are now scattered in every corner of the world, and who in seeing such marvels will be matured to accept this Teaching that the MESSIAH has come, and that the Scriptures have been fulfiled.'

Palestine was indeed a kind of alter ego for the Welsh, familiar as they were not only with the Biblical narratives, but with later historical material detailing the destruction of Jerusalem by the Romans in 70 AD, the subsequent exile of the Jews from the Holy Land, and the occupation of Palestine by the Turkish Ottoman empire. The main source material for the descriptions of the destruction, of which many examples can be found in Welsh literature, was the work of the Jewish historian Josephus, who had an ambivalent attitude towards his own people. He enjoyed the patronage of the Roman conquerors and reviled what he saw as the fanaticism of the Zealots who had insisted on defending Jerusalem until the bitter end, while he was at the same time protective of Jewish religious identity. His account tells of how the Romans, as part of a campaign between AD 66 and 73, laid siege to Jerusalem, eventually capturing it, massacring the inhabitants and destroying the Temple. It was a catastrophe for the Jews, losing them their nationhood, the centre of their worship and their holy city. It was the beginning of nearly two thousand years of exile for them.

To Christian authors, Josephus's material was readily adaptable to fit the interpretation that the destruction of Jerusalem was God's punishment of the Jews for their rejection of Christ a few decades earlier. It provided supposed historical justification for regarding the Jews as accursed wanderers in need of redemption. There was a considerable amount of poetry produced in Wales on this subject. For example, Iorwerth Glan Aled published his well-received winning eisteddfod *pryddest* in 1851 on the subject of 'Palestina', which gave a typical account of the destruction of Jerusalem. Then in 1855, the poet and editor David Owen, known as 'Brutus' (a name derived from another popular and widespread myth of Welsh noble descent: that they had descended from Brutus of Troy who supposedly gave his name to the island of Britain) published in his volume *Brutusiana*, a long poem entitled '*Y Wyryf Israelaidd*', 'The Virgin of Israel'. In this, translated here, he depicts, sympathetically, a Hebrew girl bemoaning the fate of her people:

> But now the Almighty's chosen race
>   Are scattered here and there,
>   Are wanderers in every place
> Are outcasts everywhere.
>
> Will they once more fair Canaan grace,
> Once more reclaim their state?
> Shall they once more their Father praise
> Within Jerusalem's gate?

The author then intervenes with some well-meant encouragement:

> Be still, thou maiden pure of face,
>   Put by your bitter tears;
> A sea of joy awaits your race,
>   In fullness of the years.
>
> The time of God's design is near,
>   Is nearer every day;
> The promised time is nearly here,
>   When tears are wiped away.
>
> Your Prophets, faithful to the Lord,
>   In Holy Writ foretell
> That you shall one day be restored,
>   Returned to Israel.

He goes on to prophesy the Jews' conversion. The work of Cardiganshire poet Daniel Evans (1792-1846), *Golwg ar Gyflwr yr Iueddewon*, 'A Look at the Condition of the Jews', is another example of this widespread Welsh response to Jewish history. This interest and identification, although motivated largely by a conversionist motive, nonetheless prepared the ground for Christian sympathy with 19th and early twentieth vcentury Zionist aspirations to establish a Jewish home in Palestine, a project in which the Welsh played an important part, as we will see in the chapter 'Promised Land'.

Even though Christian observance in Wales has declined sharply during the last century, and although the conversionist zeal has long faded, the impulse of evangelicalism has had sufficient momentum throughout this century to ensure that many Welsh people have been particularly sensitised to Jewish interests.

GEORGE HERBERT (1593-1633)

One of the greatest religious poets in the English language, George Herbert was born to a prominent noble Anglo-Welsh family with strong Montgomeryshire connections. An able scholar and man of affairs, and onetime Member of Parliament for Montgomeryshire, he sacrificed the attractions of a life at court in order to follow his calling as a country priest. His poetry, nearly all of it published after his untimely death in his fortieth year, depicts a man in a profound, though often troubled, relationship with God. The following poem shows Herbert recognising the Christian debt to the Jews, and, while desiring their conversion, nonetheless regarding their state with compassion rather than condemnation.

THE JEWS

Poore nation, whose sweet sap and juice
Our cyens have purloin'd, and left you drie:
Whose streams we got by the Apostles sluice,
And use in baptisme, while ye pine and die:
Who by not keeping once, became a debter;
  And now by keeping lose the letter:

Oh that my prayers! mine, alas!
Oh that some angel might a trumpet sound;
At which the Church falling upon her face
Should crie so loud, until the trump were drown'd,
And by that crie of her deare Lord obtain,
  That your sweet sap might come again!

From Ed. C.A. Patrides, *The English Poems of George Herbert*, 1974

HENRY VAUGHAN (1621-95)

The influence of George Herbert, author of the previous poem, can be felt considerably on the work of Henry Vaughan, a Breconshire poet and doctor descended from a noble Welsh family. He fought with the Royalists in the English Civil War, and, following the defeat of the political and religious establishment he had supported, he retired to a country life through which he experienced God via an intense and visionary form of nature mysticism. He was a Welsh speaker who chose to write in English, which was rapidly becoming the language of his class. His religious poems are characterised by a breathtaking ability both to perceive and to communicate the sense of the eternal. The following poem, not among his best-known, nor, it must be said, among his best, shows him desiring the conversion of the Jews.

THE JEWS

> When the fair year
> Of your deliverer comes
> And that long frost which now benumbs
> Your hearts shall thaw; when Angels here
> Shall yet to man appear,
> And familiarly confer
> Beneath the oak and juniper:
> When the bright Dove
> Which now these many, many springs
> Hath kept above,
> Shall with spread wings
>
> Descend, and living waters flow
> To make dry dust, and dead trees grow;
>
> O then that I
> Might live, and see the olive bear
> Her proper branches! which now lie
> Scattered each where,
> And without root and sap decay
> Cast by the husband-man away.
> And sure it is not far!
> For as your fast and foul decays
> Forerunning the bright morning-star,

Did sadly note his healing rays
Would shine elsewhere, since you were blind,
And would be cross, when God was kind:
  So by all signs
Our fullness too is now come in,
And the same sun which ere declines
And sets, will few hours hence begin
To rise on you again, and look
Towards old Mamre and Eshcol's brook.
  For surely he
Who loved the world so, as to give
His only Son to make it free,
Whose spirit too doth mourn and grieve
To see man lost, will for old love
from your dark hearts this veil remove.

Faith sojourned first on earth in you,
You were the dear and chosen stock:
The Arm of God, glorious and true,
Was first revealed to be your rock.

You were the eldest child, and when
Your stony hearts despisèd love,
The *youngest*, even the Gentiles then
Were cheered, your jealousy to move.

Thus, Righteous father! dost thou deal
With brutish men; Thy gifts go round
By turns, and timely, and so heal
The lost son by the newly found.

From Ed. Alan Rudrum, *Henry Vaughan*, 1976

THOMAS OLIVERS (1725-99)

Nowhere in the worship of the English-speaking Church is there a hymn so steeped in Jewish imagery and feeling as this one, the work of the Montgomeryshire-born Wesleyan Methodist preacher Thomas Olivers.[2] He wrote it after a visit to the Great Synagogue in Duke's Place in London in around 1770. There he heard the cantor Meyer Lyon, whose liturgical name was 'Leoni', singing the Yigdal, a hymn of praise written in 1404 and based on the 13 articles of Jewish faith drawn up in the twelfth century. Olivers translated the hymn from Hebrew to English, paraphrased and Christianised it, and set it to one of the tunes given him by Lyons, in whose honour he named the tune 'Leoni'. Olivers also provided Biblical references, most of them Old Testament, for almost every line of his hymn, which can still be found in many denominations' modern hymnbooks, often, in the Anglican church, as a processional hymn. It has been translated into Welsh as *'Duw Abram, Molwch Ef'*, although the successive revisions of the translation have tended to Christianise it further and deprive it of the frisson of Jewish authenticity which Olivers' English version retains. I like to think that Olivers' background as a Welshman is partly responsible for his sensitivity to cultural difference and also to his choice of the haunting Hebrew melody to which he set this most Jewish of Christian hymns.

A HYMN TO THE GOD OF ABRAHAM

The God of Abrah'm praise
Who sits enthron'd above;
Ancient of everlasting days,
And God of Love;
Jehovah, Great I am
By earth and heav'n confest;
I bow and bless the sacred Name
For ever bless'd.

The God of Abrah'm praise,
At whose supreme command
From earth I rise – and seek the joys
At his right hand:
I all on earth forsake,
Its wisdom, fame and power;
And him my only portion make,
My Shield and Tower.

The God of Abrah'm praise,
  Whose all-sufficient grace
Shall guide me all my happy days
  In all my ways:
    He calls a worm his friend!
    He calls himself my God!
And he shall save me to the end
  Thro' Jesu's blood.

He by himself hath sworn,
  I on his oath depend,
I shall on eagle's wings up-borne
  To heaven ascend;
    I shall behold his face,
    I shall his power adore,
And sing the wonders of his grace
  For evermore.

Tho' nature's strength decay
  And earth and hell withstand,
To Canaan's bounds I urge my way,
  At his command:
    The wat'ry deep I pass,
    with Jesus in my view;
And through the howling wilderness
  My way pursue.

The goodly land I see,
  With peace and plenty bless'd;
A land of sacred liberty,
  And endless rest.
    There milk and honey flow,
    And oil and wine abound
And trees of life for ever grow
  With mercy crown'd.

There dwells the Lord our King.
  The Lord our Righteousness
(Triumphant o'er the world and sin)

The Prince of Peace:
  On Sion's sacred height,
  His kingdom still maintains;
And glorious with his saints in light
  For ever reigns.

He keeps his own secure,
  He guards them by his side,
Arrays in garments, white and pure
  His spotless bride;
    With streams of sacred bliss
    With groves of living joys –
With all the fruits of Paradise
  He still supplies.

Before the great Three-One
  They all exulting stand;
And tell the wonders he hath done
  Thro' all their land:
    The list'ning spheres attend,
    And swell the growing fame;
And sing, in songs which never end
  The wondrous Name.

The God who reigns on high,
  The great arch-angels sing,
And 'Holy, Holy, Holy,' cry,
  'Almighty King!
    Who was and is, the same;
    And evermore shall be;
Jehovah – Father – great I am!
  we worship thee'.

From Ed. Ian Bradley, *The Penguin Book of Hymns*.

SAMUEL ROBERTS (1800-85)

Samuel Roberts from Llanbrynmair in Montgomeryshire was an Independent minister, and a radical author who supported, through his journalism, a host of progressive causes, such as universal suffrage, temperance and the abolition of slavery. He was also a pacifist and an opponent of imperialism. In the following passage, he can be seen engaging on the side of justice in the debate in the middle of the nineteenth century over whether Baron Rothschild should, as a Jew, be allowed to take his place in the Houses of Parliament after having been elected several times for the City of London seat. It was only in 1858, two years after this article was published, that Baron Rothschild was finally allowed to take his place in Parliament, swearing loyalty on the Old Testament rather than on the New, as he had previously been required, and had refused, to do.

BARON ROTHSCHILD

Lord John Russell and the Government could establish a law in a few minutes to make the way completely clear for the Baron to take his place in Parliament immediately following his election. The Baron is completely content to take the vows upon the Old Testament, and he testifies solemnly that that is the most effective method for his conscience; and it is truly disgraceful that Lord John Russell and Sir Robert Harry Inglis and their friends are wasting so much of the valuable time of the country and Parliament, to boast their Christianity and their conscience and to bicker like fools and argue stubbornly about such a case.

Baron Rothschild is far more honest, and magnanimous, and conscientious, than they have ever been, and it is an everlasting shame to our country that the Baron, after having been elected for such a long time for the city of London, should be shut out of Parliament. He was elected more than once by the same people who elected Lord John. It is as fair for the sons of Abraham to have a voice in Parliament as it is for the sons of Gomer, and the bastards of Hengist. Eternal shame on Lord Russell that he should quibble minutely and fake sighs instead of undoing the lock of captivity, and letting his rich and co-elected compatriot come in to join him in the court of Parliament. We have heard that some of the Parsons of the Church of England in Wales have sent petitions to Parliament against the enfranchisement of the Baron and his people; but we have not heard that they have refused the Baron's tax towards the maintenance of the Church. – *August, 1850.*

Translation from *Gweithiau Samuel Roberts*, 1856

JOHN MILLS (1812-73)

The conversionist attitudes of the poets quoted earlier were largely merely theo-retical, and did not result in any missionary activity as such. It fell to John Mills from Llanidloes in Montgomeryshire to try to put those ideals into practice. He was a minister of the Calvinistic Methodists, and, during his period in London, engaged enthusiastically in the task of trying to convert London's Jews. He learned Hebrew, steeped himself in Jewish history, and made as many contacts as he could with London Jewry in order to further his aims. He even undertook a trip to Palestine to report on the condition of the Jews there. It seems he had little, if any, visible success for his long labours; indeed, it seems that in writing his pioneering books in Welsh and English on the subject of the Jews, and in lecturing tirelessly on Jewish subjects, he actually did more to promote Judaism to Christians than vice versa. The following extracts depict aspects of this curious crusade. The first is from a biography of John Mills written by Richard Mills and the Rev N. Cynhafal Jones in 1881, and is characterised by a some-what harsher attitude towards the Jews than was displayed by Mills himself. The second extract is a more human and poignant one, taken from John Mills's own book, *Palesteina*, in which he gives an account of his encounters with the Jews of the Holy Land.

from THE LIFE OF THE REV JOHN MILLS

It is probable that there is no nation under heaven so difficult to draw close to, and to bring the light and power of the gospel to bear upon, as the Jewish people. It has shut itself up in such seclusion from everyone else; has accustomed itself to look down with such disdain on the nations, and has raised such thick walls of prejudice around itself, that it is almost impossible for anyone to get through to it in any way, excepting only to do business. And as for Christianity, to the Jews it is not a new religion, with its novelty something to be explored and experienced; but something which he has already pre-judged and condemned as an accursed thing, and every Jew has bound himself never to look upon it, and to close his ears to those who would seek to teach it. It therefore required the greatest wisdom, patience and determination in the person who would seek to draw near to them in the character of a Christian missionary. But those elements met together to an uncommon degree in Mr Mills – so much so that he was able to make his way into the secrets of the nation, and to be heard by them, more so than any other gentile in Britain, and, possibly, in the world. Some of his brothers in Wales supposed, as we shall have occasion to see later, that he was not having success in the task he was sent to perform, and he had to suffer a good deal of grumbling and accusation from men whom it was obvious had no idea of the difficulties under which he was labouring, and who could not see the success that followed his endeavours. As he did not succeed in gathering together a church of converted Jews, this group thought he had failed to achieve anything. He believed that the best way to succeed was through reducing their prejudice, and soothing their enmity towards Christ and Christianity, and to get them to look at the Messiah of the New Testament so as to form an opinion for themselves as to who he was; through joining with the Jew to acknowledge the splendour of the Jewish religion, and to stand for the authority and Divinity of the writings of Moses and the prophets; and then to draw them to look at the unity and consistency of the Old Testament and the New Testament – the way the one asks for the other, and the way they honour one another. And as for this great task, everyone must acknowledge that he succeeded to a very large extent; – he succeeded in getting an opportunity to speak for Christ to a people whose ears had been closed to everyone else, and to be able to write his arguments for Christianity in magazines and books which have a general readership and circulation among the nation. That was the start of a task which had to be done at some point; the future will see what will be its end.

★

Not every Methodist in Wales could see the writing of a book like *British Jews*, together with some other things the Missionary did, as Missionary work at all. The only job of a Missionary, they supposed, was to preach Christ and to get the Jews who believed the Word into the fellowship group in order to instruct them in greater detail. Perhaps they had not considered that not every group is as ready to listen to the Gospel as the Welsh, or they had not imagined the great work that would need to be done with such people until they can be got together as a congregation to listen. Those who complain because of the fruitlessness of his labour forget that 'reaping in joy' presupposes 'sowing in tears'. Some of the grumblers knew something about dealing with the soil: – What if someone had come to them, when they had been busy for weeks and months fertilising, ploughing and sowing, and had reproached them that the barns and haylofts were none the fuller for their labours and had blamed them for spending their strength in vain, would they not turn to such a one, and say that the work they had done was work which had to be done and was work which certainly, under the blessing of Heaven, would turn out successfully; and that they were now waiting for the valuable fruits of the earth, in good patience for them, until they received the early and the later rain? And yet, Mr Mills suffered complaints as unreasonable as that one. Because he could not refer to Jewish Calvinistic Methodists – well, perhaps not – but because he could not refer to Jews who had been convinced by and converted to Christianity, it was suggested that he was not doing any missionary work, or at least that it was very awkward and unprofitable work in the extreme that he was performing in his attempt to reach that goal.

★

Day by day, as regular as the sun, he went about visiting Jewish families; and he was so well-versed in everything which pertained to the land, to the history and to the religion of the Jews that he was completely prepared to take an interesting and intelligent part in the conversation, whatever direction it might take, and he almost always succeeded in convincing every Jew he met, that he 'loved their people' and sought their benefit. We could say a lot about his visits to Jewish individuals and families, the conversations that took place between them, and the counter-arguments against Christ and Christianity; but as they do not differ a great deal from the examples given earlier, we will refrain. The reader, if he wishes, can find many of those conversations if he refers to the Missionary's letters in the Treasury.

Apart from those efforts of visiting individuals and families, he had by now established a weekly meeting to lecture on Jewish subjects, and many Jews, apart from Welsh and English people, used to come together to listen. These meetings were held on a Tuesday, in a chapel in Grafton Street, Soho. Here are some of the subjects on which he lectured in the spring of this year: – The Call of Abraham; Israel in Egypt, and their deliverance; Jewish Education in Canaan; The Prophets and their message; The Babylonian Captivity and its effects; Jewish Literature up to the time of Christ; The Situation of the Nation in the time of Christ; Their Literature up to the Sixth

century; Their Literature up to the Nineteenth Century; Modern
Jews – their family customs; Modern Jews – their religious rituals.

Translation from *Buchdraeth y Parch. John Mills,*
by Richard Mills and Rev N. Cynhafal Jones, 1881

from PALESTINE

We should visit one synagogue, in order to recall one service in
particular, before we move on to another subject, as it is one of the
most remarkable things that has happened so far in the history of the
Jews of Palestine – we are referring to the respect and the magna-
nimity that was shown to the author on the occasion. On Friday, June
15, I was intending to go to the service in the synagogue of the
Askenasis. In the afternoon, my friend Hurwitz and I went to the
western wall, so that we could see it again; and from there we went to
the synagogue. As the service at the wall is exceptionally interesting,
and because I had stayed there to the end, it was high time for me to
be in the synagogue before I left the spot, and by the time we got
there several young men had come to look for us. The congregation
had come together, and the service was about to start. The service
was read on the left side of the ark, and on the right side they had,
out of respect for the strange visitor, spread a mat on a special bench
for me to sit. Next to me sat the chief Rabbi, an old man; but we can
enjoy his company in another place. The service began a minute after
I sat down, not by the Chazan, but by a young man chosen for that
evening only. I learned later that my friend had given them to understand that I was a musician, and, as on many other occasions to my
not inconsiderable discomfort, had praised me to the skies. They, as
a result, had arranged for this young man to go through the service
on this occasion, because he was an able singer. And he was indeed a
fine one compared to his brothers in general. He had talent in addition to a good voice, and if he had had a bit of education in the art,
he would have been an outstanding singer. I was paying attention to
him as best as I could, but not with the quietness of spirit I would
have wished. My position was too public. They were paying more
attention to me than to the service. In truth, the eyes of all of them
were upon me, until it made it painful. I would have suffered this very
easily if I had had an invitation, like our great Teacher before, to

address them and preach Jesus to them; but that was out of the question. There was nothing to do, but pay as much attention as I could to the young man going through the service.

About half way through, it stopped, and the old Rabbi called several ones to him, and there they were conversing for some minutes. The sight was a new one to me, and not one of the most desirable, because the congregation were looking at me and at the council every other, and when my friend Hurwitz came to me, and told me that I was the subject of the conversation, I felt myself more like one in purgatory than in a place of worship. But mercifully it did not continue long – everyone went back to their places – they had decided to offer a prayer for me, and before going further, here was the young man starting on it. And here is a translation of it – 'The One who grants salvation to kings, and dominion to princes, the One whose kingdom is an eternal kingdom, the One who saved David his servant from the edge of the sword of evildoers, the One who ordains a highway through the sea, and a path in the deep waters – may he bless, and keep, and protect, and help, and exalt, and magnify, and enrich to the highest degree our – John Mills; let his praise be exalted; let the King of kings, in his immortal mercy, grant him life, and preserve him, and save him from every trial, affliction and danger – Amen.'

It is difficult for me to depict my feelings at the time – they were extremely confused – after going to my lodging and pondering a while on the circumstances, my heart melted in pity for them. They had, indeed, honoured me beyond everything – praying publicly for a Christian minister! it was indeed, a new thing on the earth – but the thought that they knew nothing of the ideas and Christian experiences which are in prayer – the coming through Christ to the Father – caused me to pray, although far too coldly, for them. And I thought and pondered for a while, remembering how our fathers in Wales used to pray warmly for the Jews, and how that has now been almost completely forgotten, and I asked the God of all mercies to restore it to our congregations of every denomination. Oh how delightful it would be if the Jew were remembered in every service throughout Wales every Sabbath, every week! Who knows how soon the prayer of the synagogue might come to end not with Amen, but through Jesus Christ, Amen. I never had more enjoyment as I hummed the verse of the Poet of Pont Robert, than at that time –

O Lord do thou give heed
To those of Abraham's seed,
Restore their state,
The covering pull away,
From unbelief this day
Your vow do not delay,
No longer wait.

Translation from *Palestina*, 1858

THOMAS LEVI (1825-1916)

In Wales, unlike many countries, a Biblical surname is no reliable indicator of Jewish ancestry. There are many people surnamed Moses, Elias, Abraham or Isaac who have not a drop of Jewish blood and whose names are the result of the Welsh people's long predilection for Biblical first names, some of which duly became transmuted into surnames. However, in the case of Thomas Levi from Ystradgynlais, the surname is significant: he was indeed of Jewish ancestry, although he was brought up as a Christian and, actually became a minister with the Calvinistic Methodists. He was a prolific author, and he founded, and edited for fifty years, the denominational children's journal *Trysorfa'r Plant*, the 'Children's Treasury', which ran from 1862 to 1911, and which reached a circulation of 44,000 each month. It does not appear that he made any conscious use of his Jewish background, but I wonder if his ancestry had any influence on the following vivid passage, taken from *Trysorfa'r Plant* in 1875, which gives an account of his travels in the Holy Land and shows Levi and his party seeing Jerusalem for the first time.

THE FIRST GLIMPSE OF JERUSALEM

There are two ways of going from Bethania to Jerusalem, one going up next to us, over the Mount of Olives, and going down across the steep slope, opposite Stephen's gate at the top of Moriah, passing by the corner of Gethsemane, on our left, on the valley floor, and leaving the Tomb of the Virgin on our right, opposite the garden. The other way circles and avoids the high summit of the mountain, to the right, and joins the other at the Garden of Gethsemane. This is the old Jericho road. We went over both; but the first time, we went over the top of the mountain in order to have the best view of Jerusalem.

After passing the grave of Lazarus, we were keeping a little to our right; and before long, we saw the Church of the Ascension on the top of the mountain on our right. We were urging our horses on, despite the hot weather, and could hardly breathe for the over-whelming anxiety and excited hunger for seeing Jerusalem.

But as we reached the summit, suddenly, there was the whole city bare and open before us, and much closer than we had thought. It was around three o'clock on Saturday afternoon; a sunny, invigorating day, with the bright sun above the city to the west, before us, as though it was there purposely to illuminate the city so we could have a proper look at it – the same sun which hid its face at noonday when Jesus of Nazareth was hanging on the cross, between the thieves on old Golgotha yonder!

Everyone dismounted, everyone took off their hats, as though by instinct, and everyone stood silent and in awe. The men and the animals were as if they were standing to be photographed – had become instant images. The excitement was too much for an exhausted nature which had already half-roasted in the heat. But after a moment, when a rush of tears had run from our eyes, we came to feel better. It could be that the tears drew that so-powerful verse to my mind, 'When he saw the city, he wept over it, etc'.

Such a world of events flowed into our minds in a single hour as we gazed at Jerusalem. There appeared before us the history of Abraham and Isaac, David and Solomon, and a greater one than Solomon, and a greater than the temple, who walked through the streets of this city, healing its sick, teaching in its temple, and who stood on the flat summit of Moriah, on the great festival day, and cried, 'Anyone who is thirsty, let him come to me and drink'. I felt I saw his splendid person, and heard his sweet voice – 'My Lord and my God'.

I had seen many maps of Jerusalem, and knew it immediately from those maps; but there is no map that can show it like this. I could from this spot recognise a man standing on the summit of Moriah, and could count the stones in the wall. There are three great buildings in Jerusalem, and they stand almost like three rungs on a ladder: the Mosque of Omar – the best building in Palestine – in the centre of Moriah – the Church of the Holy Sepulchre, above it towards the west, and the Castle and Tomb of David, on the southern side of the city on the summit of Zion. The city looks ancient, built of grey limestone, on the rubble of the destructions of the city, without streets to be seen; only one huge heap of flat-roofed houses, abutting one another, and a kind of Mahomeddan dome on the top of most of them. The high, strong wall around them measures two and a half miles long, and has four gates in it: Stephen's Gate to the east, the Damascus Gate to the north, the Joppa Gate to the west and the gate of Zion or Bethlehem to the south. It is said that there are twenty five thousand inhabitants here, and most of them in extreme poverty. The city has been destroyed, it is said, seventeen times. It needs to be destroyed again to make something worthy of it.

The situation of the city is a very particular one. It stands in the highlands of the range of mountains which runs through the land of Canaan; it is raised upon small hills, and yet, there are hilltops around which rise higher than it, such as Scopus, the Mount of Olives, and others. And there are two narrow valleys, Jehosaphat and Gihon, cutting deeply around it, so that there is only a part of the north-east where the land outside the walls is on the same level as it; and it is from here that every attack on it is made. Previously, it was difficult for it to be taken by an enemy; today, with artillery on the summit of the Mount of Olives, it would not be possible to defend it for a day.

Yes, this is Jerusalem! 'The beauty of the land' once, and the 'delight of the whole earth'. What a trampling-place it has become for the feet of the nations! The surroundings of Jerusalem appear bleak, mountainous, and very poor from the Mount of Olives. Mountains and bare unshaded hills; narrow, dry, waterless valleys; earth without greenery; rocky outcrops rising out of dry, coarse soil; a few olive trees on the rough, steep, slope of this mountain, down to the dry bed of the Cedron, and the odd fig tree and the odd vine tree, like the people, struggling for existence, without anything to sustain it.

We had expected to see a more beautiful location, and more attractive views. Here there are no orange and lemon groves as at Joppa, nor any of the paradisal gardens of Damascus. There is not even the murmur of a river or stream to break upon the gloomy silence of the shadeless hills. Perhaps it is more fitting that way. There is no need here for romantic views. There is no need here for wooded verdure, nor orchards and flowers, nor the song of birds, in order to create interest in Jerusalem. If they were here, they would not be noticed in the presence of Zion and Calvary. Moriah and Zion, Gethsemane and Calvary, and the Tomb are more than enough here. The history of the world can be seen in Jerusalem. Yes, a history greater than the world – the history of heaven and earth! What city could stand comparison for a moment with Jerusalem? What nation can claim, like the Jews, that there had risen from among them three such great ones – a law-giver like Moses, whose laws today are the basis of the government of every land, – a king like Solomon, whose wisdom is a proverb through all the earth – and a Teacher like Jesus, whose teaching has enlightened all the civilised world?

Translation from *Trysorfa'r Plant*, Number CLXII, Vol XIV, June, 1875

EBEN FARDD (1802-63)

Ebenezer Thomas, known as Eben Fardd (Eben the Poet) won the important Powys eisteddfod in 1824 when he was only 22, with his poem '*Dinystr Jerusalem*', 'The Destruction of Jerusalem'. It was the start of his long career as a poet given to epic and heroic themes in what – as can be seen from the extract given here – appears by now to be a somewhat overwrought and high-flown style. Much of the poem is concerned with the military aspects of the siege, and some of it with the larger theological issues, but I have chosen the opening passage, which shows a picture of Jerusalem before the Roman attack, and which gives, considering the source material and the prevailing Christian interpretation of the events, a surprisingly positive picture of the Jews.

from ODE ON THE DESTRUCTION OF JERUSALEM[3]

Ah! Ruin! ruin in torrents – smashed
   are towering battlements,
And the gate-towers of the ancients,
Salem's foundations are rent.

So strong once, on the mountains – gracefully
   Soared her fortifications,
Her splendour ever sustains
This gem among the nations.

I go now to a clear place – I can see
   From the top of a cliff-face,
The whole shining city's grace,
its comings and goings trace.
Below, Jerusalem the great – at daybreak
   So beautiful her state;

The Chosen People

Her citadel and glorious gate,
The dawn's rays illuminate.

Canaan's sublime chief town – magnificent,
    Praiseworthy, holy crown
Of mighty gates and towers around
A myriad – not yet cast down!
Her favoured courts and thriving populace
Able governors, city of grace,
Her verdant slopes, glorious gateways,
Immaculate ramparts, O, splendid place!
Gentle, serene, silver palace,
Curious, joyful, skillful race;
Now from her pomp hard to displace – her,
City of splendour, I greet her fair face.

Above her walls, towers ascend to the highest,
And dwelling houses, halls of the fairest,
Hosts to be greeted, faces the cheeriest,
Active and swift in the houses of business,
They thread their way, with fair aspects, – through her,
And from her kitchens, scents of the best.

A glory of palaces, no place its equal,
And all its synagogues mighty, beautiful,
Her aspect embellished, sculpted, graceful,
Yes, so adorned are the homes of its people;
And all the houses are full – of Canaan's fruits
To feed the folk, and nothing needful.

Learned men in their honour,
Men of talent, walk through her,
This city, they expatiate,
They adorn and make her great.
The rabbis' and the nobles'
Good learning their aspect tells,
Behold, they follow virtue,
Great men, they seek what's true.
This city's resplendant stars

Are her truth-loving teachers.
Meetly, daily, they exegise,
To God's word they bend their eyes;
And study in the Scripture
True, strong, their tongue's deep law.

Translation from *Awdl Dinystr Jerusalem*, 1824

CRWYS (1875-1968)

By the time we reach the work of the Glamorganshire-born William Crwys
Williams, known as Crwys, we find a more magnanimous attitude again, more
concerned with understanding and explaining, and less with bending the Jewish
people to fit a Christian scheme. Although he was a minister with the
Independent Methodist denomination all his life, Crwys, a popular and talented
lyric poet, displays in this extract from a lengthy article in the magazine *Y
Geninen*, 'The Leek', a response which largely repudiates earlier prejudices about
the Jews, (although it does still endorse some lingering suspicious relating to
Jewish religious intransigence and supposed Jewish financial greed). Written in
January 1918, only a month after the conquest of Jerusalem by the British, which
made the Zionist project a possibility, it shows a predominantly admiring picture
of the Jewish people. One wonders how much the likelihood of the Jews having
their own nation had influenced the shift from patronising sympathy to admiration. There is a Welsh proverb '*A fynno barch, bydd gadarn*': 'He who wishes for
respect must first be strong'.

from THE JEW

Perhaps no-one has ever been hated like the poor Jew. Every manner
of man has spoken very slightingly of him through the ages. Luther
the Reformer said of him: – 'Know, beloved Christian, and have no
doubt, that you have no enemy more bitter, more poisonous and
violent, than the Jew – except Satan.' And then Lamb: – 'I do not
voluntarily feel any disrespect towards the Jew. He is a piece of stubborn antiquity, next to whom Stonehenge is in its youth. He is older
than the Pyramids. But I would not choose any too close intercourse
with anyone of his race and lineage. The Jew shall never be close to
my heart.' His history and tradition get the same treatment in legend
and drama, fair or unfair. It is true to say that things have changed

65

quite a bit since those critics declared their opinion, and that the children of Jacob have for some time moved victoriously from conquest to conquest, so that it is hard to refute the recent statement – 'that the Jew has conquered modern Europe in the intellectual sphere'. If we had to choose either side of the argument, we would give our voice to the latter.

To begin, it is possible to study and depict the Jew. Such a person exists; and when he is at hand, there is no danger of mistaking him. Anyone who is described as a nation is usually of mixed ancestry; and if one were to go into greater detail, very rare would be the pure-bred Welshman, Englishman, Irishman or Scotsman: but the Jew retains his particular characteristics and traits almost through the ages. When he inhabited his own land and country, his sin was too much intercourse with the native Amorites; but in the season of his dispersal and in the houses of his captivity, his weakness has become a strength. He has cherished his origins, and he has not impaired his particular characteristics despite wandering from land to land; and his faith today, like his blood, remains pure and undiluted. Yes, such a person as the Jew exists, and there is no device that can either estrange his hand and skin nor that can exile Galilee from his speech. He would be known in the most multitudinous Pentecost or Babel in the world.

On this side of his character, his history is not short of romance. Starting his career in a remote corner of Syria, he survived the captivity of Egypt, challenged the oppression of Assyria and Babylon, faced Greece and Alexander at their zenith, and then the foxy Romans and Caesars, to say nothing of his adventures in later periods. At times it appeared he was about to perish, and his memory be blotted out: but when these empires retreated one by one, the Jew rose like an apparition from their ashes every time. Then we find him breaking the yoke of the Turk, and defying the Teuton. He has lost his unity by now, it is true; but, despite his dispersal, he could not be shaken or conquered.

By today, he has risen to the highest offices in Britain and almost all the lands of the West. We saw him in Parliament the other day, taking part in some important debate; and we thought as we listened to him that the laws of our land today partly originate out of Zion. And as we watched and listened to him, let us not forget that he was oppressed, made anathema and scorned in almost every land and nation. And yet, despite everything, there he was, out of the fiery furnaces, having shaken off the dust of the cauldron, an ornament to the Senate House of Britain, and with the burden of its government upon his shoulders. It is, then, so true, the saying that the nature of the Jew is impervious to fire, like asbestos, and that his blood is like an oil that refuses to mix with the more watery blood of the Nations; all his customs of life are today the same as when he lived in the fortress cities of Judah; the same is his olive-coloured skin; the same is his taste for ornaments and jewellery, with his shining curly hair falling like before.

[*there follows a history of the Jews from Old Testament times to the end of the New Testament period, and then...*]

So here we are at the end of the line in the history of the Jew. From now on, it is right and fitting to describe him as the 'wandering Jew'. There are many old legends by this name. Here is one of them: – 'One Ahaseurus, a cobbler, who had done everything to betray and to bring Christ to his cross. In the end, Jesus was sentenced to the Cross. On His way to His death, the Innocent weakened, and leant His hand opposite Ahaseurus's house; and would have rested if He could. His betrayer denied Him this, causing Him to quicken his step. He turned to the merciless villain, saying: 'I go, and shall come shortly to my rest; you shall go, wandering – and shall wander until the last day.' It would be foolish and credulous to take this old legend as the literal truth. But a wanderer in lodging and tent has been the Jew from that hour to this. In Spain, Italy, Germany and Russia, a harsh treatment has been meted to the children of the ghetto through the ages. In Britain, it is pleasing to recall that the Jew has found better days, especially since the days of Cromwell, who was indeed a true Protector to the Jew, opening up to him the gates of citizenship and every British privilege and freedom. It would be difficult to find a more conclusive proof that even the 'Christian conscience' can go astray than can be found in the history and sufferings of the Jew – the object of every injustice. For his sin in Spain, and Russia, and Germany was, not so much that he was a Semite in Aryan lands, but the fact that he did not embrace Christianity as a religion. And the result was that some of the most barbaric atrocities were committed in the name of 'Conscience'. Were not the German – and demonic – 'holocausts' a violation of Conscience? Unworthy of the Aryan, and the Jew, and of civilisation. This caused one person to remark that if the Jew ever deserted his faith, he would do that not to embrace Christianity, but perhaps Mohammedanism. I find that hard to believe, especially in the face of the great joy of every Jew at the British army's entry into Jerusalem the other day.

★

So, after a hasty glance at the history of the Jew, what about his main characteristics? To begin,
(a) he is the most unconquerable and invincible creature amongst men; and it is his religion that accounts for it all. He stands for his Faith with an almost sinful conservatism. He throws his arms around the one who made Heaven and earth and demands him for himself. He sets 'a boundary upon the saints of Israel'. Indeed, the Jew does not wish for anyone else to embrace his faith, for he fears that this would lose him his privileges. This without doubt accounts for why he has never gone in for missionary ventures. On the other hand, is there not something romantic about the fact that there are now 12,000,000 of this old stubborn nation scattered abroad in the world, clinging unwaveringly to the old traditions which are more vanished than the zeal of their adherents; keeping their Pesach with unleavened bread and sour leaves, and celebrating their Pentecost and their Festival of tabernacles in booths of willow plaited together in every climate and country; and also remembering the Sabbath on a day when he could as a merchant in Britain do far better. And it is not hard to understand the loyalty, because his is a Religion with its face to the future; and it is not likely that he shall desert it until he is blessed.

On the other hand, the Jew is not a proselyte. The dark continent will have been enlightened, and idols of the nations will have been shattered, and he of the faith of Abraham would stay by the seat of Moses, and would ask the founder of every religious system, 'Are you greater than our father Jacob'? Indeed, the conservatism of the Jew has turned into a source of cruelty towards his own people before now. Perhaps the best example of his anger at broadmindedness was his behaviour towards Spinoza, the philosopher from Holland. As a philosopher, and a student of the truths of life, it would have been hard for him to remain in the old Faith without weighing it considerably.

So, he had to change his idea of God and man, and the universe, and life. And in excommunicating him and cutting him off from the privileges of Judaism, the president of the Synod told him: – 'With the judgement of the angels and saints, we excommunicate you, we curse you, and we cast you out, Baruch de Spinoza. May you be accursed by day, accursed by night; may you be accursed sleeping and accursed awaking; accursed in coming in, and accursed in going out. And may the Lord not forgive you.'

His treatment of Moses Mendelssohn, the German Jew, was hardly more gentle. Scarcely was ever born to Jewish home a greater genius than this great, frail man. He acquainted himself too much with the philosophy of Plato to be persona grata to his people. Indeed, what could be expected of a people that can not look at a girl who has married a gentile except as one already dead, and awaiting burial. However, in looking at the Jew in the light of his faith, it has to be said he is perfectly consistent with himself: and in the light of this many of his faults disappear; and one can better understand even such a greedy creature as Shylock, and reconcile oneself to the fluent argument of Portia.

(b) He is the shrewdest of all men. When Montefiore argued for better education for his people, one Russian President answered, saying, 'Heaven protect us; the Jew is already too much for us.' Financially, he rules the world. On his death bed, Meyer Anselm ordered his children – five sons, to be faithful to their religion, and to add to their wealth as much as they could. There is the Jew complete – Religion and Riches. Like Shylock, he can make his money, and produce children as numerous as the sheep of Jacob. A short time ago it was said, that if he chose, he could, through calling in all the money he had loaned out in every country, make all the nations of the world bankrupt in forty eight hours!

It would be easy to multiply examples of his shrewdness and his quick faculties. Taking all this together, one could expect him to be the most contented person under the sun: but he is not. Through the years he has stood in yearning, pouring out his tears by the 'Wailing Wall,' in Salem like one who cannot forget the old, old times; and his tears shall not be dried by ought except the hope that he shall come once more into his land. This has been his sustaining hope and dream in every age. He hoped long and hard to once more sit under his own olive tree, and to ply his oar on the Sea of Galilee, and to tend his sheep on Moriah and Tabor and Hermon, and to rejoice on Carmel and Bashan, and to worship his God once more in Salem. For nearly 2,000 years, this confidence has burned in his heart, and tempests only fan the flame higher. By today, are there not clear signs that the old dream is almost realised and that the Zionism of recent times has almost succeeded in its desire, and that the sound of the striking of the old wanderer's tents can be heard in the ends of the earth? Until that day dawns, let the Jew take comfort in remembering that it is he who has given the world the surest of all the laws; that in the vessel of his language and ancient literature has been transported the treasure of Revelation in every age; and that from his broad loins have come philosophers like Paul, and Spinoza, and Moses Mendelssohn; and poets like David and Heine; and musicians like Felix Mendelssohn; and philanthropists like Rothschild. If this is not enough, let it also be remembered that a Jew, called Jesus, is the ruler of the world; and that if every Jew returns to his land, more than seven nations will grasp at His hem, saying 'Abide with me'.

Translation from *Y Geninen*, 1 January 1918, Vol XXXVI

REES HOWELLS (1879-1950)

This is one of the more extraordinary examples of Welsh religious involvement with the Jews, extraordinary not only for how recent it is – it took place in the Second World War period – but also for its intensity. Rees Howells was a miner from Welsh-speaking Brynaman in Carmarthenshire who followed a divine vocation to become an evangelistic preacher, a leader of the evangelical movement in Wales and the founder of the Bible College of Wales. However, the most remarkable feature of his ministry was the intensity of his prayer life, in which he and those close to him experienced regular instances of apparently miraculous answers to their intercessions, in healing and financial matters particularly. His biographer, Norman Grubb, recognised the centrality of this experience of prayer to the life of his subject when he entitled his book *Rees Howells: Intercessor*. To his credit, Rees Howells did more than pray when the details of Nazi anti-semitism became known. He campaigned and raised money to bring Jewish refugees to Britain, and his community at the Bible College gave a home to 12 of them; they had been prevented by the outbreak of war from doing more. Also to his credit, his approval of the establishment of the state of Israel is accompanied by genuine concern for the fate of the Palestinian Arabs.

from REES HOWELLS: INTERCESSOR

The next burden which came on Mr Howells was for the Jews. As we follow him and the College through their months and years of intercession for Israel, it is remarkable now to see the fulfilment of the first stage of their prayer in the actual return of the Jews and the establishment of the state of Israel. How little there seemed any outward sign that this would come to pass, when the burden first came on His servant. It reminds us that no great event in history, even though prophesied beforehand in the Scriptures, comes to pass unless God finds His human channels of faith and obedience. Prophecies must be believed into manifestation, as well as foretold.

The burden first came on Mr Howells when he read of the proclamation by Italy, on September 3, 1938, that all Jews must clear out of Italy in six months. This, coupled with the anti-Semitism then so fierce in Germany, turned his thoughts towards the return of God's people to their own land. He said at the meetings:

September 3. 'I have a great burden for these people, and I want God to lay their burden on me. The devil, through Hitler and Mussolini, is being used to send them back to their own land; it is the fulfilment of prophecy; it is another sign that this is the closing of the age. I am longing to help God's people to return to their land.'

September 5. 'In Isaiah's prophecies about the second return of God's people, he says in Chapters 11 and 12 that God will draw them from the four corners of the earth. That is just what is happening today. The Holy Spirit is longing to help them through someone. I want God to touch me deeper still with the feelings of what these people are suffering.'

September 7. 'Daniel was able to prevail with God in a wonderful way for the return of God's people, after he had seen that the seventy years of captivity were ended. We must have faith and believe God's covenant with Abraham that they are to dwell in the land, and not merely have sympathetic feelings for the Jews. God moved Cyrus, the one who had held them in captivity, to supply the money to take them back! He will do this again, if someone will believe Him. I firmly believe the times of the Gentiles are drawing to a close, and the Jews must be back in their own land when the Master returns.'

September 11. 'I think of the places of intercession gained for the tramps, in the village, as a Nazarite, for the widows of India, for a consumptive, for the missionaries' children. Now God is calling us to be responsible for the Jews.'

He then began to describe how God had definitely told him to be responsible for a gift of £100,000 for the Jews, and to believe for it. Days were spent in believing prayer for this sum.

A few weeks later, however, news came of Hitler 'throwing out' several thousand Jewish children on the Polish border, and the burden on Mr Howells increased. 'The moment I read this in the paper,' he told the College, 'a great anguish came over me. Nobody knows what this must mean to their parents. The Holy Ghost is just like a father, and if I were a father of children whose home had been destroyed, wouldn't I seek a shelter for them straight away? The Holy Ghost suffers like that for all those parents on the Continent. Unless He in you makes the suffering your own, you can't intercede for them. You will never touch the Throne, unless you send up that real cry; words don't count at all.'

As usual, when he had a burden like that, he felt that God would have him do something, and as he asked what he could do the answer came, 'Make a home for them'. Mr Howells had already bought three estates by faith, but the Lord was now to call him to a new and greater venture in finance. He tried to rent the home of Sir Percy Molyneux, a friend of his who had lately passed away. He calculated that he could house fifty children in it, but the owners were not willing to let him have it. He then tried for a larger one, which would hold 250. Again he was turned down. Then one night God 'whispered' to him 'Penllergaer', the name of an estate he had heard of but never seen; he knew that it was one of the largest in the Swansea area, and that the owner was Sir Charles Llewellyn. On inquiry, he found that it consisted of 270 acres, and that the Roman Catholics had made a former offer of £14,000 for the mansion and two fields only; so he realised that it would cost him nothing less than £20,000.

The records of the meetings for the next week or two speak of constant prayer about it, until, on November 26, he came right out with the statement: 'I shall buy the new estate, probably next week, and I am willing to risk my all in order to help the Jews'.[4]

★

Through the years of the war, the Jews were never forgotten, although prayer to God was mainly for affairs of the nations; for, as Mr Howells said, 'When the war came, He changed us from the Jews to the Beast (a name he commonly gave to the devil in the Nazi system), and said, 'Get victory over him.'' But it was after the war again, in October and November 1947, that whole days were given to praying through for the Jews' return to Palestine. Mr Howells said, 'We pleaded that because of his covenant with Abraham 4,000 years ago, God would take His people back to their Land, and Palestine should again become a Jewish State.'

The challenge that came before the College was: if the Jewish people did not go back after the 1914-18 war, would they go back after this one? They saw the hand of God in the setting up of a United Nations Committee to consider the question of Palestine. There was thanksgiving when the news was published that Britain was going to evacuate the country. On eleven different days during those two months, prayer was concentrated on the coming United Nations vote. It was touch and go. On the day of voting, November 27, 1947, there was much prayer, but the news came that the partitioning of Palestine had not been carried. The College went back to intense prayer, during which they saw in faith 'God's angels influencing those men in the United Nations conference in New York to work on behalf of God's people', and had full assurance of victory. When, next day, the news came that the United Nations had passed the partitioning of Palestine by 33 votes to 13, and that the State of Israel was a fact, the College acclaimed it with rejoicing as 'one of the greatest days for the Holy Ghost in the history of these 2,000 years. During all those centuries there wasn't a single sign that the country was to be given back to the Jews, who were scattered all over the earth, but now, 4,000 years after His covenant with Abraham, He has gathered all the nations together and made them give much of the land of Palestine back to them.'

One unusual ray of light was also given to Mr Howells at that time concerning the Arabs. He said: 'God put me aside for some days to reveal the position of the Arabs. In *Genesis* 16: 12, God says of Ishmael that 'he shall dwell in the presence of all his brethren.' This is the problem. Does God mean the Arabs to dwell with the Jews? Abraham loved Ishmael and wanted him to have the inheritance; and God, who means what He says, declared: 'I have blessed him.' The Arabs only worship the One God. Did God mean them to be blessed as well as the Jews? They will afford shelter to the Jews (*Isaiah* 21: 13-15), and will be the first to come to Jerusalem to pay homage to the King (*Isaiah* 60: 7). Just as we were only burdened for the Jews when we had to make intercession for them, so the Lord wanted us to have a concern for the Arabs also. They also are the sons of Abraham. Can the Holy Ghost bring in something which will break down the barrier between the Jews and Arabs so there may be a home and blessing for both? Certainly the Arabs are the people of God, if they are to shield the Jews and live in those countries which are to escape out of the hands of the Beast'.

From Norman Grubb, *Rees Howells, Intercessor,* 1952

GWENALLT (1899-1968)

Born to a working-class Swansea Valley family, David James Jones, known as Gwenallt, moved from Christian socialism to atheist Marxism, and was imprisoned during the First World War for being a conscientious objector. Afterwards, he pursued an academic career and became a university lecturer in Welsh, and later became a convinced Christian with the Calvinistic Methodists. His poetry, hard-edged and angry, with a burning sense of social justice combined with Christian conviction, is among the most important literary work of the century in the Welsh language. A passage based on his experience of a fellow Jewish prisoner in jail can be found in the chapter 'Conflict and *Shoah*' in this book. The following extract is from his last, posthumous volume, *Y Coed*, 'The Trees', which contains a large number of poems based on a journey he made in the Holy Land late in his life. This poem is not one of the best examples of his artistry – Gwenallt's use of a conversational unadorned style sometimes failed to rise above the prosaic – but it is a good example of Welsh religious interaction with the Jews. It depicts both an instinctive human and communal sympathy tempered by a reservation based on an ideological Christian position. As such, it is a late illustration of how Welsh Christians encountering the Jews have held in tension the two responses of affinity and apprehension.

THE WAILING WALL

There was nothing left of Herod's Temple
Except the stone wall at the base,
And the Jews in former times could come once a year
To mourn for the old Temple,
To sigh for the old Throne of David,

74

And to wail for the old glory of Solomon.
We could, as nationalists, sympathise with their ancient tears,
And admire their old Monotheistic nationalism.
But, despite that, it was they who crucified the Temple of His
        Body,
And although it was buried for three days in the whale of the
        earth,
It rose as the Church of Christ despite them.
In this Temple we have a High Priest,
Who tore the curtain of the Holy of Holies,
The light, joyful sanctuary,
Where the God-Man is a sacrifice,
The sacrifice is crucified blood,
And the crucified blood is atonement, reconciliation and
        sacrament.

Translated from *Y Coed*, 1969

NOTES

1. Bridgend, Evangelical Library of Wales, 1990.
2. A close collaborator with John Wesley, he was actually buried in the same grave as him.
3. The original is in *cynghanedd*, the Welsh strict metres. In translating it, I have kept the syllable count and end rhyme pattern, but not the internal consonantal harmony.
4. He did indeed risk all. He was only able to buy Penllergaer by offering more than a rival bidder, and the Home Office would only allow the Jewish refugees to be brought in if a surety of £50 was paid for each one. To meet these combined costs involved selling all of Howells's existing three college estates. In the event, although Penllergaer was acquired, only 12 Jewish refugees were housed before the outbreak of war made further rescue efforts impossible.

THE PROMISED LAND

In the previous chapter, we saw how the Welsh had long felt an unusual interest in the land of Palestine, and how this sometimes led them to a strong identification with the history and the future of Palestine and with the Jews who claimed it as their home. Those religious considerations spilled over into real political results when the British conquest of Palestine in the First World War opened the way for the Jews to return there.

Wales had a major role to play in this historic drama. When British troops seized Jerusalem from the Turks on December 9, 1917, there was particular and justified pride in Wales. Not only had Wales long identified with the land of Israel, but the redemption of the holy city had been achieved under the leadership of a Welsh Prime Minister, David Lloyd George, and through the prowess of Welsh troops, as the 53rd (Welsh) Division had played a leading part both in the military action which freed the city and in the victory march which followed.[1] The Welsh press gave considerable coverage to the event: the *Western Mail* of December 11 1917 led with the headline: 'Capture of Jerusalem. Another Triumph for Allenby. Enemy Driven Back by Welsh Troops'. It reported how Bonar Law had told the House of Commons of the victory, and how special mention had been made (no doubt with a view to Lloyd George's home constituency) of the Welsh role. Further on, the paper reported 'Rejoicing in Jewry' and carried interviews with Britain's Chief Rabbi and with Leo Joseph, the lay leader of Cardiff's Jews, in which they welcomed the news and its implications for their people. In the National Eisteddfod at Neath in 1918, the *Western Mail* sponsored a special competition for an English poem on the theme of 'Wales in the War'. One of the joint winners was Wil Ifan[2], whose heroic poem, in rather stagy blank verse, celebrated the conquest of Jerusalem. The following extract from the poem describes the moment immediately after the Turkish surrender, when Welsh troops break into a well-known hymn about 'Caersalem', Welsh for 'Jerusalem'. Hackneyed though it is, the passage still gives an idea of the popular conception of this triumph in Wales:

> The Welshman's lines curved round a stalwart youth
> Who, with brown hand for baton, gave calm pulse

To their full-blooded harmony, 'O fryniau
Caersalem!' How the walls made answer loud,
Frightening the hollow echoes of '...Akbar,'
That still clung to the ancient stones! The hymn
Drew first the children from the narrow lanes,
And then the old, upon whose parchment face
Seemed writ the endless story of Israel.
How could they fear a foe who sheathed his blade
In melody? 'Caersalem!'.[3]

The magazine *Welsh Outlook* funded by the industrialist David Davies, also carried a celebratory article on the capture of Jerusalem, pointing out the Welsh contribution and condemning the British refusal at that time to allow Zionists to fight for the Allies under their own colours.

The following extracts from Welsh responses to the land of Palestine begin with a Welsh episode in the promotion of Zionism, and move through some Welsh reactions to the capture of Jerusalem, through to later responses to Israeli independence following the end of the British mandate period.

SIMON CRAMMER (1903-1991)

The following article appeared in *CAJEX*, the journal of the Cardiff Jewish community, in September 1983. It tells the story of how Dr Theodor Herzl, the founder of modern Zionism, came to the Welsh capital in 1895 to promote his ideals. *Daniel Deronda* is mentioned in the narrative; the Welsh connections of George Eliot's novel of that name are examined in the next chapter. This passage, being a self-contained article, needs little introduction. It may, however, need a postscript: Colonel Albert Goldsmid, who is shown in this article receiving Dr Herzl in Cardiff, was later involved in a survey of El Arish in Egyptian Sinai in 1903 as part of a plan for a Jewish state there. The plan was abandoned after Egyptian opposition. The compass used by Colonel Goldsmid on that survey is on display at the Herzl museum in Jerusalem.[4] The author of this account of Dr Herzl's visit was born in Sheffield, studied French and German at that city's university and came to Cardiff as a young man where he taught French and German at Canton High School for 45 years. There he taught several generations of many of the Jewish Community until his retirement at the age of 65. He was an active member of the Jewish Community, particularly *Bnai Brith*. In his later years he joined Cardiff Reform Synagogue.

The Chosen People

THE DAY DR HERZL CAME TO CARDIFF

In the summer of 1895 Dr. Theodor Herzl, the Paris correspondent of the Viennese newspaper *Neue Freie Presse* and the founder of modern political Zionism began his diary with these words:

> For some time now I have been working on a task of limitless dimensions. Today I do not know whether I shall complete it. It looms before me like a tremendous vision. But for days and weeks it has possessed me, pervading even my unconscious. It accompanies me everywhere, haunts my normal conversation, looks over my shoulder at my ridiculously petty journalistic work, disturbs and intoxicates me. What will become of it I cannot even guess. Only my experience tells me that it is extraordinary even as a vision and that I shall write it down, if not as a memorial for mankind, then at least for my own pleasure and recollection later on. And perhaps, also, between these two possibilities, for Literature. If no action emerges from the novel, then perhaps a novel will emerge from the action.

Though he never claimed to be a prophet and was never regarded as one even by his most ardent supporters and admirers, his vision kindled the imagination of many kindred spirits among the spiritual and lay readers of World Jewry and, not surprisingly, among the oppressed and under-privileged Jewish masses in Eastern Europe.

In the second volume of his diary, Herzl records that in 1895 – only two years before the First Zionist Congress in Basle – he arrived in Paris where he met among other distinguished Jewish leaders, Baron Hirsch, Baron Rothschild and Dr Max Nordau.

Nordau advised him to go to London and contact the leaders of the Anglo-Jewish community to obtain the publication of his ideas about the proposed Jewish State in the *Jewish Chronicle* and the Hebrew paper *Ha-magid*.

His ideas were received with some caution and reserve, but it was agreed that they should all meet on November 24th at the dinner of the Grand Order of the Maccabeans, when Dr. Herzl would make a speech. It was pointed out to him that it was most important that he should meet a certain Colonel A.A.W. Goldsmid, the Commanding Officer of Maindy Barracks in Cardiff. Little was known about Colonel Goldsmid in Jewish circles at the time, but he was regarded as a person of some influence and most importantly he had certain ideas about the restoration of the Jews to their ancient Homeland.

Zangwill sent a telegram to Colonel Goldsmid in Cardiff inviting him to the Maccabean Dinner but he was unable to attend. Herzl was prepared to go to any lengths to further his plans and lost no time in contacting the mysterious officer in Cardiff.

The following day, November 25th, Herzl arrived in Cardiff. He was met at the station by Colonel Goldsmid who was wearing his uniform. Herzl describes him as 'of Anglo-Jewish appearance, medium height, with a small black moustache and clever dark eyes.'

Outside the station a small horse-drawn shooting brake was waiting. Herzl climbed into the brake, the Colonel mounted his own horse, and together they drove through the streets of Cardiff to 'The Elms', the house where he and his family lived.

During the drive they exchanged a few words of conversation, which must have been somewhat disjointed since the colonel changed his position occasionally, riding now in front now behind the brake. With a smile of satisfaction he remarked to Herzl: 'We shall work for the liberation of Israel.' *En passant* he explained that he was the C.O. of the Cardiff and District Garrison.

At 'The Elms' Mrs Goldsmid was waiting to greet them. Dr Herzl describes her as 'a refined-looking, slim English lady'. She welcomed him with a few friendly words and introduced her two young daughters, Rachel and Carmel. Herzl was made to feel at home immediately.

During the afternoon Herzl read out his plan for the establishment of the Jewish State. As Colonel Goldsmid's German was not very good the explanation dragged somewhat but eventually Goldsmid said: 'That is the idea of my life'. He could not undertake the direction of the Cause because it was political and as an officer he must not engage in active politics. If the Movement succeeded then he would leave the British Army and enter the Jewish Army. Actually, he said, he preferred to speak of the Israelites rather than the Jews, because the term Israelites included all the Twelve Tribes and showed Herzl the flag of Chovevei Zion with its insignia of twelve stars! In return Herzl unrolled his own flag with its seven blue stars on a white ground! (To an outsider this dramatic scene with its symbolical overtones must have seemed a trifle absurd in its setting of the drawing room of an ordinary Victorian villa). Nevertheless the two men understood each other and Herzl thought that Colonel Goldsmid was a wonderful man.

After dinner they were joined in the drawing-room by another colonel and a number of ladies and a little later Colonel Goldsmid asked to be excused and invited Herzl to accompany him into the smoking-room where Herzl heard the following remarkable story:

'I am Daniel Deronda,' the Colonel explained, 'I was born a Christian. My father and mother were baptised Jews.' When he made this discovery as a young man in India – he was born in Poona in 1846 – he decided to return to the people of his ancestors and as a lieutenant in the Indian Army he was converted to Judaism. 'My family,' he went on, 'were furious. My wife at that time was also a Christian of Jewish origin. We eloped and were first married in Scotland and later we were married again in a synagogue. I am an orthodox Jew. It has done me no harm in England. My children, Rachel and Carmel, have been brought up to be strictly religious and learnt Hebrew as small children.' If Goldsmid mentioned any more specific details of his revelations Herzl did not record them.

All this and the Colonel's stories about Jewish colonisation in South America sounded like a novel to Herzl. He was deeply impressed. The Colonel had visited South America on behalf of Baron Hirsch and had first-hand knowledge of the conditions there. Only Palestine, he said, could seriously be considered as a future home for the Jewish people. The devout Christians of Great Britain would help them if they went to Palestine, for they (the Christians) expect the coming of the Messiah after the return of the Jews to their ancient Homeland.

The two men then returned to their fellow guests in the drawing-room. On that very evening of November 25th the Austrian-Jewish pianist, Moritz Rosenthal, happened to be giving a concert in Cardiff. Dr. Herzl had written to him to meet at 'The Elms' and after the concert he duly arrived and played for the Goldsmid family and their guests. Dr. Herzl commented in his diary: 'Rachel and Carmel listened to the music in graceful attitudes. Here were two Jewish aristocratic ladies of the future. Sensitive creatures with Eastern features, gentle and pensive! On the drawing-room table stood a Torah scroll in a silver case.'

The following day, on November 26th, Dr. Herzl said good-bye to Colonel Goldsmid and his family and returned to London. He confided in his diary: 'I have grown fond of him like a brother.'

Herzl's subsequent activities and Colonel Goldsmid's involvement in the development of the Zionist Cause are now part of history. Neither Herzl nor Goldsmid lived to see their dream realised. Herzl died in 1904 at the early age of 44 exhausted and burnt out by his labours, but his spirit still broods over his tomb in the capital of the State of Israel, in Jerusalem. By a strange coincidence, Colonel Goldsmid died in the same year. I do not know where Colonel Goldsmid lies buried but his name is inscribed on the foundation stone of the Synagogue in Cathedral Road, Cardiff. Two thousand miles separate the two memorial stones, but their names are linked in their deaths as they were in their lives.

From *CAJEX*, Vol 33, No. 3, September 1983

T. ap SIMON[5]

The monthly journal *Cymru* was set up in 1891 by O.M. Edwards, who edited it until his death in 1920. The magazine was only one of the numerous influential projects begun and sustained by Edwards, an educationalist and author who was an indefatigable promoter of every aspect of Welsh culture. We will have the opportunity to consider his career in the chapter on 'Conflict and *Shoah*', when we examine some surprisingly credulous and prejudiced remarks he published about the Jews in 1889. However, the following passages show him publishing two very positive views of the Jews two decades later. They are from a contributor to *Cymru* in 1918, T. ap Simon, who was a serving officer in Palestine at the time and who had taken part in the Jerusalem campaign. They express admiration for the achievement of the early Zionist colonists in Israel, an appreciation of the legacy of Jewish culture and religion to the world, a repudiation of antisemitism, and a hope that the Zionist project aided by the British army and its Welsh soldiers, will succeed.

The first article was written when British forces had just forced their way into Palestine from the direction of Egypt, and it looks forward with a remarkably generous attitude to the way the coming battles will further the return of the Jews to Palestine. While the following passages display a laudable and high-minded concern with the religious implications of the campaign, it must be remembered that this was also a hard military affair and that soldiers like ap Simon faced very real dangers. The Turks were not going to vacate Palestine at the wave of a nonconformist hymn-book. T. ap Simon's own brother was killed in the war. The first attempt to gain entry to Palestine, the first battle of Gaza in January 1917, had ended in defeat for the Allies, costing the Welsh Division 397 dead, 200 missing and 2,900 wounded, by far the largest number of casualties of the Allied forces engaged. The second battle of Gaza, in April, had also ended in defeat and another 6,500 Allied casualties.[6] Beersheba was eventually captured in October after General Allenby had taken over command of a reinforced Allied army, and Gaza fell at the third attempt on November 7, clearing the way for an attack on Jerusalem itself.

The second extract (published prior to the above article, probably because of its likely popularity in the euphoric public mood surrounding the conquest of Palestine) deals with the actual liberation of Jerusalem. Both passages display and assume a familiarity with the Bible that seems very alien from the perspective of the beginning of the twenty first century. However, such a perspective was very much valid for the participants in he campaign at the time. Welsh soldiers from places like Bethesda, Bethel, Carmel or Bethania could hardly be ignorant of the historical significance of the landscape in which they now found themselves. Indeed, a chaplain with the Welsh Division circulated pamphlets among the troops, encouraging them to see themselves as modern-day crusaders, and stressing the Biblical significance of their actions. As these passages show, the historical and religious dimension was very real for the men risking their lives against a redoubtable enemy on the hard earth of Palestine in 1917.

from FROM GAZA TO BEERSHEBA

Now we had reached the threshhold of the Promised Land. Our rest would be brief, but let us get our breath for a moment, and remember a few things. Almost three and a half thousand years ago, another general called Joshua was on the threshhold of the eastern side of the land, with his intention, like ours, to possess it. If his people had listened to the Lord, then it is likely enough that the way we travelled from Egypt would have been their course. But everyone knows the history. 'Just be strong and brave' was all that was asked of them at the start of their campaign, and that indeed was the biggest and most important part of our work too. Is our host like the host of Joshua a chosen instrument to redeem the land from its Turkish oppressor? Is perhaps the time drawing near when the old nation will come back again to its land for ever? The old godly people of Wales used to sing so often in their missionary prayer meetings, –

> The prophecies will be fulfiled
> All the promises will be made complete.

And the return of the seed of Abraham to his land was a strong element in their petitions. If we have the privilege of preparing the way for the old nation to return then we will have done something to be proud of. And remember that young Welsh people are doing their part.

Between those who take every word of the prophet literally and those who seek to spiritualise every promise, it is difficult indeed for an ordinary man to know for certain what will happen, and especially what will happen in our time; but the centre-ground of opinion gives a strong basis for a belief that the Jews will return to their land and to their privileges as an independent nation. Others insist that the promises were fulfiled when the nation was brought back from the great captivity in Babylon. But that does not satisfy anyone, especially the Jews of the dispersal. The effect of that was partial and imperfect at best. When it happened, the success and independence of the nation was brief. The definite promise of a permanent return runs through all the prophecies like a vein of gold. The returns which have taken place in the history of the nation do not correspond to the richness of the promises. What do you make of a promise like this: 'And He shall raise up a banner for the nations and shall gather the scattered ones of Israel and shall collect the wanderers of Judah from the four corners of the earth,'? (*Isaiah*, xi, 12) That has not yet been fulfiled. And as God is never less than his word we have a strong reason to hope that we will see Palestine a land full of Jews who love their country, their language and their fellow-man. There is a great deal of enjoyment to be had from turning over the prophecies.

There are other signs which draw attention. One sign is the awakening there has been in the Jewish world during the last fifty years: and one of the most obvious fruits of that awakening is the comparatively recent movement known as Zionism. This movement is full of all kinds of hopes about the future of the nation and the land. The war has brought it into the compass of practical statecraft. Its aim is to regenerate the Jews in Palestine through starting up agricultural and rural colonies. By now it has received the official sponsorship of the British Government, which means that Zionism has been made one of the nations' war aims. Mr Lloyd George said that 'the national rights of Palestine must be recognised', and that means, whatever may be decided in a peace conference about the land's political future, Britain will make sure that the words of Mr Lloyd George and the promise of Mr Balfour on November 2 are fulfiled.

Now, the question which arises is this – Are the Jews ready to justify their right to a national home in the old land? Can they work together and continue together in unity? Zionism has arisen to answer that question. The movement's greatest motive was the Jews' instinctive opposition to letting their nation be swallowed by the nations among whom they dwell. We Welsh can sympathise with a

feeling like that. It is interesting that Michael D. Jones, round about
the time that the Jewish Awakening began, was working hard to send
the first party in the *Mimosa* to Patagonia.[7] As far back as 1862 (the
Mimosa set off in 1865) a German Jew called Moses Hess published
a book called *Rome und Jerusalem* in which he bitterly exposed the
tendency which was flourishing among his brethren to assimilate
with the nations; he preached the essential nationhood of the Jew and
foretold the re-establishment of a national state under the patronage
of the French. A little later, a Russian Jew did similar work and
stressed the importance of Palestine as a centre, and the resurrection
of Hebrew as an indispensable matter. In 1870 the dream started to
be made into reality. An agricultural college was set up in Joppa and
an agricultural colony in Galilee. A little later, the Jews of Jerusalem
started a small colony they called the 'Door of Hope' on the banks of
the river Audja.

But it was the persecution and cruelties in Russia in 1880-81 that
was the greatest spur for the Zionist movement. The societies of the
'Lovers of Zion' were established in Russia, and they were a great
help in strengthening the young colonies that were growing in
Palestine. By 1895 there were around twenty of them. The movement
and its ideals took an increasing hold on the Jews scattered in every
land. A Viennese Jew called Herzl caused some controversy by
arguing that something 'big' was needed, something that would earn
recognition from the great nations: a strong establishment in a new
country with enough space to develop: not small colonies here and
there across the land of Palestine. This disturbed the Zionist movement considerably for some time, but in 1897, in a Zionist Congress
in Basle, Herzl's ideals were rejected and it was decided to keep the
movement within its former limits. Some secular Jews and some of
the millionaires are still siding with Herzl, but the large majority of
Jews in every land are in favour of the original plan. However, Herzl
had still done great good by bringing Zionism to the attention of the
world, and through his broad ideals.

When the present war broke out, the agricultural communities had
grown to more than forty, and the little 'Door of Hope' of the Audja
river had grown to become the largest of them. There are 12,000 Jews
in these colonies, and their chief work is cultivating vineyards and
plantations of almonds and oranges and crops of wheat. The muddy
land has been dried and made fertile. The work of replanting the land

with trees has begun on a small scale. In the towns, the Jewish population has grown quickly, and many of them are surrounded by extensive gardens. Proof of the revival can be seen in the fact that banks, agricultural colleges and experimental sites are being established to promote the farmers' work. A kernel of workers, who are also smallholders, is being formed. Problems such as local government, administration of laws, and self defence are being met ably. A start has been made on a General Council of representatives of every establishment. The Movement – the Yishub as it is called – is increasingly coming to realise its character and its national significance. One thing is sure to interest Wales, the Hebrew language as the mother tongue of the children is taking the place of the mixture of other languages in the Hebrew schools of all kinds which have been established, especially in the art and craft schools. The first steps have been taken to setting up a Hebrew university, and it is likely that it will be built on the Mount of Olives. In a word, there is scarcely an aspect of national life, except for foreign affairs, that the Jews have not ventured upon through the medium of the Yishub. The national life is flowing strongly, although within narrow limits. It has shown beyond all argument the ability and the determination of the Hebrew people to 'raise the old country once more', and to return the nation to its ancient home.

Considering all this, is it not a sign that Zionism is a medium for preparing the way for the return of Israel to God and to their land, the land He covenanted to them?

There are other signs. One is our presence in the land as representatives of Britain. There's no other country under the sun in whom the inhabitants put so much trust as Britain. Mr W.T. Massey puts it like this –

> Our soldiers get the most heartening welcome as they go through the villages. The women sit back according to their custom to talk and gossip while drawing water from the wells; they have no fear in time of war. Peace and security surround them. They all know that an end has been put to violence, oppression and theft in the name of military necessity; a week has made a huge difference in the happiness and contentment of the natives. They well know what British ideals of freedom are; the worthy conduct of our soldiers has intensified the idea they had about Britain's work for the sake of civilisation.

We do not have to rely upon other signs, such as the inexhaustible marvel of the survival of the identity of the Jew in every land, in every age and through every kind of oppression and cruelty. We are too apt to believe that the Jew's home is in the world of commerce, wealth and materialism. There was never a greater mistake. The truth is that the intellectual world is his appropriate domain. Religion, ethics, ideals – those are his affairs. It is still true that 'his is the adoption, the glory, the covenants, the giving of the law, and the service and the promises.' This is his inheritance and his legacy in the world, whether under the shadow of a curse or the sunshine of blessing. Even his corruption has been of more benefit to the world than the success of many a country. The majority of Jews in every land are poor, and their millionaires are only a minority. It is true that there are some important blemishes in their character – deception, profiteering – but what but the merciless oppression of the nations was responsible for much of that? Zangwill gives a charming description of their brotherhood, their equality, their childlikeness and their innocence in their ghettos. What of them, in every land from far Siberia to the far west of America? It is simply this, that there is an instinct in the depths of the soul of every Jew for return. Not in vain does God place this instinct in the bosom of the impoverished Jews – his covenant people. And perhaps we can cherish the hope that the ancient nation shall be regenerated in Palestine, perhaps in our own time. In that idea there is nothing contrary to the ideas of those who believe that a restoration of God's Kingdom of earth is intended by the promises. The two ideas can co-exist without tension.

With thoughts of that kind, we face the splendid adventure to which we have been called. That other general was a worthy man, an unrivalled leader, who feared God, and feared nothing else. Is it just a coincidence that our general is a man of that kind? Perhaps that fact is a sign.

Translation from *Cymru*, June 1918

from CAPTURING JERUSALEM

December 8. It was decided that our final attack should take place today. The Welsh Detachment, together with the cavalry who had been with them while in Birseba, had moved in the direction of Hebron since the fourth. They were not opposed, and by the sixth the column was ten miles north of Hebron. The infantry were to reach Bethlehem by the seventh. By the dawn of the eighth we had a line of men three miles south of Jerusalem. It poured down on the seventh; mist arose on the mountains, and our supplies were threatened because the roads had been made impassable by the rain. Because of this, it was very difficult to surround the city, but by the afternoon of the eighth, the London Regiment had reached two miles from the north of Jerusalem. The London men, fair play to them, performed with great valour. On the ninth they were four miles to the north while a Welsh regiment took up position in the direction of Jericho on the eastern side of Jerusalem. In this way the holy city was surrounded without being damaged. She escaped, like Hebron and Bethlehem, dear and sacred names, without any damage at all. At midday on the ninth the mayor of the city sent messengers to us to arrange for the city to be surrendered to us.

December 10. The first and most important part of our campaign has concluded successfully. Through the actions of the last few days we have taken 12,000 prisoners, a hundred big guns, a huge amount of machine guns and around twenty million pieces of ammunition for guns and a quarter of a million cannon shells. Our losses, to compare with those of the enemy, are only very light. The strategy of our shrewd general is to be thanked for that.

Today we took official possession of the city. I wonder if there has ever been in the history of the world a conqueror more unassuming, humble and respectful of his enemies than our general?

JERUSALEM, December 11. The oppression of the Turk which has persisted unbrokenly for four hundred years is over. Midday today, with a representation of around 150 of our army, and to their tremendous honour, a party of Welsh among them, and in the most prominent place;[8] and with representatives also of the French, the Italians, the Americans, and the Mohammedans in India, the general went in through the Acre gate, not on horses, not with pomp and ceremony, but with the most fitting simplicity, on foot. A dignified spectacle, worthy of Great Britain and of every high ideal for which Britain stands.

★

The land has had terrible losses through the war; but it has also received several benefits as well. Instead of the old roads that were no better than narrow tracks, there is now a network of hard and broad roads, and of railways, connecting every part of the land with one another, and with Syria and Egypt. The swift advance of the British saved the whole land of Judea; there is every reason to hope that Samaria and Galilee will be saved in the same way and with similar energy. That would mean the exceptional success of the 'colonies' would be an earnest of the similar success of the whole land, and that the Jew will once again be seen dwelling under his own vine and under his own fig tree. Our soldiers liked being billeted in these colonies, with their cosy, clean houses; the fruit gardens were very delightful to us after marching through rough places. They are very different to the mud houses of the Arabs. The colours of the East and the bright glare of the sun impart an enchantment to everything. It is a good sign that the Synagogue is the most prominent place in every town and village.

But the signs of war damage can be seen. Everywhere is full of refugees from Joppa and Jerusalem. You cannot find a farmer who has not lost property, horses, agricultural equipment or a market, or whose wife has not lost all her poultry. In many a colony one can see that the forest of olive trees has been destroyed – the fruits of years of planting, watching and hoping rendered vain in a single day.

It is the brotherly love of the Jew which is the explanation of the success of the colonies. They have a proverb that 'all Israel is responsible one for another.' They have lived according to this principle since the start of this war. Under the inspiration of that principle the rich Jew extends help to the man who is in his debt. All the resources of the colony have been handed over to the hands of the Institute's Governing Council to be used for the benefit of the inhabitants of the village; and the people of the surrounding area take part by sheltering and feeding the refugees. The gentleness and the care of that first prophet for the poor and those in danger of dying has come to the surface four thousand years since the law was laid down. Perhaps this enlightened age has something to learn from Moses yet.

Everything portends a fine future for the land after the war. The

Utopia of the prophets will be seen as a fact before long in Palestine. The Hebrew schools are alive, and the Hebrew language is being taught despite the opposition of the atheists and the millionaires. The local government, similar to our parish and town councils, is an obvious success. The Jew has proved, before the world, his ability and his suitability to form a national life. Hail to him, and may he succeed.

Translated from *Cymru*, 54, No 323, June, 1918

DAVID LLOYD GEORGE (1863-1945)

The greatest Welsh politician in history, Welsh-speaking David Lloyd George rose from humble origins in north west Wales to become first a radical reforming Chancellor of the Exchequer, then the British Prime Minister credited with winning the First World War, and finally an international statesman who helped draw up the Versailles peace treaty.

It is interesting to note in passing that before the First World War, Lloyd George had been involved in what was probably the last time a supposed Jewish conspiracy became a major *cause célèbre* in British public life. This was the Marconi Affair of 1912, when, as Chancellor of the Exchequer, Lloyd George was accused of what would now be called 'insider dealing'. He and the Jewish Attorney General, Rufus Isaacs, bought shares in the American Marconi Company on the advice of Isaac's brother Godfrey, who was a director of the company. This was shortly before the British Marconi Company was given an exceedingly lucrative wireless telegraphy contract by the British government, and the Chancellor was very quickly accused of having profited by inside knowledge of the deal. As Kenneth O. Morgan details in his book *Lloyd George*, while Rufus Isaacs made a handsome profit on the deal, the Welshman actually lost money. However, the affair brought highly damaging criticism on to the Government at a critical time, and certain sections of the press were happy to point out that two of the three 'conspirators' were Jews. Northcliffe in the *Daily Mail* attacked the 'Welsh solicitor and the Jew barrister', using the racial origins of each as an insult. The neo-Catholic authors Hilaire Belloc and G.K. Chesterton pursued the Jewish conspiracy theory of the Marconi affair obsessively, and Lloyd George was lucky to keep his job. He offered his resignation and was only saved because the Government could not afford the damage that would follow from his admitting his fault. They made it a party issue and forced through a committee report which whitewashed the Chancellor. It saved his career and allowed him to progress, in 1916, to the position of Prime Minister, where his involvement with the Jews takes on a more significant aspect.

During the war, Lloyd George came under the influence of Chaim Weizmann, a Manchester chemist who had helped him solve a problem in the supply of chemicals for explosives. Lloyd George became convinced by the

Zionist case and undertook to promote it. One of his first acts after becoming Prime Minister was to telegraph the Commander in Chief of the British forces in Egypt telling him that military successes in the middle east were much required. The following year, in November 1917, it was Lloyd George who authorised the Balfour Declaration which stated:

> His Majesty's Government view with favour the establishment of a national home for the Jewish people, and will use their best endeavours to facilitate the achievement of this object, it being clearly understood that nothing shall be done which may prejudice the civil and religious rights of existing non-Jewish communities in Palestine, or the rights and political status enjoyed by the Jews in any other country.

It would be too much to claim that the declaration was entirely due to Lloyd George's altruism. It also served several war aims at a point when the outcome of the First World War was far from certain: firstly, Weizmann had argued that it would win wavering American public opinion, with its influential Jewish lobby, over to wholehearted support for the Allies; secondly, it would similarly work upon Russian Jewry and influence Russia to continue in the conflict. In the event, it did neither, but the declaration had been made, and following the Allied victory the Zionists lost no time in holding the British to their word.

It has to be remembered that a victory in Palestine was by no means a certainty. The Turks were tough opponents who had already inflicted humiliating and disastrous defeats on the Allies in Mesopotamia and Gallipoli, and Allied forces available for the Palestine campaign were not large. However, Lloyd George was determined to succeed, and he summoned General Allenby to Downing Street from France in June 1917, gave him command of a reinforced army and told him he wanted Jerusalem as a Christmas present for the British nation. The reinforcements contained a very substantial contingent of Welsh units, strengthening the already considerable Welsh presence in the existing British force in the region.[9]

A grateful state of Israel later honoured Lloyd George's contribution by naming streets after him and even by naming a kibbutz in his honour.[10] However pragmatic may have been the motives for the Balfour Declaration, there is certainly a large element of truth in the Welsh affinity with the Jews which Lloyd George, after the war, stressed as one of the motives for his support for Zionism when he gave his own account of these world-shaping events. The extract given here is from Lloyd George's speech to the Jewish Historical Society of England in 1925, which took the form of a vote of thanks to a speaker who had just given a lecture on Napoleon's attitude to Palestine.

PALESTINE

We have just heard a very fascinating and entrancing lecture, rendered all the more interesting and attractive by the mordancy of its wit and the brilliance of its phrasing. The topic itself is a very absorbing one, and I confess that there were a good many facts quite unknown to me, although I made a considerable study, at the time when Palestine was invaded, of the whole of that story. I was very interested in the passage, which I think Mr. Guedalla quoted from Napoleon himself, as to his conception of the strategy by which he was to conquer his enemies in Europe. It shows there is nothing new under the sun. His idea was to take Europe in the rear, attack Constantinople, then to proceed to attack Austria, at that time the most formidable enemy he had, as Germany was ours. That was the strategy that was successfully carried out by the Allies in the late war.

I am here treading on very controversial ground. There are three or four parties in the House of Commons, but there was a very formidable division between two very powerfully entrenched parties at that time. One was called the Westerners and the other the Easterners. I inclined towards the Eastern party. The Western Front was so very powerfully entrenched, there being only a very limited front you could attack, defended by the most powerful, force that the world had ever seen, in numbers, in formation, in training, in leadership (because it is no use underestimating your foes – indeed, Marshal Foch told me that the German army that invaded France was the most formidable military force, in leadership, in organisation, in equipment, and, in everything that constitutes an army, a very formidable and redoubtable force), that there were many of us who said: 'The weakness of the enemy is on their Eastern front.' Ultimately the Turk was attacked from Mesopotamia – that did not produce very much impression upon his military power. There were some of us who were very strongly of opinion he ought to be attacked from Egypt – Dr Weizmann knows very well the controversies that went on at the time – and that that would help to break him up. There was another attack made upon Bulgaria, with the possibility of a lateral attack on Constantinople. It ultimately succeeded. The Turk was broken up in Palestine, then the Bulgarian was broken up, and Constantinople was menaced. And then Austria saw she was to be taken from behind. There is nothing that demoralises an army more than the knowledge that something is coming from behind, while held by formidable foes in front. There they had to face the Italians, and when they knew that the forces of the Allies had broken in from behind, from Palestine, from Constantinople, the morale of the

Austrian army broke up, and when the Germans, who were the most formidable, realised they would be taken in the rear, their forces lost their morale.

And thus you see the Napoleonic conception, read out by Mr. Guedalla, was actually carried out by the Allies as a piece of triumphant strategy to win the great victory. We also made an appeal to your great people. Unlike Napoleon – let us be quite frank – our motives were mixed. It was undoubtedly inspired by natural sympathy, admiration, and also by the fact that, as you must remember, we had been trained even more in Hebrew history than in the history of our own country. I was brought up in a school where I was taught far more about the history of the Jews than about the history of my own land. I could tell you all the kings of Israel. But I doubt whether I could have named half a dozen of the kings of England, and not more of the kings of Wales. So that you must remember that was very largely the basis of our teaching. On five days a week in the day school, and on Sunday in our Sunday schools, we were thoroughly versed in the history of the Hebrews. We used to recite great passages from the prophets and the Psalms. We were thoroughly imbued with the history of your race in the days of its greatest glory, when it founded that great literature which will echo to the very last days of this old world, influencing, moulding, fashioning human character, inspiring and sustaining human motive, for not only Jews, but Gentiles as well. We absorbed it and made it part of the best in the Gentile character. So that, therefore, when the question was put to us, we were not like Napoleon, who had never been in a Sunday school and had probably read very little of that literature. We had all that in our minds, so that the appeal came to sympathetic and educated – and, on that question, intelligent – hearts.

But I am not going to pretend there was not a certain element of interest in it, too. You call yourselves a small nation. I belong to a small nation, and I am proud of the fact. It is an ancient race, not as old as yours, and although I am very proud of it, I am not going to compare it with yours. One day it may become great; it will perhaps be chosen for great things. But all I know is that up to the present it is small races that have been chosen for great things. And there we were, confronted with your people in every country of the world, very powerful. You may say you have been oppressed and persecuted – that has been your power! You have been hammered into very fine steel, and that is why you can never be broken. Hammered for centuries into the finest steel of any race in the world. And therefore we wanted your help. We thought it would be very useful. I am putting the other side quite frankly. We had had already very great help. I personally owe a deep debt of gratitude to Dr. Weizmann, and I am his proselyte. In the Ministry of Munitions, I was confronted with one of the most serious crises with which I was ever beset. It was one of those unexpected things that come upon you like a cavalry charge coming up against a chasm. And I found such a chasm. As I marched from gun to gun, from shell to shell, I suddenly found that we had not got one of the great motive powers to make cordite – wood alcohol. I turned to Dr. Weizmann. Alcohol had to be made out of wood, and he trained little animals – I don't know through how many generations – to eat sugar, and the alcohol was made out of maize, and then there was plenty of 'corn in Egypt,' and we were saved.

I felt a deep debt of gratitude, and so did all the Allies; to the brilliant scientific genius of Dr. Weizmann. When we talked to him and asked him, 'What can we do for you in the way of any honour?' he replied : 'All I care for is an opportunity to do something for my people.' It was worth anything to us in honour, or in coin of the realm, but all he asked for was to be allowed to present his case for the restoration of his people to the old country which they had made famous throughout the world. Acetone converted me to Zionism. So the case was put before us, and when the War Cabinet began to consider the case for the Declaration, it was quite unanimously in favour. I think we secured the co-operation of the French at that time, and the famous Balfour Declaration was made. But there is no man with a greater part in the conversion of the Gentiles running the war than my friend Dr. Weizmann. I am glad of it, both on the ground of sympathy and of interest. I was a very strong advocate of the conquest of Palestine. Some day I shall be able to tell the story of how near a thing that was, when we organised all our forces, took all our guns and munitions for the final attack with the idea of capturing Jerusalem, but the danger on the Western front very nearly forced us to take the troops away.

If that had happened, I think Palestine would still have been in the hands of the Turk. Because it is idle to say that in the terms of peace you could have insisted on clearing Palestine. The Turk has not retired from any country from which he was not driven before the armistice. He has a way with him of signing documents. Say to him. 'Give up Palestine,' he simply says: 'Where shall I sign?' Say to him: 'You must give up Constantinople,' and his pen is ready. The Turk will sign any document you can present to him and he will never honour one of them. The Turk signed everything after the armistice, but he has never retired from a single yard of territory from which we had not driven him at the point of the bayonet. If anything had gone wrong, if we had not stuck to it at some risk and insisted on the conquest of Palestine and driven the Turk out, he would have been there still – writing documents.

But I came here to preside over this lecture and not to make a speech myself. The Zionist movement is a great conception. But let me say one word about the Arabs. It is not our conception, and I am certain it is not the conception of the Zionists, that anyone should be driven out of Palestine who does not want to go. We have men of every race in this country – including mine – and it is one of the glories of the British Empire that it is an Empire of all races. It is not an English Empire and it is not a Scotch Empire. But you have in every corner of it a variety of races – in Africa Dutchmen, in Canada Frenchmen, and so on. There is no greater variety of races in the world under the same crown than you will find in the British Empire, and that is what constitutes the greatness of Greater Britain – it is inhabited, not by one race or two races, but by scores of races speaking hundreds of languages, not all incomprehensible like mine – to uninstructed people who don't understand them. That is what makes its greatness. And Palestine was never a land exclusively of Jews. Every race was admitted there. Now let that be your glory. Everybody willing to work with you side by side should be there, and any policy of expropriation or anything that suggests it will only make difficulties in the path of Zionism. There are about 600,000 Arabs in Palestine, which once held millions. There is undoubtedly room for a very considerable population there, and if the Arabs like to work there, why should they not? But that is no reason why Jews should be kept out of their country and not be permitted to fertilise a land, the topic of song and poetry – the very reading of which makes you think of the land flowing with milk and honey, of its beauty and fertility.

I do not know whether Napoleon promised it to the Jews. I listened carefully to Mr. Guedalla. I do not know what conclusion to come to. I am not quite sure what conclusion he came to. But it does not matter. I will tell you the difference between the Balfour Declaration and Napoleon's promise. An oppressed race has one vice and one great, very great, gift. The great vice is over-suspicion. They are driven to it. But one of their strengths is: they understand human nature, and when Napoleon promised them Palestine they knew how far to trust him. Napoleon never kept faith if it did not suit him. He promised Poland to the Poles, and Poland sent her best sons to fight for him. He never redeemed the promise, and the Jews knew he was not the sort of man to risk their lives for. The Poles were left in the lurch with the Russians after them, and the Jews were not going to be left in the lurch with the Turks after them. They are much too shrewd a race. I remember an old Governor of the Bank of England, a very shrewd man, at the beginning of the war, when we were considering Bills of Exchange, and when specimens with all-sorts of queer signatures written across them, dirty pieces of paper, but all covering great sums of money, were shown me. I asked him: 'How do you know which of these papers you can trust?' He said: 'I smell 'em.' That is the instinct that makes people know what signature they can accept. The Jews knew the signature of Napoleon was not of much use, but they also know the British signature is invariably honoured. We fought the greatest war we have ever been engaged in and lost nearly a million of our sons, and were saddled with a debt of thousands of millions because we signed a piece of paper to Belgium and honoured it. And the Jews knew that breaking faith is not one of the weaknesses of Britain. I venture to say that whatever party is in power – I care not, whether it is Conservative, Labour, Liberal, or anything you could conceive of – they would each of them say: 'The name of Britain has been appended to that solemn declaration to the Jews of the world, and Britain will stand by its bond!'

From 'Napoleon and Palestine,' a lecture delivered in 1925
to the Jewish Historical Society of England

T.E. LAWRENCE (1888-1935)

It is one of the strange accidents of history that two Welshmen were at opposite poles of British policy in the middle east in the First World War. While Lloyd George was making promises to the Zionists about the future of Palestine, Thomas Edward Lawrence, 'Lawrence of Arabia', was trying to realise largely conflicting promises made by the British to the Arabs. Lawrence was born during his family's brief residence at Gorphwysfa, Tremadog, in north west Wales, only a few miles from Lloyd George's childhood home of Llanystumdwy. This accident of birth was sufficient for Lawrence to enter Oxford on a scholarship for Welsh students to study at the traditional Welsh college, Jesus. It appears he made some attempt to acquire a knowledge of Wales befitting his position, although it would be misleading to claim that his Welsh connection went much further than what has been noted here. Nonetheless, as a curiosity of history, it is worthy of record, particularly as it allows us to take a different perspective on Zionism.

During the First World War, Lawrence, due to his knowledge of the region and of the Arabic language gained on archaeological expeditions, was given the task of promoting a revolt among the Arabs against Turkish rule in the middle east. In doing this, he had remarkable success as a guerilla leader and a diplomat. As his autobiography, *Seven Pillars of Wisdom*, shows, he had to tread an uneasy line between his loyalty to British interests and his identification with the desire of the Arabs for independence both from the Turks and from the Western empires. However, after the victory over the Turks, he became disillusioned with the policy of the Allies in the region, when it became apparent that conflicting promises had been made to different interest groups. The following passage from *Seven Pillars of Wisdom* shows Lawrence giving an overview of the pattern of settlement in Palestine during the war. He was not anti-Jewish; elsewhere in *Seven Pillars of Wisdom* he refers to the 'everlasting miracle of Jewry'. But this typically acerbic passage is valuable because it reveals that the land was a far more complex ethnic and religious mix than was admitted, or known, by many of the Zionists and their Western supporters, and because it views many of the early Zionist colonists with a less than idealistic eye.

from SEVEN PILLARS OF WISDOM

Mixed among the Ansariyeh were colonies of Syrian Christians; and in the bend of the Orontes had been some firm blocks of Armenians, inimical to Turkey. Inland. Near Harim were Druses, Arabic in origin; and some Circassians from the Caucasus. These had their hand against all. North-east of them were Kurds, settlers of some generations back, who were marrying Arabs and adopting their politics. They hated native Christians most: and, after them, they hated Turks and Europeans. Just beyond the Kurds existed a few Yezidis,

Arabic-speaking, but in thought affected by the dualism of Iran, and prone to placate the spirit of evil. Christians, Mohammedans, and Jews, peoples who placed revelation before reason, united to spit upon Yezid. Inland of them stood Aleppo, a town of two hundred thousand people, an epitome of all Turkey's races and religions. Eastward of Aleppo, for sixty miles, were settled Arabs whose colour and manner became more and more tribal as they neared the fringe of cultivation where the semi-nomad ended and the Bedawi began. A section across Syria from sea to desert, a degree further south, began in colonies of Moslem Circassians near the coast. In the new generation they spoke Arabic and were an ingenious race, but quarrelsome, much opposed by their Arab neighbours. Inland of them were Ismailiya. These Persian immigrants had turned Arab in the course of centuries, but revered among themselves one Mohammed, who in the flesh, was the Agha Khan. They believed him to be a great and wonderful sovereign, honouring the English with his friendship. They shunned Moslems, but feebly hid their beastly opinions under a veneer of orthodoxy. Beyond them were the strange sights of villages of Christian tribal Arabs, under sheikhs. They seemed very sturdy Christians, quite unlike their snivelling brethren in the hills. They lived as the Sunni about them, dressed like them, and were on the best terms with them. East of the Christians lay semi-pastoral Moslem communities; and on the last edge of cultivation, some villages of Ismailia outcasts, in search of the peace men would not grant. Beyond were Beduin. A third section through Syria, another degree lower, fell between Tripoli and Beyrout. First, near the coast, were Lebanon Christians; for the most part Maronites or Greeks. It was hard to disentangle the politics of the two Churches. Superficially, one should have been French and one Russian; but a part of the population, to earn a living, had been in the United States, and there developed an Anglo-Saxon vein not the less vigorous, for being spurious. The Greek Church prided itself on being Old Syrian, autochthonous, of an intense localism which might ally it with Turkey rather than endure irretrievable domination by a Roman power. The adherents of the two sects wore at one in unmeasured slander, when they dared, of Mohammedans. Such verbal scorn seemed to salve their consciousness of inbred inferiority. Families of Moslems lived among them, identical in race and habit, except for a less mincing dialect, and less parade of emigration and its results. On the higher slopes of the hills clustered settlements of Metawala, Shia

Mohammedans from Persia generations ago. They were dirty, ignorant, surly and fanatical, refusing to eat or drink with infidels; holding
the Sunni as bad as Christians; following only their own priests and
notables. Strength of character was their virtue: a rare one, in garru-
lous Syria. Over the hill-crest lay villages of Christian yeomen living
in free peace with their Moslem neighbours as though they had never
heard the grumbles of Lebanon. East of them were semi-nomad Arab
peasantry; and then the open desert. A fourth section, a degree south-
ward, would have fallen near Acre, where the inhabitants from the
seashore, were first Sunni Arabs, then Druses, then Metawala. On the
banks of the Jordan valley lived bitterly-suspicious colonies of
Algerian refugees, facing villages of Jews. The Jews were of varied
sorts. Some, Hebrew scholars of the traditionalist pattern, had developed a standard and style of living befitting the country, while the later
comers, many of whom were German-inspired, had introduced
strange manners, and strange crops and European houses (erected
out of charitable funds) into this land of Palestine, which seemed too
small and too poor to repay in kind their efforts: but the land tolerated
them. Galilee did not show the deep-seated antipathy to its Jewish
colonists which was an unlovely feature of the neighbouring Judea.
Across the eastern plains (thick with Arabs) lay a labyrinth of crackled lava, the Leja, where the loose and broken men of Syria had
foregathered for unnumbered generations. Their descendants lived
there in lawless villages, secure from Turk and Beduin, and worked out
their internecine feuds at leisure. South and south-west of them
opened the Hauran, a huge fertile land; populous with warlike, self-
reliant and prosperous Arab peasantry. East of them were the Druses,
heterodox Moslem followers of a mad and dead Sultan of Egypt. They
hated Maronites with a bitter hatred; which, when encouraged by the
Government and the fanatics of Damascus, found expression in great
periodic killings. None the less the Druses were disliked by the
Moslem Arabs and despised them in return. They were at feud with
the Beduins, and preserved in their mountains a show of the chival-
rous semi-feudalism of Lebanon in the days of their autonomous
Emirs. A fifth section in the latitude of Jerusalem would have begun
with Germans and with German Jews, speaking German or German-
Yiddish, more intractable even than the Jews of the Roman era, unable
to endure contact with others not of their race, some of them farmers,
most of them shopkeepers, the most foreign, uncharitable part of the

whole population of Syria. Around them glowered their enemies, the sullen Palestine peasants, more stupid than the yeomen of North Syria, material as the Egyptians and bankrupt. East of them lay the Jordan depth, inhabited by charred serfs; and across it group upon group of self-respecting village Christians who were, after their agricultural co-religionists of the Orontes valley, the least timid examples of our original faith in the country. Among them and east of them were tens of thousands of semi-nomad Arabs, holding the creed of the desert, living on the fear and bounty of their Christian neighbours. Down this debatable land the Ottoman Government had planted a line of Circassian immigrants from the Russian Caucasus. These held their ground only by the sword and the favour of the Turks, to whom they were, of necessity, devoted.

From *Seven Pillars of Wisdom*, 1926

JONAH JONES (b.1919)

The victory in the Great War left the British rather uneasily holding the Mandate for Palestine, charged with administering a region in which tensions between native Arabs and immigrant Jews were becoming increasingly unmanageable during the inter-war period. It was what might be termed a 'no-win' situation. Allowing Jewish settlement outraged the local Arabs, who feared – with justification as it transpired – that they would lose their land. Clamping down on Jewish immigration outraged Jewish opinion both inside and outside Palestine, and when this policy was enforced even during the Nazi persecution of the Jews, it inevitably earned Britain lasting condemnation. It was an uncomfortable position either for such an abstract entity as a government, or for the ordinary British soldiers charged with keeping the peace in the region. One of these soldiers was the sculptor Jonah Jones, born in Durham of Welsh ancestry, who met and married Judith Maro (whom we will consider further in the chapter on Welsh Jewish writers) while he was helping uphold the British Mandate in Palestine. As well as being a sculptor, Jonah Jones is also an author. The following extract from one of his autobiographical pieces shows how humanity and love can find expression even in such fraught and bitter circumstances as those of wartime Palestine.

THE VOYAGE OUT FROM INNOCENCE

The discovery of this worn-out old notebook certainly brings back that voyage. The first mention of Mount Carmel touches me, because later I was to become very much acquainted with it, there making many friends at No 1 Army Formation College, an educational establishment for undergraduates in the ranks about to be demobilised. There they were given a month's course of Liberal Studies to ease their return to academic life. And there I met the girl who was to become my wife. Courtship was clandestine. Judith Maro was recently demobilised from our own ATS, but as far as our army was concerned she thereby reverted at once to the hostile native Jewish population, since we were implementing our League of Nations Mandate, standing neutral between Arab and Jew and loathed by both officially. Judith and I were married in great secrecy at a charming private ceremony by the District Commissioner, Mr Lowe, who exercised the correct discretion that it was none of the Army's business and did not inform them. When I returned after lunch to camp a married man and announced to the Commandant that I had married that day, he was astounded. 'Who to, for God's sake?' he asked. 'To Judith,' I replied cheerfully, and his reaction was a prompt handshake and a libation, for Judith had indeed been a most popular member of our college community and nothing could have been as artificial as the non-fraternisation ban we were supposed to exercise towards those who had only yesterday been colleagues and friends in our own forces. Among the Staff at the College were Michael Stewart, later a Foreign Secretary in a Labour Government, Willie Hamilton the ardent Republican, and Huw Wheldon. The Commandant was an amiable academic, Allan Champion. None of us saw any reason to give up friendships we had forged with the local people, whether Jew or Arab. But the Holocaust was not far behind us. Many of us had witnessed in Europe those pathetic columns trailing out of the labour and concentration camps. As for the Jews themselves, they were determined that nothing should prevent them establishing their own homeland in Palestine. The seeds of the present Middle East crisis were sown then, if not earlier. The British stood in the middle and it was an unenviable task. When, in 1948, we decided to withdraw and leave the Jews and Arabs to fight it out between themselves, there was immense relief in Britain, and especially among the evacuating forces.

From *The Gallipoli Diary*, 1989

The Promised Land

MICHAEL FOOT

Following the end of the British Mandate in 1948, and the formal establishment of the State of Israel, the new young nation became the focus of a new form of secular pilgrimage. This extract from Michael Foot's admiring biography of the great left-wing Welsh Labour politician and architect of the National Health Service, Aneurin Bevan, shows such an instance. Bevan is here shown visiting Israel in early 1954, and displaying sympathy with the Jewish cause in the early years of Israel's independence.

ANEURIN BEVAN IN ISRAEL

He had been told that difficulties might occur in crossing from Transjordan to Israel, but when he arrived at the Mandelbaum Gate in Jerusalem, all went smoothly – except a new brush with the British press. A *Daily Express* reporter wrote in his paper on 5 January that 'under his arm Mr Bevan clutched a bottle of whisky – unopened'. In fact it was a bottle of perfumed rose water which had been given to Jennie after she had admired the delicacy of the flavouring of the tea they had drunk with leading Arab priests before crossing to Israel. Prophetically Bevan had said to the reporters: 'My mind is a blank, and I hope what you write on it will be interesting.'

Nothing he and Jennie saw in the Arab lands, however, could compare with the impact of their first experience of Israel; the meeting with a young friend, Yigal Allon, with whom they were to become increasingly affectionate and intimate, on his kibbutz in Upper Galilee; the whole stirring spectacle. 'For the Jew,' wrote Bevan on his return, 'the immediacy of his remote past is an intimate reality. He is living among places whose names are enshrined in his racial literature and they make sweet music to his ears. From Dan to Beersheba, he can now make the journey – Nazareth, Galilee, Jerusalem, all these and so many more belong to him in a special sense, for they whisper in his blood, and evoke memories of a time that was, before he was compelled to seek shelter in reluctant lands. When therefore the Arab says that the Jew should find a home anywhere except in Palestine he asks something the Jew cannot concede without mutilating his racial personality beyond endurance. It is no answer to say that many centuries have passed into history since the Jew was at home in Palestine. If he had been permitted the security of a safe home elsewhere, the answer might do. But, as we know, it was not so.'

He was almost a Zionist. Certainly some of his very best friends were Zionists, dating back to the pre-1939 days, when he had been on intimate terms with Israel and Becky Sieff or the late 1940s when Ernest Bevin had driven him near to resignation. Friendships could influence his outlook and it did possibly have an effect that he had no friend among the Arabs to equal Yigal Allon.

From Michael Foot, *Aneurin Bevan 1945-1960*, 1975

GWENALLT (1899-1968)

This short poem by David James Jones, 'Gwenallt', is the product of a Welsh Christian poet visiting one of the holy places of Jerusalem in the 1960s, and dealing with what is by this time a history of Jewish success over the Arabs in Palestine. Biographical details of Gwenallt have already been given in the preceding chapter.

THE WALL OF WAILING

The Jews possess the Wailing Wall
After driving the men of Jordan from the old Jerusalem:
The soldiers rush to it, and some of them kiss it,
This, the most sacred screen, part of the old Temple rampart
That was left when the Romans destroyed the city.
For centuries they have wept, and prayed and yearned
For the Temple of Solomon, and the city King David built.
And the priest comes there and blows the Shofar,
The horn of the ram that was sacrificed instead of Isaac on
          mount Carmel,
Every Abraham in Israel was ready to sacrifice Isaac,
Unhindered by the ram, to repossess the city.
Although so old, the history of the Jews is so alive,
Only a year ago was David buried in his tomb,
And three months back Judas Maccabeus conquered the
          enemies of his people.
There is no more need to wail at the wall, and to yearn
For the Temple, and for Jerusalem, the Zion of their Psalms.

Translated from *Y Coed*, 1969

The Promised Land

ELWYN EVANS (b.1912)

The following two impressive sequences of poems arise out of a Welsh poet's encounter with Israel stemming initially from his four years of service in the middle east with British forces during the Mandate period. This experience leads to a love affair with a Jewish girl, to a concern with both Arab and Jew in the troubled condition of Palestine, and to a later return journey to Israel where these issues are sympathetically explored from a recognisably Welsh perspective. The author was the eldest son of Wil Ifan, one of whose poems is given in the final section of this book and an extract from whose work describing the capture of Jerusalem was quoted in the introduction to this chapter. The poems are self-explanatory; suffice it to say that they are among the best Welsh literary treatments of the subject of Israel that I have found.

JERUSALEM DIVIDED

Summer
The Voice of the City:

I am called the City of Peace. I lie like a gem
In the hollow between two bare breasts. And through the days
There burns on me the lustful gaze of men

Which makes the hot air tremble. When evening falls,
A breeze down from the hill country gently curls
And in unquiet squares with fountain water plays

And lightly shakes my secret gardens' vines.
I am called Queen: on high-days countless times
They come to seek my face, the singing tribes.
But here's a different evening. A harsh breeze came
Upon the orange-stoned and grand Jerusalem.
My face is scarred, a crack-disfigured gem.

A Middle-Aged Jew:

The road snakes up to the high city from the strand
And the plain hills open up on either hand.
I remember the months when death squatted in them.

103

The Chosen People

A city under siege: our company tried
To reach it through the bullets. And they died,
Joel and she, peace to these in Jerusalem

And to the other hundreds. On a heat-harsh pasturage
Along the hillside where there was such costly passage
The tanks and broken lorries slowly rust,

And on the reddened metal I can see
the wreaths adorning vehicles just
as skeletal as they. What would they think, Joel and she

If they could see the city split this way?
Was it for this such gifts were made,
The glorious body of my love a sacrifice, a prey?

Winter
An Old Arab:

The door of heaven is closed, but between it and the threshold
There's still a flickering line of scanty gold,
Across the rushy western slopes, a yellow stain is rolled.

We rode across the slopes one time, and stayed
Among my father's servants while they strayed,
To lead as all his bleating wealth an endless pilgrimage made.

A lad upon the hills I heard the voice
Of birdsong rising to the azure skies:
For such an hour I'd forego Paradise.

I journeyed to Mecca so I might implore
That before I die I'd tread my land once more
But Allah did not answer: closed is heaven's door.

The Promised Land

A Young Arab:

I never saw the city more given to night
But its intestines are a riot of bright
Appliqué lightning which drags until first light.

The dun-coloured face grows harsher still and greyer
As it watches the alien race below the wire
There's a hatred there that's purer than gunfire.

My beggar's candle stammers a lying fate:
Thin are the arms that guard my son's estate:
And, mixed with mother's milk, he sucks in hate.

The wind grows cold that flees the naked hill.
The old men in their flimsy tents grow chill
And their shivering shanty children that a cough could kill.

But in the dawn of vengeance we shall see
The Arab peoples like one man agree
And rise and drive their enemies to the sea.

Spring
A Young Jew:

It's Sabbath morning – my bearded grand-dad's day
The Orthodox one. My little cousins obey
And dressed in black to synagogue sweat their way.

Their greasy locks of hair, their cheeks so pale –
In Israel! Aged before their time, they quail
And lug their ghetto with them – like a snail.

In Auschwitz too it's Sabbath. These don't ask why
Their ghetto's God did not descend from high
To save these blameless, pious ones whom hatred doomed to
       die.

The Chosen People

And it's us who feel the guilt! As though our great
Inexorable march to Eretz Israel were somehow reprobate –
Coming quicker than Messiah, before God could open the
  gate.

Someone had to act: if not God, us.
The Rabbi can say what he likes: he's out of date.
The Nation's saved through the actions of the just.

It's Sabbath in New York and London; where the exile thrives
And from his wealth to Israel gives a crust.
Just don't let exiles tell us how to run our lives.

It's the day of Sabra. As long as we're alive,
We will not yield an inch of ground. We've done with all
That Jewish cringing. From now on, we stand tall.

Another Voice:

And it's Easter morning. Like a quarter century past
We saw the clamorous lanterned hundreds pass
To seek the Holy Sepulchre and hear the sacred mass.

But different then. With zeal for God aflame
From forgotten village, from valleys with no name,
The remnants of Christendom on donkeys came.

And rushed without restraint into her womb.
Climbing the Hill of Sufferings they come,
and burst into the temple, a godly rugby scrum.

But these are cautious tourists that draw near
The gate between the old and new, and peer
At the silent armed men guarding heaven here.

I gazed at Olivet a day or so ago,
Its white and stony ribs, its scanty growth,
Remembering the prayer, the spears, the unkept oath.

But we, the Welsh, we keep a careful distance.
Between us and the garden, the barbed-wire fence:
A new scar men have put upon that back without defence.

So often here the crisis, so often famine's dread.
So often the ecstatic slaughter, the rape among the dead:
Burning of house and temple, and the marble stained with red.

And now it's No Man's Land, where weeds of hate grow free
And choke the heart, and grow a poison tree,
(Be far the bomb from this most holy place).

She's witnessed every tenderness and grace,
But bayonets now are ranged round Calvary.
How long, O Lord? She was called the city of peace.

Translation from *Amser a Lle*, 1975

RETURN JOURNEY

1
And this is the girl who decided -
Having had enough of half-living between two lives,
Between Howells School, God Save the Queen and the Urdd
On the one hand and on the other the Synagogue
(Her father under the eaves of a silk hat
Reading the chapter
And more of a shine on his hat than his Hebrew;
Then on the holy pavement of Cathedral Road
Mrs Cohen's chronicle
Of the undoubted success of her nephews in New York;
When the other girls of the Sixth were playing tennis
With their retinue or setting waves in their hair
On their Sabbath-less Saturday) –
She decided
To make an existential choice à la Sartre; and as
She was not irreligious enough to turn Christian
To put an end in a different way to a lifetime of translation,

Of suffering the many surreptitious glances and the gaps in
    conversation,
Of defending Charlie Clore and Sherman's Pools.

And now here she is with her serious, thin-haired lover
(And Mrs Cohen stealing a march on *hiraeth*,
Her cheeks dewy with emotion and champagne)
Ready to fly to an uncomplicated land
Of rather dubious Promise, and the kibbutz in the sand.
Good luck to her and blessings upon her bed
Because of her foolish hope and her cheerful pallour –
And because she is so similar,
In body, in face, in open sensual look,
To the one I saw, how many lives ago,
As through the crowds of Jerusalem her melting way she took.

2
An awkward soldier-man –
A man of book and lesson
I crossed over Jordan
In a high-spirited van
Our journey complete
Through the desert's heat:
Shouldering rifles,
Sweat on our temples,
Camping under hills,
Swift burials.
Leaving behind dust
And mistrust
And the vulture of silence
of the desert's expanse,
And the breast of this one
Was my Afallon.

3
When I was shaving yesterday there was a blemish on the glass
And in stooping and making faces to see better
I remembered suddenly many a whistling struggle
And the too-small piece of mirror I carried in my pack
When I prepared on light-headed evenings

The Promised Land

To meet her in Jerusalem and then
On the perfumed Mountain of Carmel.

The sugary smile of the Evening Star was less polished
Than the bronze crown on my right wrist;
My uniform was the colour of cream, crackling with starch.
I went to seek her past the pomegranate grove
Praising the strike.
She too wore the livery of the King of England –
A beautiful Judith or Esther in khaki drill.
Frequently we laughed at table, in that savoured twilight,
In the garden of the Panorama Hotel, with the strip of sea
I spied between the hotel wall and the perfect turn of her cheek
Gradually darkening, but without ever being able to match
The thrilling blackness of her hair.

About Wales and Israel we reasoned diligently,
And in sweet unreason talked about ourselves.

Strolling then through the birch groves
And the thousand long-shadowed pines
On every side of the great monastery.
In the branched gloom when we lounged
Her body spread itself like a pale white cloud, but it was
As solid as a ship beneath me: no sound
But our breathing, and the incomparable tenderness
Of her hoarse voice: sometimes, but seldom,
We heard the distant sound of the sea, billowing,
And casting itself on an unseen shore;
Sometimes
The close-by slip-slap of some Arab's sandals
On his tired way home to his little village
In the folds of the mountains.

She stirred herself at last like a lazy tigress
On the short dry grass or the carpet of rotten needles.
Twice there was a quarrel between us, and twice I wondered
At the symmetrical beauty of her haughty, sculpted face
And the uncontrolled swell of her noble breasts.

5

Israel at last.
'You'll notice great changes', said the taxi man,
It was a true word. Under the shadow of Carmel,
a shattered mosque beside the sea
And the door hanging on one hinge. No more
Comes the sacred shriek from the minaret
To the faithful in the slender overcrowded houses
Before daybreak: 'Prayer is better than sleep'.
Where are the godly old men? And the straight-backed, pretty
          girls
Swaying delicately in their black cloaks.
Where are the graceful youths
Happy-exhausted? Here in their place
Have come the busy immigrants from Bucharest and Vienna,
Hasty walkers. Their homes are beginning
To disfigure all my Mountain. I see them
Like chalk heaps along the fields of Wales,
On the second ridge defacing the gentle spot
I knew,
When Europe was on fire, made glorious by spring.

7

It was so strange to see the girl from Cardiff
In a blue, cheap frock not ironed too well,
Her legs brown and bare, and the hair on them
More apparent than before, and her feet in sandals.
But she still had the same manner of shaking the hair
From her eyes, and the same was the youthful awkwardness of
          her welcome.
She was expecting me with her husband
(Eager spectacles, bruised knees and big shoes)
In one of the wooden huts...incredibly ugly,
Of chocolate colour.
Across the wasteland either side of the new road
Blow dust and sand and the odd piece of paper.
Inside there was a table, three chairs, a Hebrew Grammar,
A double bed and happiness.

Not far away fields are starting to ravage
The desert, and their earth is starting to separate from the
          sand.
Two feet above the ground, a network of rusty pipes
And their hundreds of little fountain-heads moisten the land
And urge it to bud. By the gate of the kibbutz
A giant pipe is being dragged from a lorry
By men sweating quarts and cursing in an old new language.
The work of the brave and cautious
Crew who dwell here is culturing and enclosing and irrigating
And turning once more to garden and to a fertile sanctuary for
          ever
The land that was given to their fathers by their God.

But beyond the mist that rises to the white-hot heavens
The desert like the Arab is waiting its chance.

8
The voice of my beloved
Crackled to my hearing in the hotel phone box:
The tone sharper than I remember
Her English more accented. The next day
Her letter (on official paper). Rather curt.
I'm welcome to call and here's her address.

That night I reconnoitred the place.
After finishing in the College I walked
To the top of the mountain, with the breeze
Cooling my forehead; up the dusty white road
And the black stain in front of me, and the starlight trembling
          like before.
Arrived at the newest houses and her dark flat,
And her tree-filled sloping garden, and waited.
Then climbed through the empty pastures
Until I could see the moon at last
Lighting theatrically the noble remains of the pines,
And returning untidy and parched
To the sleepy forced welcome of the night porter.

But today, painfully clean, twice-shaved,
And in a taxi I go to meet her. After all
It is a special experience for a man to visit the girl
It had been convenient for him to leave when he left her country.
(And wise of course; kind in the long term.
It would have been hard, would it not,
For her to accustom herself to the Welsh Way of Life?).

Alighting from my taxi with my heart appropriately pounding:
Going to the door and ringing the bell.
An endless moment, and I felt rather than saw,
In a spell of blessedness, that her face bore a smile
Completely disillusioned, haughty, and extraordinarily tender.

Her hard, complicated look. How on earth
Did I imagine there could be anyone on earth like her?

9
When a man returns to his homeland
From wandering far and wide
He knows in fullness of his joy
Each hill, each valley side.

He recollects the hidden ways
The smooth slopes and the glade.
So do I feel as I draw near
The glory of this maid.

10
My one, my goddess, my delight,
My poison in my blood.
My open wound, my healing,
My oil for head and foot.
My gentle tigress, rainstorm,
My field of verdant grass,
My puzzle, my solution,
My heart, my Hebrew lass.

11

The sparks thrown up into the sky
By god of Greek or Jew,
So cold they burn, so far beyond
The thousands, and we two.

Two sounds that break the silence
With heaven's peace above:
The small cicadas in the trees,
The accents of my love.

12

That dulcet hoarseness I once loved:
And every whispered word
Is like the ninth wave's soft caress
On shingle seashore heard.

That hoarse impassioned night-time voice:
Its murmur comes to me
From far and near, embracing all,
Insistent like the sea.

It holds me in its motion;
I float upon its face.
Entranced, I plumb its gentle depths
And drown in her embrace.

Translation from *Amser a Lle*, 1975

HARRI WEBB (1920-1994)

The establishment of Israel and her subsequent survival, seemingly against all the odds, proved an inspiration for Welsh nationalists. If the Jews could overcome the incalculable obstacles on the road to their independence and the restoration of their language and culture, then might not Wales do the same? Details of Harri Webb's life and work are given in the first chapter of this book. In the passage that follows, from his verse drama, 'The Homecoming', which tells the story of Theodor Herzl's Zionist vision, Webb displays a noteworthy imaginative identification with the motives of Zionism. The whole work is imbued with an unspoken wish that a similar vision might be vouchsafed to, and realised in, Wales.

from THE HOMECOMING

HERZL: I know I am near my end.
My whole life is before my eyes.
I see myself as a child in Budapest, a young man in Vienna,
The smell of printer's ink and greasepaint, the excitement
Of deadlines and first nights. It was a good life. Then
Suddenly a voice spoke to me in the night
After a day of shame and anger when the mobs
Rioted in Paris, baying for our blood.
A calm proud voice. Once it spoke to me. Never again.

HER: Never till now. Your journey is done,
I have come to take you across the last river.

HERZL: You were with me at the time.
You kept your promise.

HER: And you yours.
And now I will show you how it will be with our people
When you are at rest.

HERZL: I know how it will be.
I know the steep lift out of history, the sickening lurch
Out of the fetters of sense, the giddy overhang
Above time, that men call prophecy, poetry, madness.
And I saw the near horrors and the far victory.

HER: You saw the Land.

HERZL: The Land so many nations have desired
And so intensely the ardour of their longing
Has parched her beauty. I have seen the Land
From the snows of Hermon to the sands of Sheba's Well.

HER: 'A pleasant land, a land of hills and valleys.
That drinketh the water of the rain of heaven.'

HERZL: Parched, all parched, cracked, salt, bone-dry,

Poisoned, cluttered with garbage, hatred and greed.
I have smelt the stinking alleys of the City
That men call Holy, but through the screeching
Clamour of the bazaars I have heard the ram's horn
Ring out from the ramparts of David to proclaim
The acceptable day of the Lord, the ingathering
Of all his scattered children.

HER: Open the gates
That the righteous nation that possesseth truth
May enter in.

HERZL: And I must die here in Austria.

HER: As he died who led Israel through the wilderness
And never lived to drink the waters of Jordan.

HERZL: I must be content then to come as far as this.

HER: I will take you a little further.

HERZL: Where? When?

HER: Years hence. After the holocaust. You know the place.

HERZL: I know the place. It's Rome. The Pope, the King of Italy,
How well I know the proud smooth travertine
Of the palaces where I pleaded, bargained, waited.

HER: Look closer, what do you see?

HERZL: The peaceful ruins, the soft Italian autumn –
And the Arch! The abhorrent Arch of Titus the destroyer.
Why do you show me such a hated sight?
For all the eighteen centuries it has stood
No Jew has ever passed beneath its shadow,
It stands under the ban of all Israel,
The symbol of our scattering as a people,
Carved with the spoils of Zion. Read those stones:

115

The Chosen People

      The Victor in his chariot, and the march
      Of a people into captivity and exile, carrying as slaves
      The plunder of the Temple, the seven-branched Menorah,
      The golden tables and the silver trumpets
      That were never to sound again. The curse of God

HER: Has been lifted. Look again. Look and listen.

HERZL: I see a crowd of people. I hear footsteps,
      The soft shuffling footsteps of a crowd
      Not hurrying, not dawdling, just people walking,
      A lot of people, walking like normal people.

HER: Walking under the Arch. They're your people,
      Walking as people everywhere who walk as they please,
      Under the Arch of Titus, which is now no more
      Than an ancient monument of a forgotten victory
      The living people move by the carven captives,
      The two triumphal marches pass in counterpoint
      Of flesh and marble. And the shadow of the Arch
      Is only a shadow, and its stones are only stone.

HERZL: And I am not there with them.

HER: You are there.
      You are there in the heart of each of them,
      You who planted a seed where there was only sand,
      You who fenced a field where there was wilderness,
      You who dug foundations where there was rubble,
      See, the walls are rising and the firm streets laid
      Where our people walk as they will.

From Ed. Meic Stephens, *Harri Webb: Collected Poems, 1995*

TWELI GRIFFITHS

Earlier in this chapter, we remarked upon the coincidence which saw Lloyd George and T.E. Lawrence, both hailing from villages within a few miles of one another in north west Wales, playing conflicting roles in the First World War settlement in Palestine. The following passage from a book by Welsh television journalist Tweli Griffiths based on his experiences with the *Byd ar Bedwar* series, tells the story of another remarkable coincidence, although its consequences are more domestic than historic. This time, it involves two Welsh-speaking women of a similar age, both called Susan; one, from Porthmadog, next-door to T.E. Lawrence's birthplace Tremadog, has emigrated to Bethlehem and married an Arab, becoming Susan Diek; the other, from Pwllheli, next-door to Lloyd George's home village Llanystumdwy, has emigrated to an Israeli kibbutz at Negba and married a Jew, becoming Susan Jablonski. Both then became caught up on opposing sides in the Palestinian *intifada* of the late 1980s and early 1990s. In the television programme recorded here, the women, who never knew one another in Wales, are brought together for the first time. It gives a domestic insight into the reality of life in the divided land of Israel.

THE TWO SUSANS

Before the end of the year, Susan, after a few weeks' holiday in Porthmadog, and some Welsh-medium education for Adam and Natalie, has returned to Bethlehem. There, in December 1991, she maintained that she was far more at home now in Israel than in Wales. 'I've had such a welcome here from the start,' she said. 'There aren't many foreigners in Bethlehem. They call me the British Girl. I'm pretty famous here, to tell the truth. But I speak Arabic fluently; no-one would believe I was a Welshwoman. Of course, the intifada has changed a lot of things. Before that, there were many more things to do, more places to go, plenty of fun. But I can't go to parties now. It wouldn't be right when people are getting shot. So we go to friends' houses. But I love it here; it's a completely different way of life – the pace is slower, like it was in Wales, probably, fifty years ago. I like to go back to 'Port' on holiday – to see my parents and friends, and to have a little break – but it's here that I like to live.'

While Natalie attends classes in the local Catholic school, Adam is in a private school – the best school in Bethlehem – and has an excellent education, according to his mother. Although Arabic is his first language, he also has lessons in English and French. 'The government schools aren't as good,' says Susan: 'We can send Adam to this school because Tony works hard and earns enough of a salary, but it's hard for other people. Wages here are quite a bit lower than they are in the Israelis' territory.'

In the Negba kibbutz, Susan Jablonski is delighted with the provision for her children. Rebecca and Tamar were born in Bangor, and Keren and James David in Israel. 'The kibbutz is a great place for children,' she says. 'It's completely safe for them here. They can move around the kibbutz as they wish; it's much safer than somewhere like Bangor. There are plenty of hobbies, plenty for them to do, and the education's good.' As we film Rebecca's school class, the children are having a lesson about the attack by Israeli special forces on Entebbe airport.

In the meantime, Susan Jablonski is looking forward to meeting the other Susan. 'All I know about her is what you've told me. I have celebrated several Christmases in Bethlehem over the years – sleeping out in the Manger Square and so on – without knowing she was there.'

The rain is pouring down as we go by car to pick up Susan Diek, Adam and Natalie. This is the big day when the two Susans will meet one another for the first time ever. Susan Diek doesn't often travel to the 'other side', and she is not used to mixing with Jews. 'We don't get many of them in Bethlehem. We're more used to Arabs. But from what I've heard they're nice people, you know.'

The other Susan was waiting for us in the rain at the gate of Negba kibbutz. Despite the wetness, the welcome was exceptionally warm. Not unexpectedly, when they remember their Welsh backgrounds, the first talking point was the weather. 'Make yourself at home, now,' says Susan J as she leads her guests in to dinner in the kibbutz dining room. This is where the population of six hundred have their meals. 'We share all kinds of things,' says Susan J. 'Sometimes, other people will wash my clothes, and I'll do the ironing for them, and so on. We work together for one another. Sometimes I will teach other people's children, and the other day I worked in a spa kibbutz up the road – like the Dead Sea, you know. I also work in the canteen and the Children's House.'

'What are wages like here?' was Susan D's question.

'Not like they are outside', was the answer. 'We get paid every three months for our work, and another sum every three months for saving or buying something big. Some things are free of charge, of course, like the food here, but there's a place to buy extra things like sweets and so on.'

Adam and Natalie were enjoying themselves wandering around the kibbutz farm, and Nir, one of the workers, was explaining with great pride that the cattle are milked three times a day. At the end of the afternoon, Susan J went to collect James David from the Children's House. She said this was the first kibbutz to allow children to sleep in the same house as their parents. Before that, they had to spend the night in the Children's House. Susan admitted that not everything was perfect. 'For example, if there's someone who doesn't fit in properly, it's difficult to tell them – especially if they are a friend.'

Over a cup of tea in Susan J's home, Susan D said she was not sure what to make of it all. 'The landscape's so flat here,' was her first comment. 'Everything's green. In Bethlehem everything's brown. And the way of life is so different; everyone living together and eating together. Terribly interesting, of course, and everyone appears very happy too. I would find it difficult myself, but perhaps if I lived here I would get used to it.'

The following day, the two walked down one of the streets that leads to Manger Square in Bethlehem, and it was Susan D's turn to describe everyday life on the west Bank. 'There aren't any pubs here,' of course, she said. 'So we meet in one another's homes. Food is pretty cheap in the market – fruit and vegetables particularly. The expensive things are things from outside – tinned food, ketchup – a packet of Cornflakes costs three pounds!'

As we are walking, stones start flying over our heads towards the soldiers who were guarding the square, and we had to take shelter quickly in a cafe. Naturally, our talk turned to the intifada. It started in a refugee camp in Bethlehem, one of eighteen in the occupied territories which were a home to twelve thousand Palestinians who lost their homes when their houses were seized by the Jews. In March 1991, as we tried to film the camp, a hand was put over the camera and we were arrested by soldiers. What angered our Jewish cameraman more than anything was that the soldiers could not spell his name in Hebrew!

It was quite obvious that the Israeli soldiers did not have much of an idea about life on the West Bank. I had further experience of their lack of knowledge and their lack of sensitivity. In Manger Square, I asked a soldier for directions how to reach the Lutheran Church.

'There's a church over there. Perhaps that's it,' he said, pointing at the Church of the Nativity.'It was terrible here during the intifada,' said Susan D. 'They shot a lad by that house over there. In his head. He died instantly. The week after in the paper, the soldiers claimed it was self-defence, that the lads had attacked them with iron bars. That wasn't true, but because I live here, I couldn't make a fuss. Another time, I was walking down the street with the children, down the steep hill by the market, and we were caught between the lads behind us throwing stones at the soldiers in front of us, who were shooting back. Everyone dived into the shops straight away.'

Susan J referred to the Arab terrorism which was making life dangerous too in Israel itself. 'If I go on a bus, I don't know if its going to be hi-jacked or not, and people are killed even on the beaches – as happened the other day.' She described how an Arab once grabbed her from behind in the old city in Jerusalem. Thanks to some judo training, she gave him a blow in the stomach and managed to escape unharmed. Susan J is a member of one of Israel's peace movements, and has taken part in public protests. The slogan of these movements is Land for Peace, which is to return the occupied territories to the Palestinians on condition that they promise peace and security to Israel. 'Everyone wants peace,' she said, 'but it depends what the price is. Some would be willing to give back the West Bank, but the policy of the Shamir government of continuing to build new Jewish homes there isn't a positive thing at all.'

The two Susans agree that the greatest problem is the extremism of both sides. 'You have people like Hamas and Jihad. They don't want peace,' says Susan D. 'They want the whole of Israel and everything – they want all the Israelis out. Sometimes they cause strikes in Bethlehem, and people are afraid. If they don't obey and shut the shops, they get Molotov cocktails through the window. But that's not everyone's feeling – it's just this small group which shuts the whole of Bethlehem.'

Arm in arm, the two walk in through the little door of the Church of the Nativity, where Susan D and Tony were married. These were their last words in the programme: Susan D – 'The place is very special to me. Every time I come in I get a very nice feeling. I wouldn't live here if I thought the trouble was going to go on for ever. I just hope things will be settled pretty quickly, so we can all live like we did four years ago. It was a fine life, lovely, safe – completely different.'

Susan J – 'Everyone wants peace. We have to start discussing around the table, and it has to develop into something. And if it develops into peace – Amen! Our children have played well together on the kibbutz. I hope that can continue.'

Susan D – 'It was lovely to see someone from Pwllheli. To have a chat, see how she lives, and her to see how we live. I look forward to us meeting again often, and her often coming to Bethlehem.'

Susan J – 'Our lives are completely different – like night and day. She's happy the way she is, I'm happy the way I am. I'm glad to have met her. She's a very nice girl.'

Translation from *Tra'n Teithio*, 1993

NOTES

1. It being the Holy City, General Allenby chose to make his entrance through the Jaffa Gate humbly, on foot. The occasion, showing the Welsh troops heading the march, is commemorated in a painting by Sir Frank Brangwyn (1867-1956), 'Entry of the Welsh Troops into Jerusalem,' in the National Museum of Wales in Cardiff. Begun in 1920 and completed in 1931, the painting was commissioned by the museum's War Memorial Committee.

2. One of Wil Ifan's poems can be seen in full in the final section of this book. His son, Elwyn Evans, served in Palestine in the Second World War, and some of his poems are collected in this section and, again, in the final one.

3. 'Wales in the War', *Cyfansoddiadau Eisteddfod Castell-Nedd, 1918*, (London, Cymdeithas yr Eisteddfod Genedlaethol), 1919. The hymn quoted in the poem is a well-known one, and is written from the standpoint of one who has finally reached the Holy City. Translated, it begins: 'From the hills of Jerusalem can be seen/All the journey through the wilderness.'

4. Also on display in the same museum is the concession drawn up in 1903 at the office of David Lloyd George for the alternative plan for a Jewish state put forward after the failure of the Sinai proposal. This alternative plan was for a state in Uganda. It was presented by Dr Herzl to the 6th Zionist Congress in Basle that year, where it proved highly controversial and, of course, unacceptable.

5. The author was a captain with the British forces in Palestine and wrote a series of articles, illustrated with photographs, for *Cymru* throughout the Palestine campaign. He was the son of Thomas ap Simon, whose obituary notice appeared in *Cymru*, in November 1919, (p168) and the grandson of Simon Jones of Bala.

6. Ifor Wynne Jones, *Wales and Israel*.
7. Michael D Jones organised the first Welsh emigration to Patagonia in Argentina. Seeking cultural and religious freedom, the emigrants sailed in a ship called the Mimosa and established the colony which still has Welsh-speaking families to this day.
8. The honour of forming the first Christian guard at the Citadel in Jerusalem since the Crusades went to a platoon of the Welch Regiment. But they were not the first Welsh troops to have occupied the Holy City: an army of 3,000 Welshmen, signed up during Gerald of Wales's well-documented preaching and recruitment tour of Wales in 1187, formed a major contingent in the Third Crusade which recaptured Jerusalem in 1192. (Ifor Wynne Jones, *Wales and Israel*).
9. The original force comprised two mounted divisions and the 53d (Welsh) Infantry Division, which was made up of three battalions of the Royal Welch Fusiliers, two of the Welch Regiment, and seven English battalions. The support units for the force were also Welsh and included the 2nd Welsh (267th) and 4th Welsh (266th) Royal Field Artillery Brigade; the 1st Welsh Howitzer Brigade; the 1st Welsh Field Company Royal Engineers; the 53rd Welsh Divisional Signal Company; the 1st, 2nd and 3rd Welsh Field Ambulance units and the 53rd Welsh Divisional Cyclist Company. Allenby's reinforcements included two more battalions of the Royal Welch Fusiliers and another of the Welch Regiment, (Ivor Wynne Jones, *Wales and Israel*.)
10. The Ramat David kibbutz, between Nazareth and Haifa, set up in the 1930s. It was visited by Lloyd George's daughter in 1954.

THE LANGUAGE OF EDEN

This short chapter deals with one specific aspect of Welsh-Jewish relations, namely attitudes towards the Hebrew language. As a people whose native language has been under threat ever since the first Act of Union with England forbade its usage in public life in 1536, the Welsh have long been sensitised to linguistic matters. As was shown in the opening chapter, in a bid to borrow prestige for their threatened tongue, some Welsh writers claimed it was descended from Hebrew, the language spoken in the Garden of Eden, thereby appropriating a nobility and lineage to which the more recent arrival, English, could never aspire. However, retaining the language while living as the next door, and entirely politically subservient, neighbour of the most successful empire and most widespread language the world has ever known, has always been an uphill struggle. In the twentieth century, those Welsh people who sought to retain and promote the Welsh language were therefore glad to be able to point to an example of a language which had suffered an even greater eclipse, but which had miraculously been revived. However, before considering the Welsh debt to the Hebrew revival, this chapter starts with the less well-known story of the debt which the revival of Hebrew owes to Wales.

GEORGE ELIOT (1819-1880)

It might appear to be stretching a point to include George Eliot in a study of Welsh writers. This would certainly be true were it not for the specific context of a study of Welsh relations with the Jews, for it is only in this regard that George Eliot's Welsh connections have anything more than curiosity value. She was born as Mary Ann Evans to a family in Warwickshire who, although they were working-class, cherished the memory of their descent from noble Welsh stock. Mary Ann's father Robert was so concerned to establish the truth of his ancestry that he had searches made in parish registers and paid the College of Arms to trace his genealogy and coat of arms. They found that his forebear Thomas Evans had lived in Northop Hall in Flintshire in the early seventeenth century. As George Eliot's biographer, Ina Taylor, points out: 'Robert Evans's children grew up with the belief that they came from good stock, with a pedigree equal to many of the gentry... This was the high point in the family's history they were all keen to remember and was to provide inspiration for some of Mary Ann Evans's earliest literary efforts.'[1]

So George Eliot, from her earliest years, had been affected by the sense that her ethnic origins were remote, alien, and prestigious. It is not too daring a supposition to suggest that this sense informs, at least partly, her creation of the character of Daniel Deronda in her 1875 novel of that name. Deronda is brought up a Gentile, but gradually discovers that he is really a Jew, and is inspired through his contact with the Jewish visionary Mordecai to recover his Jewish heritage via learning the Hebrew language and living in Palestine. The book, hugely sympathetic towards early Zionism, was naturally eagerly welcomed by Jews, and one of its most far-reaching results was due to the deep understanding it showed for the role of language in forming a national and religious identity. Its depiction of the value of Hebrew inspired Eliezer Ben Yehuda (1858-1922) to work for the revival of the language.

The success of that vision can be examined in subsequent Welsh responses to the phenomenon later in this chapter. But first, we can look at some of the passages in Daniel Deronda which Ben Yehuda found so inspiring. In the first extract, Mordecai, employed as a tutor in a Jewish home, seeks to inspire his young charge with his ideals of Jewish fulfilment by exposing him to the influence of the Hebrew language, which he believes might influence his soul even if it is not understood by his mind. In the second extract, Mordecai has fixed on Deronda as the chosen vessel to carry on his vision, and the Hebrew language plays an important role in their revelatory meeting.

from DANIEL DERONDA

Of late the urgency of irredeemable time, measured by the gradual choking of life, had turned Mordecai's trust into an agitated watch for the fulfilment that must be at hand. Was the bell on the verge of tolling, the sentence about to be executed? The deliverer's footstep must be near. The deliverer who was to rescue Mordecai's spiritual travail from oblivion, and give it an abiding place in the best heritage of his people. An insane exaggeration of his own value, even if his ideas had been as true and precious as those of Columbus or Newton, many would have counted this yearning, taking it as the sublimer part for a man to say, 'If not I, then another,' and to hold cheap the meaning of his own life. But the fuller nature desires to be an agent, to create, and not merely to look on. Strong love hungers to bless, and not merely to behold blessing. And while there is warmth enough in the sun to feed an energetic life, there will still be men to feel, 'I am lord of this moment's change, and will charge it with my soul.'

But with that mingling of inconsequence which belongs to us all, and not unhappily, since it saves us from many effects of mistake, Mordecai's confidence in the friend to come did not suffice to make him passive, and he tried expedients, pathetically humble, such as happened to be within his reach, for communicating something of himself. It was now two years since he had taken up his abode under Ezra Cohen's roof, where he was regarded with much goodwill as a compound of workman, dominie, vessel of charity, inspired idiot, man of piety, and (if he were inquired into) dangerous heretic. During, that time little Jacob had advanced into knickerbockers, and into that quickness of apprehension which has been already made manifest in relation to hardware and exchange. He had also advanced in attachment to Mordecai, regarding him as an inferior, but liking him none the worse, and taking his helpful cleverness as he might have taken the services of an enslaved Djinn. As for Mordecai, he had given Jacob his first lessons, and his habitual tenderness easily turned into the teacher's fatherhood. Though he was fully conscious of the spiritual distance between the parents and himself, and would never have attempted any communication to them from his peculiar world, the boy moved him with that idealising affection which merges the qualities of the individual child in the glory of childhood and the possibilities of a long future. And this feeling had drawn him on, at first without premeditation, and afterwards with conscious purpose, to a sort of outpouring in the ear of the boy which might have seemed wild enough to any excellent man of business who overheard it. But none overheard when Jacob went up to Mordecai's room on a day, for example, in which there was little work to be done, or at an hour when the work was ended, and after a brief lesson in English reading or in numeration, was induced to remain standing at his teacher's knees, or chose to jump astride them, often to the patient fatigue of the wasted limbs. The inducement was perhaps the mending of a toy, or some little mechanical device in which Mordecai's well-practised fingertips had an exceptional skill; and with the boy thus tethered, he would begin to repeat a Hebrew poem of his own, into which years before he had poured his first youthful ardours for that conception of a blended past and future which was the mistress of his soul, telling Jacob to say the words after him.

'The boy will get them engraved within him,' thought Mordecai; 'it is a way of printing.'

None readier than Jacob at this fascinating game of imitating unintelligible words; and if no opposing diversion occurred, he would sometimes carry on his share in it as long as the teacher's breath would last out. For Mordecai threw into each repetition the fervour befitting a sacred occasion. In such instances, Jacob would show no other distraction than reaching out and surveying the contents of his pockets; or drawing down the skin of his cheeks to make his eyes look awful, and rolling his head to complete the effect; or alternately handling his own nose and Mordecai's as if to test the relation of their masses. Under all this the fervid reciter would not pause, satisfied if the young organs of speech would submit themselves. But most commonly a sudden impulse sent Jacob leaping away into some antic or active amusement, when, instead of following the recitation, he would return upon the foregoing words most ready to his tongue, and mouth or gabble, with a see-saw suited to the action of his limbs, a verse on which Mordecai had spent some of his too scanty heart's blood. Yet he waited with such patience as a prophet needs, and began his strange printing again undiscouraged on the morrow, saying inwardly –

'My words may rule him some day. Their meaning may flash out on him. It is so with a nation – after many days.'

Meanwhile Jacob's sense of power was increased and his time enlivened by a store of magical articulation with which he made the baby crow, or drove the large cat into a dark corner, or promised himself to frighten any incidental Christian of his own years. One week he had unfortunately seen a street mountebank, and this carried off his muscular imitativeness in sad divergence from New Hebrew poetry after the model of Jehuda ha-Levi. Mordecai had arrived at a fresh passage in his poem; for as soon as Jacob had got well used to one portion, he was led on to another, and a fresh combination of sounds generally answered better in keeping him fast for a few minutes. The consumptive voice, originally a strong high baritone with its variously mingling hoarseness, like a haze amidst illuminations, and its occasional incipient gasp, had more than the usual excitement, while it gave forth Hebrew verses with a meaning something like this:

'Away from me the garment of forgetfulness,
Withering the heart;
The oil and wine from presses of the Goyim,
Poisoned with scorn
Solitude is on the sides of Mount Nebo,
In its heart a tomb:
There the buried ark and golden cherubim

Make hidden light:
There the solemn faces gaze unchanged,
The wings are spread unbroken:
Shut beneath in silent awful speech
The Law lies graven.
Solitude and darkness are my covering,
And my heart a tomb;
Smite and shatter it, O Gabriel I
Shatter it as the clay of the founder
Around the golden image.'

In the absorbing enthusiasm with which Mordecai had intoned rather than spoken this last invocation, he was unconscious that Jacob had ceased to follow him and had started away from his knees; but pausing he saw, as by a sudden flash, that the lad had thrown himself on his hands with his feet in the air, mountebank fashion, and was picking up with his lips a bright farthing which was a favourite among his pocket treasures. This might have been reckoned among the tricks Mordecai was used to, but at this moment it jarred him horribly, as if it had been a Satanic grin upon his prayer.

'Child! child!' he called out with a strange cry that startled Jacob to his feet, and then he sank backward with a shudder, closing his eyes.

'What?' said Jacob, quickly. Then, not getting an immediate answer, he pressed Mordecai's knees with a shaking movement, in order to rouse him. Mordecai opened his eyes with a fierce expression in them, leaned forward, grasped the little shoulders, and said in a quick, hoarse whisper –

'A curse is upon your generation, child. They will open the mountain and drag forth the golden wings and coin them into money, and the solemn faces they will break up into ear-rings for wanton women! And they shall get themselves a new name, but the angel of ignominy, with the fiery brand, shall know them, and their heart shall be the tomb of dead desires that turn their life to rottenness.'

The aspect and action of Mordecai were so new and mysterious to Jacob – they carried such a burthen of obscure threat – it was as if the patient, indulgent companion had turned into something unknown and terrific. The sunken dark eyes and hoarse accents close to him, the thin grappling fingers, shook Jacob's little frame into awe, and while Mordecai was speaking he stood trembling with a sense that the house was tumbling in and they were not going to have dinner any more.

But when the terrible speech had ended and the pinch was relaxed, the shock resolved itself into tears; Jacob lifted up his small patriarchal countenance and wept aloud. This sign of childish grief at once recalled Mordecai to his usual gentle self. He was not able to speak again at present, but with a maternal action he drew the curly head towards him and pressed it tenderly against his breast. On this Jacob, feeling the danger wellnigh over, howled at ease, beginning to imitate his own performance and improve upon it – a sort of transition from impulse into art often observable. Indeed, the next day he undertook to terrify Adelaide Rebekah in like manner, and succeeded very well. But Mordecai suffered a check which lasted long, from the consciousness of a misapplied agitation; sane as well as excitable, he judged severely his moments of aberration into futile eagerness, and felt discredited with himself. All the more his mind was strained towards the discernment of that friend to come, with whom he would have a calm certainty of fellowship and understanding.

It was just then that, in his usual mid-day guardianship of the old book-shop, he was struck by the appearance of Deronda, and it is perhaps comprehensible now why Mordecai's glance took on a sudden eager interest as he looked at the new-comer. He saw a face and frame which seemed to him to realise the long-conceived type. But the disclaimer of Jewish birth was for the moment a backward thrust of double severity, the particular disappointment tending to shake his confidence in the more indefinite expectation. Nevertheless, when he found Deronda seated at the Cohens' table, the disclaimer was for the moment nullified: the first impression returned with added force, seeming to be guaranteed by this second meeting under circumstances more peculiar than the former; and in asking Deronda if he knew Hebrew, Mordecai was so possessed by the new inrush of belief, that he had forgotten the absence of any other condition to the fulfilment of his hopes. But the answering 'No' struck them all down again, and the frustration was more painful than before. After turning his back on the visitor that Sabbath evening, Mordecai went through days of a deep discouragement, like that of men on a doomed ship who, having strained their eyes after a sail, and beheld it with rejoicing, behold it never advance, and say, 'Our sick eyes make it.' But the long-contemplated figure had come as an emotional sequence of Mordecai's firmest theoretic convictions; it had been wrought from the imagery of his most passionate life; and it inevitably reappeared –

reappeared in a more specific self-asserting form than ever. Deronda had that sort of resemblance to the preconceived type which a finely individual bust or portrait has to the more generalised copy left in our minds after a long interval. We renew our memory with delight, but we hardly know with how much correction. And now, his face met Mordecai's inward gaze as if it had always belonged to the awaited friend, raying out, moreover, some of that influence which belongs to breathing flesh; till by-and-by it seemed that discouragement had turned into a new obstinacy of resistance, and the ever-recurrent vision had the force of an outward call to disregard counter-evidence, and keep expectation awake. It was Deronda now who was seen in the often painful night-watches, when we are all liable to be held with the clutch of a single thought – whose figure, never with its back turned, was seen in moments of soothed reverie or soothed dozing, painted on that golden sky which was the doubly blessed symbol of advancing day and of approaching rest.

Mordecai knew that the nameless stranger was to come and redeem his ring; and, in spite of contrary chances, the wish to see him again was growing into a belief that he should see him. In the January weeks, he felt an increasing agitation of that subdued hidden quality which hinders nervous people from any steady occupation on the eve of an anticipated change. He could not go on with his printing of Hebrew on little Jacob's mind; or with his attendance at a weekly club, which was another effort of the same forlorn hope: something else was coming. The one thing he longed for was to get as far as the river, which he could do but seldom and with difficulty. He yearned with a poet's yearning for the wide sky, the far-reaching vista of bridges, the tender and fluctuating lights on the water which seems to breathe with a life that can shiver and mourn, be comforted and rejoice.

★

In ten minutes the two men, with as intense a consciousness as if they had been two undeclared lovers, felt themselves alone in the small gas-lit book-shop and turned face to face, each baring his head from an instinctive feeling that they wished to see each other fully. Mordecai came forward to lean his back against the little counter, while Deronda stood against the opposite wall hardly more than four feet off. I wish I could perpetuate those two faces, as Titian's 'Tribute

Money' has perpetuated two types presenting another sort of contrast. Imagine – we all of us can – the pathetic stamp of consumption with its brilliancy of glance to which the sharply-defined structure of features, reminding one of a forsaken temple, give already a far-off look as of one getting unwillingly out of reach; and imagine it on a Jewish face naturally accentuated for the expression of an eager mind the face of a man little above thirty, but with that age upon it which belongs to time lengthened by suffering, the hair and beard still black throwing out the yellow pallor of the skin, the difficult breathing giving more decided marking to the mobile nostril, the wasted yellow hands conspicuous on the folded arms: then give to the yearning consumptive glance something of the slowly dying mother's look when her one loved son visits her bedside, and the flickering power of gladness leaps out as she says, 'My boy!' – for the sense of spiritual perpetuation in another resembles that maternal transference of self. Seeing such a portrait you would see Mordecai. And opposite to him was the face not more distinctively oriental than many a type seen among what we call the Latin races: rich in youthful health, and with a forcible masculine gravity in its repose, that gave the value of judgment to the reverence with which he met the gaze of this mysterious son of poverty who claimed him as a long-expected friend. The more exquisite quality of Deronda's nature – that keenly perceptive sympathetic emotiveness which ran along with his speculative tendency – was never more thoroughly tested. He felt nothing that could be called belief in the validity of Mordecai's impressions concerning him or in the probability of any greatly effective issue: what he felt was a profound sensibility to a cry from the depths of another soul; and accompanying that, the summons to be receptive instead of superciliously prejudging. Receptiveness is a rare and massive power, like fortitude; and this state of mind now gave Deronda's face its utmost expression of calm benignant force, an expression which nourished Mordecai's confidence and made an open way before him. He began to speak.

'You cannot know what has guided me to you and brought us together at this moment. You are wondering.'

'I am not impatient,' said Deronda. 'I am ready to listen to whatever you may wish to disclose.'

'You see some of the reasons why I needed you,' said Mordecai, speaking quietly, as if he wished to reserve his strength. 'You see that

I am dying. You see that I am as one shut up behind bars by the wayside, who if he spoke to any would be met only by headshaking and pity. The day is closing – the light is fading – soon we should not have been able to discern each other. But you have come in time.'

'I rejoice, that I am come in time,' said Deronda, feelingly. He would not say, 'I hope you are not mistaken in me,' – the very word 'mistaken,' he thought, would be a cruelty at that moment.

'But the hidden reasons why I need you began afar off,' said Mordecai; 'began in my early years when I was studying in another land. Then ideas, beloved ideas, came to me, because I was a Jew. They were a trust to fulfil, because I was a Jew. They were an inspiration, because I was a Jew, and felt the heart of my race beating within me. They were my life; I was not fully born till then. I counted this heart, and this breath, and this right hand' – Mordecai had pathetically pressed his hand against his breast, and then stretched its wasted fingers out before him – 'I counted my sleep and my waking, and the work I fed my body with, and the sights that fed my eyes – I counted them but as fuel to the divine flame. But I had done as one who wanders and engraves his thought in rocky solitudes, and before I could change my course came care and labour and disease, and blocked the way before me, and bound me with the iron that eats itself into the soul. Then I said, 'How shall I save the life within me from being stifled with this stifled breath?" Mordecai paused to rest that poor breath which had been taxed by the rising excitement of his speech. And also he wished to check that excitement. Deronda dared not speak: the very silence in the narrow space seemed alive with mingled awe and compassion before this struggling fervour. And presently Mordecai went on –

'But you may misunderstand me. I speak not as an ignorant dreamer – as one bred up in the inland valleys, thinking ancient thoughts anew and not knowing them ancient, never having stood by the great waters where the world's knowledge passes to and fro. English is my mother-tongue, England is the native land of this body, which is but as a breaking pot of earth around the fruit-bearing tree, whose seed might make the desert rejoice. But my true life was nourished in Holland, at the feet of my mother's brother, a Rabbi skilled in special learning; and when he died I went to Hamburg to study, and afterwards to Gottingen, that I might take a larger outlook on my people, and on the Gentile world, and drink knowledge at all sources.

I was a youth; I felt free; I saw our chief seats in Germany; I was not then in utter poverty. And I had possessed myself of a handicraft. For I said, I care not if my lot be as that of Joshua ben Chananja: after the last destruction he earned his bread by making needles, but in his youth he had been a singer on the steps of the Temple, and had a memory of what was, before the glory departed. I said, let my body dwell in poverty, and my hands be as the hands of the toiler; but let my soul be as a temple of remembrance where the treasures of knowledge enter and the inner sanctuary is hope. I knew what I chose. They said, 'He feeds himself on visions,' and I denied not; for visions are the creators and feeders of the world. I see, I measure the world as it is, which the vision will create anew. You are not listening to one who raves aloof from the lives of his fellows.'

Mordecai paused, and Deronda, feeling that the pause was expectant, said, 'Do me the justice to believe that I was not inclined to call your words raving. I listen that I may know, without prejudgment. I have had experience which gives me a keen interest in the story of a spiritual destiny embraced willingly, and embraced in youth.'

'A spiritual destiny embraced willingly – in youth?' Mordecai repeated in a corrective tone. 'It was the soul fully born within me, and it came in my boyhood. It brought its own world – a mediaeval world, where there were men who made the ancient language live again in new psalms of exile. They had absorbed the philosophy of the Gentile into the faith of the Jew, and they still yearned toward a centre for our race. One of their souls was born again within me, and awaked amid the memories of their world. It travelled into Spain and Provence; it debated with Aben-Ezra; it took ship with Jehuda ha-Levi; it heard the roar of the Crusaders and the shrieks of tortured Israel. And when its dumb tongue was loosed, it spoke the speech they had made alive with the new blood of their ardour, their sorrow, and their martyred trust.. it sang with the cadence of their strain.'

Mordecai paused again, and then said in a loud, hoarse whisper –

'While it is imprisoned in me, it will never learn another.'

'Have you written entirely in Hebrew, then?' said Deronda, remembering with some anxiety the former question as to his own knowledge of that tongue.

'Yes – yes,' said Mordecai, in a tone of deep sadness; 'in my youth I wandered toward that solitude, not feeling that it was a solitude. I had the ranks of the great dead around me; the martyrs gathered and listened. But soon I found that the living were deaf to me. At first I saw my life spread as a long future. I said, part of my Jewish heritage is an unbreaking patience; part is skill to seek divers methods and find a rooting-place where the planters despair. But there came new messengers from the Eternal. I had to bow under the Yoke that presses on the great multitude born of woman... family troubles called me – I had to work, to care, not for myself alone. I was left solitary again; but already the angel of death had turned to me and beckoned and I felt his skirts continually on my path. I besought hearing and help. I spoke; I went to men of our people to the rich in influence or knowledge, to the rich in other wealth. But I found none to listen with understanding. I was rebuked for error; I was offered a small sum in charity. No wonder. I looked poor; I carried a bundle of Hebrew manuscript with me; I said, our chief teachers are misleading the hope of our race. Scholar and merchant were both too busy to listen. Scorn stood as interpreter between me and them. One said, 'The Book of Mormon would never have answered in Hebrew; and if you mean to address our learned men, it is not likely you can teach them anything.' He touched a truth there.'

The last words had a perceptible irony in their hoarsened tone.

'But though you had accustomed yourself to write in Hebrew, few, surely, can use English better,' said Deronda, wanting to hint consolation in a new effort for which he could smooth the way.

Mordecai shook his head slowly, and answered –

'Too late – too late. I can write no more. My writing would be like this gasping breath. But the breath may wake the fount of pity – the writing not. If I could write now and used English, I should be as one who beats a board to summon those who have been used to no signal but a bell. My soul has an ear to hear the faults of its own speech. New writing of mine would be like this body' – Mordecai spread his arms – 'within it there might he the Ruach-ha-kodesh – the breath of divine thought – but men would smile at it and say, 'A poor Jew!' – and the chief smilers would be of my own people.'

Mordecai let his hands fall, and his head sink in melancholy: for the moment he had lost hold of his hope. Despondency, conjured up by his own words, had floated in and hovered above him with eclipsing wings. He had sunk into momentary darkness.

'I feel with you – I feel strongly with you,' said Deronda, in a clear deep voice which was itself a cordial, apart from the words of sympathy. 'But – forgive me if I speak hastily – for what you have actually written there need be no utter burial. The means of publication are within reach. If you will rely on me, I can assure you of all that is necessary to that end.'

'That is not enough,' said Mordecai, quickly, looking up again with the flash of recovered memory and confidence. 'That is not all my trust in you. You must be not only a hand to me, but a soul – believing my belief – being moved by my reasons – hoping my hope – seeing the vision I point to – beholding a glory where I beheld it!' – Mordecai had taken a step nearer as he spoke, and now laid his hand on Deronda's arm with a tight grasp; his face little more than a foot off had something like a pale flame in it – an intensity of reliance that acted as a peremptory claim, while he went on – 'You will be my life: it will be planted afresh; it will grow. You shall take the inheritance; it has been gathering for ages. The generations are crowding on my narrow bridge. What has been and what is to be are meeting there; and the bridge is breaking. But I have found you. You have come in time. You will take the inheritance which the base son refuses because of the tombs which the plough and harrow may not pass over or the gold-seeker disturb: you will take the sacred inheritance of the Jew.'

From *Daniel Deronda*, 1875

LEWIS VALENTINE (1893-1986)

We first encountered Lewis Valentine in the opening chapter to this book, where he was in jail in 1937 for his part in the Welsh nationalist protest at Penyberth. His career as a Baptist minister subsequent to his release from jail was less eventful, although he remained true to the ideals of Christianity, pacifism and Welsh nationhood which had led him to prison in the 30s. Both the following two extracts show how he was inspired by the success of the revival of Hebrew, and how he recognised the role played by George Eliot in its inception. They also show the first stirrings of a Welsh desire to emulate the feat of restoring an ancient tongue to its former glory. Both passages are taken from *Seren Gomer*, a journal whose name derives from the belief in the descent of the Welsh from the Jews, as was discussed in the first chapter of this book.

RESTORING HEBREW TO PALESTINE

The great wonder of the Union[2] this year was the welcome of Cwm Rhondda. Wales is refusing to die in this dear old valley, whose people, in the days of their fame and greatness, had no equal, and this was displayed in the Welsh and Christian welcome that was received. It's something of a miracle that there is any Welsh here at all when we remember its former hardship and scars, but, truly, this was one of the Welshest Unions for a long time, in its language as well as in its welcome. Even in these dry days we had testimony from one of its most prominent men of letters that the greatest purity in the Rhondda today is Welsh and Welsh-language. Before I started off for the Union, I threw into my bag the book of the Welshwoman George Eliot, *Daniel Deronda*, and before I went to sleep one night I read the part where the old man, Mordecai, soliloquises mournfully as he contemplates his people's fate: 'The life of a people grows,' the old man says, 'It is knit together and yet expanded in joy and sorrow, in thought and action, it absorbs the thought of other nations into its own forms, and gives back the thought as new wealth into the world... There may come a check, and arrest: memories may be stifled, and love may be faint for the lack of them, – the soul of a people, whereby they know themselves to be one, may seem to be dying for want of common action. But who shall say the fountain of their life is dried up, they shall forever cease to be a nation?' Who shall say it? Not he who feels the life of his people stirring within his own.' Then Mordecai turns to teaching Hebrew to the lad Jacob, and he, poor thing, unable to understand a word of it, just as the Scripture was taught in Welsh to the children of Cwm Rhondda for the children's service, and they unable to understand it. 'But', says Mordecai, 'My words may rule him some day. Their meaning may flash out on him.' It is interesting to think that this book written by George Eliot, who had her roots in Flintshire, gave strength to Ben Yehuda to struggle and strive to restore Hebrew to Palestine, and to succeed! Who shall put Welsh once again on the tongues of the children of Cwm Rhondda? The impression I had was that there was some strange inner strength in the Welsh-speaking Christian remnant in the valley, and, with God on their side, perhaps they can bring back faith and spiritual life to the old valley. For goodness sake, depose your present trivial leaders and give that common people brave Christian leadership once again.

Translation from 'Nodiadau'r Golygydd', *Seren Gomer* Vol XLIV, No 2, Summer 1952, collected in Ed. John Emyr *Dyddiadur Milwr, ac ysgrifau eraill gan Lewis Valentine*, 1988.

GWYNFOR EVANS (b. 1912)

By the time the following passage was written, the Welsh desire to copy the revival of Hebrew was beginning to crystallise into a firm plan of action. The language movement in Wales had been born in its modern form in 1962 in the wake of Saunders' Lewis's *Tynged yr Iaith*, 'Fate of the Language' speech in which he warned that the language was in danger of dying unless radical action were taken. By 1969, when this passage was written, the movement for civil rights for Welsh speakers was in full swing. The author of this article is Gwynfor Evans, the leading Welsh nationalist of the second half of the twentieth century. He was Plaid Cymru's first MP, elected in 1966, and led the party to the point where it was a force to be reckoned with in Welsh and Westminster politics. In the early 1980s, when the Conservative government reneged on an election pledge to establish a television channel for Welsh-language programmes, he threatened a hunger strike to the death until the pledge was honoured. The government backed down and duly established Sianel Pedwar Cymru, which quickly became more of a success story than its most enthusiastic advocates could have foreseen, and which played a major part in the revival of the language in the late twentieth century. However, that success was still in the future when Gwynfor Evans was writing the following article in 1969 in the hope that Jewish determination might be emulated in Wales. Three years later, Shoshana Eytan, of the education department of the Jewish International Agency, was addressing members of UCAC, the Welsh-language teachers' union, and others in Cardiff, to recount her experience of the success of the *ulpan* intensive language tuition methods. Chris Rees, a driving force in the successful subsequent establishment of the *ulpan* system in Wales, reported on the meeting, concluding like this:

> If there were a means for us in Wales to process some thousands of new speakers each year through a system such as the 'ulpan', we would then have the thousands of new readers that are needed for Welsh books and the thousands of new viewers which are needed for Welsh television. The key to everything is to boost the number of speakers, and we will not get sufficient success without 'language factories' of the kind mentioned. Let Israel be an example to us, and let the word 'ulpan' become as familiar a part of our vocabulary as the word 'kibbutz'.[3]

The *ulpan* system was soon established in Wales and has since become a familiar feature of the adult education scene, having brought many learners to fluency. But it needed vision such as that offered by Gwynfor Evans below to bring such a scheme to reality.

IT HAPPENED IN ISRAEL

Shortly before Christmas, Mr Avraham Harman, the President of Jerusalem University, came to the House of Commons to address a gathering of MPs under the chairmanship of Sir Barnett Janner (a former pupil of Barry County School) on the political situation in Israel. Before he was appointed to this academic post, Mr Harman was the Israeli ambassador in Washington. I asked him not only about the political situation in Israel but about the position of the Hebrew language in the University. It was a surprise to many an MP, but not to me, to hear from him that every subject, without exception, in that great and famous University is taught through the Hebrew language, and that the position is the same in the country's four other universities and in all its schools, primary, secondary and technical.

A great achievement has been realised in Israel with every thoroughness. It is true that a combination of factors which do not pertain in Wales made the revival of Hebrew possible; despite that, Wales has a great deal to learn from the story. The National Eisteddfod Council would do an immeasurable service to the Welsh language if it were to send a commission of suitably qualified Welsh people to Israel to study the situation and bring back a report. The commission should include schoolteachers and university teachers, lawyers and Hebrew scholars. If Wales had a government, or even a university which served it, this would have happened years ago. Indeed, we would have studied the linguistic, social and economic situations of many countries in order to learn from others in many fields, to the benefit of our economy and society. All wisdom is not to be found in England.

Hebrew is the only language which has been successfully revived as a spoken tongue after it has ceased to be a vernacular. We have to take this experience very seriously. One of the great heroes of the story was a Polish Jew, Ben-Yehuda. His son, who was born in Palestine in 1882, was the first child in our time to be raised with Hebrew as his mother tongue.

The first thing Ben-Yehuda did after getting to Palestine in 1880 was to appeal passionately for Hebrew to be made the language of the country's Jewish schools. Ten years earlier, English had been made the only language of the schools of Wales, which every child was forced to attend.

Hebrew had been the language of the Jews for around 1,400 years before it died out completely as a spoken language around 200 AD. In 1870, Welsh had been the language of the Welsh people for around the same long period. At this time, the contrast between the situation of the two languages was very favourable towards Welsh, for at the end of this long period, there were more Welsh speakers than there had ever been in the history of Wales, while the sound of Hebrew, after a 1,400-year period, had become silent on the lips of Jewish children. The silence continued for 1,700 years. Despite that, the first thing Ben-Yehuda did, and before the birth of his son, was to call for Hebrew education.

The revival of Hebrew is an aspect of the Jewish national revival. Increasingly they had been assimilating into the lives of the other nations just as the Welsh had been assimilating into the life of England. The massacre in Russia in 1880 brought this to an end. They were forced to live as a nation because other nations had refused to assimilate them. This is the source of Zionism. But the Jews instinctively knew that it was not possible to restore their nationhood without restoring their language. The campaign for the language was led by the writers, and the period following 1880 is considered to be the classical period of their literature.

However, Ben-Yehuda was right. The only way to revive Hebrew was through Hebrew education – that is, education in a language which was not understood by any of the children, and a language that all the teachers had to learn as a second language. Welsh faces no such obstacles as those which burdened the heroic men who were determined to revive Hebrew; and yet Welsh education is as essential to us as was Hebrew education to the Jews. The only ten-year-old children who speak Welsh today, with a few exceptions, are those who have received Welsh education. And let us remember that only 14% of the children of Wales speak the language.

In 1888, a primary school was opened where every subject was taught through Hebrew. In 1892, the teachers in the Jewish schools in Palestine called for Hebrew to be the only language used in these schools, in an Arabic-speaking country. In 1913, some German Jews arranged to open a German-language technical school. The majority of the Jewish population opposed it fiercely, and as part of their protest, thousands of children and teachers left their schools and held their classes in the open air. The German Jews had to give way and make Hebrew the medium of instruction of the technical school.

By 1918, 40% of the Jews outside Jerusalem (34,000 in all) spoke Hebrew. That number is around 3% of the number of Welsh speakers at the same time – a miraculous increase. Since 1882, and the birth of the first child to be raised in Hebrew, the number of speakers of the language had increased to 34,000. And what was most important was that the proportion of children who spoke the language in 1918 was 54%, and in Tel Aviv and the villages it was as much as 77%. How different to the history of the Welsh language in the same period, which saw such a disastrous fall in the proportion of children who could speak the language.

When Palestine was put under the authority of England by the United Nations in 1921, Hebrew was recognised as one of the country's three official languages. From then on, it was used in public administration, the post and so on. (Bear in mind that the total number of speakers was 3% of the total number of Welsh speakers and that Welsh was refused official recognition in these fields.)

In 1925, Jerusalem University was established, with Hebrew, of course, as its medium of instruction. This practice was not deviated from even though there was a great increase in the number of subjects for which there were no Hebrew terms or books. English scientific terms, and English and German textbooks were used, but Hebrew terms were coined in many ways, especially by the Hebrew Language Academy, an excellent establishment which developed, with government help, in 1949 out of the Hebrew Language Council. But Hebrew was the language of the lecturers, and in Hebrew the students wrote. When lecturers arrive from a foreign country, they have a year or two in which to learn the language.

The astonishing difference between the National University of Wales and Jerusalem University is underlined by words spoken by H.J.Roth, the Rector of the University, in 1941,

> 'The University', he says, 'trains the Hebrew language to speak in the languge of the sciences...We will not allow the language an excuse. 'The language cannot' – what does that mean? It must. If it is not willing we will compel it until we find it obedient to what we desire. The University teachers are people who force the claims of science upon the language.'

The success of the policy of Hebrewising education was sweeping, and no-one can say that it has hindered the development of the students nor the economic or political development of the country. Whether the policies of the state of Israel are always good is another matter. Professor Chaim Rabbin can say this,

> After eight years in a Hebrew school, young people leave having become used to speaking Hebrew to one another, whatever may be the language their parents speak to them. In time, these pupils married amongst themselves, establishing families in which speaking Hebrew was the natural thing.

By 1958 he could write a sentence that should put us to shame, 'Hebrew is now spoken by more people than speak Welsh'. In the middle of the eighties, one little child spoke it.

Only a generation after the beginning of the effort to revive Hebrew, the majority of people said the pioneers' efforts were in vain. In 1948 it was in a strong enough position to assimilate a million immigrants to Israel who did not have a word of Hebrew. Today it is the language of the country to all intents and purposes, in politics, administration, education, literature, commerce and the military, as was Welsh five hundred years ago. Every week, dozens of Hebrew books come from the presses on all kinds of subjects.

The language was revived as the main tradition of the nation. This marvel was not the result of a movement to save the language its own, but of a movement to secure full Jewish nationhood. To quote Chaim Rabbin again,

> The main reason why almost the whole population agreed with the supremacy of Hebrew was the fact that it was the language of the nation's cultural heritage, that it was the language of the literature in which the character and aspirations of the Jewish people were expressed, and especially that it was the language of the Hebrew Bible.

The national values of the Jew, and his determination to incorporate them in the life of a free country – this is what gave him the tenacity to revive the national language. Can we achieve the far less daunting task of Cymricising the life of this nation afresh? I say the task is far less daunting. That is because the Welsh language has never died as a spoken tongue, and because 35 people speak Welsh today for every one who spoke Hebrew a hundred years ago. But we face huge difficulties which the Jew never had to face – the host of Welsh people who have been deracinated and the host who have been corrupted by the materialism of the age. Getting on in the world: sustaining or enriching the economy; these are the main aims of education for the great majority of our councillors and education officers, as well, alas, as of the parents. In vain do we curse that their attitudes verge upon the barbaric. However pathetic their condition may be, it is they who are in authority.

The only hope is a national spiritual revival that will demand full nationhood for Wales. For only the strength of the national spirit can put into authority in our education committees, in the colleges and in the University, those who desire to give our national language its proper place. I wonder if that revival is afoot in Wales in these days?

Translation from *Barn*, April 1969.

NOTES

1. *George Eliot:Woman of Contradictions*, (London, Weidenfeld and Nicolson, 1989)
2. The Baptist Union had held its annual convention in the Rhondda that year.
3. Translation from 'Language Schools for Adults', *Yr Athro* (The Teacher) January 1973.

CONFLICT AND *SHOAH*

It is a tragic fact that no book about the Jewish experience can avoid the subject of anti-semitism and particularly the horror of the Holocaust, known to Jews as the *Shoah*. This next chapter looks at Welsh involvement in, and responses to, this most painful subject. It begins with some Welsh examples of anti-semitic prejudice. In this category, I have included all the relevant material I can find, with the exception of a few passing references. The examples are mercifully few, and all pre-date the Nazi persecution; however, they are there, and they need to be confronted honestly. The chapter then leads on to Welsh literary responses to the Holocaust. In this category, far from including all the examples I could find, I have had to be be highly selective, as there is a vast quantity of material, poems particularly, both in Welsh and English, which deal with the Holocaust. Very many of these tend to deal with the Holocaust as a general example of inhumanity, or as a metaphor for the human capacity for cruelty and hatred. I have excluded this generalised material and have confined myself to material which is either informed by personal experience, and which is valuable testimony as a result, or which has something to say about the Holocaust victims specifically as Jews, not merely as abstract victims of persecution.

RAYMOND WOOLFE (1918-1957)

It was shown earlier how a great deal of Welsh evangelical Protestantism cherished a conversionist attitude towards the Jews, but that this was confined largely to the realm of theory. It was also shown that the one example of a serious Welsh attempt to proselytise among the Jews, that of John Mills in the nineteenth century, ended in a polite impasse when the Jews would not take the bait of conversion. The following passage, however, shows what happened when evangelical zeal would not, unlike John Mills, take a Jewish 'no' for an answer. The sensational 'Jewess Abduction Case' shows how prejudice and deceit could corrupt evangelical belief. The account of the case here is given as found in *CAJEX*, the journal of the Cardiff Jewish community, in a form combining elements of the short story and the historical article, and is thereby brought within the remit of a literary anthology.[1] However, two things about this story must be pointed out. Firstly, as will be seen from the text, it is a partisan account, committed to the Jewish version of the case. However, that is not a major problem, because, as the Assize court decided, and as the vast majority of public and press opinion at the time – both Jewish and

Gentile – agreed, the Jewish parties to the case were undoubtedly in the right. Secondly, and more importantly, it is incomplete. A far fuller account can be found in the chapter devoted to the case in Ursula Henriques' study *The Jews of South Wales*.[2] The main ommissions from Lyons's narrative, as Henriques points out, are twofold: firstly, the fact that the short story relies almost entirely on the 1868 correspondence relating to the incident and does not tap the huge source of material contained in the reports of the 1869 trial; secondly, the short story does not mention the Thomas's later successful appeal against the Assize court verdict. However, the essence of this tragic case is contained within the short story, which shows how religious zeal can tip over into deception and prejudice.

THE ABDUCTION OF ESTHER LYONS

Barnett Lyons was a well-known and respected member of the Cardiff Jewish Community who lived with his wife and family of eight children at No. 11, Mount Stuart Square. He was a prosperous shipbroker, and he and his wife brought up their children well, if rather strictly. On the evening of Monday March 23rd in the year 1868, he returned home from business which had kept him away several days, at the late hour of 11 p.m.

He found his home in a turmoil. His second oldest child, Esther, who managed his shop in Roath, had not yet returned home.

Esther Lyons was eighteen years old, but looked much younger. She was fond of fruit and cheap novels. Probably through no fault of her own she did not mix with the younger Jewish set. Her mother made her help with the home; whilst her father taught her to look after his shop. Until recently she had been sleeping at the Roath shop, but at her mother's request had, for the past week been sleeping at home. This particular evening she had not yet returned from the shop.

Enquiries were made immediately by Mr. Lyons and his eldest son Reuben. They saw the police, they went to the shop and woke up the neighbours. They searched frantically the whole of the night and the next day.

The next afternoon Barnett Lyons made an important discovery. One of his neighbours in Roath had seen Esther, accompanied by a Sarah Carver, her assistant at the shop, going into 'Croome Villa,' the house of the Rev. Nathaniel Thomas, a Baptist Minister, who lived not far away. This was on Monday afternoon. Barnett Lyons immediately called on Mr. Thomas, who regretted that he had no knowledge of Esther or her companion, and could not help in the search.

Mr. Lyons was not satisfied: his informant was reliable. He pressed Mr. Thomas for news of Esther, without success. He went away, and returned with the police, but in vain. He asked to see Mrs. Thomas, but was informed that she was away visiting friends, and would not return until the 30th.

He and his family searched for the whole of that week, but succeeded only in confirming his suspicions that Mr. Thomas knew more than he cared to tell.

On the following Sunday, the 29th, Barnett Lyons could stand it no longer. His wife's health was seriously affected; he could not attend to his business; the police seemed helpless. He called again on Nathaniel Thomas, and faced him point-blank with his suspicions. Thomas laughed at him. 'Your suspicions are groundless,' he said, 'I do not know where your daughter can possibly be.'

'Perhaps your wife could help me?'

'I don't think so. She is away, and does not return until to-morrow.'

'May I call on her then, tomorrow? Perhaps she may be able to recall my daughter's visit.'

'I tell you your daughter did not call here. You are wasting your time.'

'In any case, I should like to see her.'

'Oh, very well.'

The next day Barnett Lyons called to see Mrs. Thomas. Explaining the purpose of his call, he continued:

'I have received strong information that on the evening of Monday last she was harboured by you.'

Mrs. Thomas shook her head without replying.

He continued in a harsher voice, 'This will be a magistrate's case if I cannot get any satisfaction.'

Mrs. Thomas paused, then said in a low voice that steadily gained crescendo, 'I am a great friend to all the Jews. If it were not for the Jews I would not have that book on the table.' She pointed to one which lay there – 'I am continually praying for the Jews. I have been praying for you and your family for three months in particular....'

Mr. Lyons interrupted, 'What about Esther?'

There was another long silence. Then – 'Your daughter was here last Monday night,' she whispered. 'I gave her a night's shelter.'

Barnett Lyons' suspicions were confirmed.

'Where is she now?' he demanded.

'I do not know.'

'When did she leave?'

'The next morning, the 24th.'

'Did she not tell you where she was going?'

Mrs. Thomas, her thin lips white, crouched in a chair. 'You – you – ask – me – too – strong – questions'

He controlled himself. 'She slept in your house one night,' he said in a low deliberate voice, 'and yet you did not ask her when she left where she was going?'

'You ask me too strong questions,' Mrs. Thomas repeated, 'I have told you she was here one night. I can say no more.'

Again, Barnett Lyons called the police, who were unable to get any further information from her.

2

The search for Esther Lyons continued unabated for six weeks. No further clues to her whereabouts were discovered; no reason for her sudden and complete disappearance came to light, although her father moved Heaven and earth to find her.

On May 14th he wrote to Mrs. Thomas, for he was convinced that she at least knew where his daughter was. He could not fathom Esther's silence, and could not understand why she had not communicated with him. He did not know if his daughter had come to harm, he did not know in what part of the country she might now be.

Barnett Lyons wrote to Mrs. Thomas, assuming that she knew where Esther was, suggesting that Mrs. Thomas grant him at least an interview with his daughter, saying that if this were refused he would advertise for the girl, and if necessary take proceedings in a court of law with a view to her recovery. Mrs. Thomas replied with the following letter.

Croome Villa,
Roath,
Cardiff, 25th May.

My Dear Sir,
I promised to reply to your letter of May 14th on Monday. Before considering your proposal as to seeing your dear child, I must make one or two remarks.

You seem to imply that I have acted deceitfully, and assert that the whole of the time I have said I know nothing about her.' This is not true.

I never said so. I told you I did not know where she was, and I spoke truly. I told the police officer I was wilfully ignorant of her whereabouts. This was also true, and is true now. I thank God I fear falsehood, nor have I uttered any to you or either of the other querists. I was placed in a very difficult position, for I had to shield your child while I replied to your and others' many questions. The dear girl came to me for refuge, having left a *very wretched home*. I of course took her in, but, fearing our house was not safe, I advised her to leave us. She did so, and I took care the hands she fell into were of the very safest and best in all ways. Of course I shall never betray these, which is why I halted in your examination of me, and hinted to you that I had said enough, though I volunteered to you the information that she had slept at our house, and was NOT obliged (as you say) to acknowledge that I gave her shelter, etc. Perhaps this is your awkward way of putting it, however, and not meant as an implication in any way?

And now for your threats and accusations, etc. I can only say my conscience is perfectly clear; that I should act the same over again, and that I am not at all afraid of any punishment you can inflict. I am a FRIEND and NO ENEMY of yourself and family; would not harm a hair of your heads, and would do and suffer a very great deal for your welfare and salvation, and that of your nation, and pray (oh! how fervently) that the veil may be removed, and that with joy you may see and adore the blessed Messiah who died for you on Calvary, and LOOK upon Him you have pierced, and mourn and bathe in the fountain open for sin and for uncleanliness, and be saved! The Lord, even Jesus, bless you and all yours. And now for your proposal.

I don't know where your dear girl is, but I can find out, if I desire so to do. She could be brought to Cardiff to see you, but this would incur heavy expense, for it would need the farway travelling expenses of herself and a friend here and back again, and it must be first-class travelling. She was destitute of clothing, so that much expense has been incurred by her friends as you may suppose, and she is dearly loved by all who have had to do with her, I hear; and one friend remarked, 'What a mine of wealth in her loving heart her mother has lost.' Now, are you willing to pay down £10 for expenses of the interview? Any overplus you should of course have returned, and you could bring any of your friends to meet her, and she shall have a few of hers present also.

You would then see that she was *not detained* or *influenced* by anyone from the first moment of her flight from your roof, and if she likes she can go back with you, and if not, as I understand, you give a pledge to leave her to her own choice? If you give this pledge, and wish the interview, and will hand over the money, I shall then endeavour to find her out, and she can have the plan laid before her.

I am, Sir,

Yours faithfully,

L.E. A. THOMAS.

The hypocrisy and refined cruelty of this letter leave nothing to be added to a portrait of the character of Mrs. Thomas. She emerges as the evil spirit behind the catastrophe which fell upon the entire Jewish Community of the Cardiff of 1868.

Barnett Lyons, however, in his anxiety to find his daughter, was ready to accept any offer, to grasp at any straw to bring about her recovery. He accepted Mrs. Thomas's terms. A few days later he received a reply. It came in the form of a document, entitled,

'CONDITIONS OF A PROPOSED INTERVIEW' between MR. BARNETT LYONS and his DAUGHTER ESTHER who has LEFT HER HOME.'

Following a series of arrangements and terms the document was signed by Mr. Thomas.

Had it not been for the stark reality of Esther Lyons' disappearance without trace, the receipt of such a document as this might have lent a comic-opera atmosphere to the whole situation. However, such was Barnett Lyons' state of mind that he would readily have forwarded the £10, which he counted as a small price to pay for his daughter's return.

Yet by the following post he received a further communication from Nathaniel Thomas. In this letter he cancelled his proposal for the interview, and requested Mr. Lyons to call to see him. To this end Mr. Lyons lost no time: he called on Mr. Thomas the next day.

At the meeting Mr. Thomas was full of bitterness. He reproached Mr. Lyons for having brought the police into the matter – this, he said, had caused Esther to be sent away from Cardiff (a clear admission that he had sent her off!). Mr.Lyons' continued and unrelenting search for his daughter had caused complications which had been unforeseen.... Barnett Lyons was at a loss to understand Mr.Thomas's attitude. First, his daughter had disappeared after having been seen entering this house – then the Thomas's had denied all knowledge of her. Then they admitted having abducted her and sending her away from Cardiff. They showed no remorse, no regret. He saw that there was nothing for it but to seek legal aid in the recovery of his child. He appreciated by now the fact that she had fallen a victim to the proselytism of two fanatics, and since they would not grant him even a personal interview with his daughter he must go to law to get her back.

Mr. Thomas's bitterness began to subside.

'Mr. Lyons,' he said, 'You must either admit that your daughter is eighteen years of age, or under sixteen, by the production of a certificate of her birth.'

'What is your motive?'

'I wish to protect myself from the law.'

Mr. Lyons was taken by surprise. 'Oh!' he cried, 'that you feared the laws of God as much as you do the laws of Man!'

3

It was now the end of May. On this day Mr. Lyons received a letter from Sarah Carver, his late assistant. Together with a covering note, there was enclosed a letter which Esther Lyons had sent to Sarah Carver, which she had forwarded on ' for his perusal.' The letter is far too long to be reproduced fully here, but extracts must be quoted.

> I can ... make your mind easy by telling you that I am in good hands, with one who is a kind mother to me, surrounded by every comfort, indeed, I may say, luxury. I am quite happy, happier than I ever was in my life before. My kind friends try to teach me to be tidy, useful, and to cultivate my mind, and make me fit for some position in life, which you know has never been done before. I can also say that I am truly happy in the love of my Saviour ... he has given his precious life for me, and you ... my dear girl, seek Jesus ... my dear girl, I always pray for you, and ask the Lord to keep you out of temptations ... we may not meet again very soon on earth ... it is far more important to meet in that glorious kingdom where all will be peace, joy and love – no unkind, cruel parents – no unhappy homes, no disappointments – none, none whatever ... have you seen my parents lately? Are they really sorry to have lost me? I would be a comfort to them if I could, but I dare not trust them, though I now forgive them for all the sad past ... I owe it to the Lord to forgive all those who try sometimes to make us unhappy, or harm us unwillingly, for they know not what they do. Always seek to forgive those who do you harm. It will be a good example for them. They may profit by it, as I trust my parents will.

One can but imagine the feelings of Barnett Lyons as he read this letter. No Jewish parents, however strict, could possibly warrant the writing of it. To the reader it will appear the letter of an immature emptyheaded schoolgirl, dictated, for the most part, by a fanatic, enjoying his – or her – visions of the mental anguish he is about to cause.

This letter, and a note received from Thomas on 3rd June, stating that he had heard from Esther Lyons, and she had declined an interview with her family, convinced Mr. Lyons that he had better seek legal advice without any further delay. Accordingly, Mr. Lyons sought the legal advice of Messrs. Sampson Samuel & Emanuel, solicitors in London.

4

On the 9th July Mr. Oppenheim, the counsel instructed by the solicitors, applied for a writ of 'habeas corpus,' directing Mr. Thomas to bring Miss Esther Lyons into court, thereby to ascertain whether or not she was under restraint.

At the hearing of the application Mr. Justice Blackburn said he had no doubt in his own mind that Mr. and Mrs. Thomas had smuggled the girl away; that they knew where she was, and that they had acted improperly, but that as she was over eighteen years of age the writ of 'habeas corpus' could not be granted.

Mr. Oppenheim submitted that there was strong proof that the girl was held against her will. He asked his lordship to grant a summons calling upon Mr. and Mrs. Thomas to 'show cause why the writ should not issue.' This summons was granted, for the 16th July.

On the 16th, when the case came again before Mr Justice Blackburn, Mr. Thomas applied for a postponement, saying that there had not been time to prepare affidavits in reply. His lordship waved aside this weak excuse, and directed Mr. and Mrs. Thomas to produce Esther Lyons in court, otherwise the writ would be issued against them. The summons was adjourned until Tuesday, July 21st.

Tuesday the 21st July saw the court once more convened. A Mr. Dodson now appeared on behalf of the Thomas's. He produced two long affidavits from his clients, admitting that they had received the girl into their house on the evening she left home; that before that day they had not known her; than on the very next day they had placed her at a ladies' school in Cardiff, and *that since that time they had not known, nor did they then know, where she was.*

★

Mr. Justice Blackburn, bound as he was by the legal position, began to lose his temper. He said outright in as many words that he did not believe the affidavits in so far as they stated that they were not able to obtain further information about Esther Lyons. Yet, by law, the most he could do at that stage was to say that unless Mr. and Mrs. Thomas stated positively, in separate affidavits, that they neither knew, nor could by any means in their power learn where the girl was, the writ should be issued.

Before the summons was again adjourned, Mr. Oppenheim handed his lordship two supplemental affidavits which had been filed on Mr. Lyons' behalf. One was by Mr. Jacobs, Minister to Cardiff Hebrew Congregation. In it he said that as late as the 13th July he had received a written proposal, the contents of which he had been asked to convey to Mr. Lyons. These were to the effect that a promise should be made that 'if the girl were brought into court no violence should be used upon her.'

The other affidavit was by a Mr. David Goodman of Pontypridd. In it he stated that he had recently attended the chapel in which Mr. Thomas was minister, and had been present when Mr. Thomas had addressed his congregation (in Welsh), acquainting them with the whole Esther Lyons case insofar as he was implicated, telling them that he would have to produce the girl in court the following Tuesday, and appealing to the congregation for their support.

Mr. Justice Blackburn then adjourned the summons until the following Tuesday.

★

And on the following Tuesday the Thomas's produced the affidavits, and again denied all knowledge of Esther Lyon's whereabouts.

It was stalemate. Mr. Justice Blackburn could do no more. He pointed out that since the girl was over sixteen years old the writ of 'habeas corpus' could not be issued until it was proved that she was held against her will.

5

Barnett Lyons returned from London a broken man. So far, the devil had won. He did not know what to do next. It was Bank Holiday... the weather was very hot, the hottest of the year. He sat down in the stillness of that summer's afternoon, no joy in his heart, and wrote the whole sad story down in a very long letter, which he addressed to the *Cardiff and Merthyr Guardian*, the newspaper of the time:

'Sir,' (he wrote) 'With aching heart, and a mind deeply agitated, I venture to address you and my fellow townsmen....'

He wrote down the whole story, and appealed for advice, the last gesture of despair. And as if by the will of the Almighty Himself, fate took a hand.

Public opinion was whipped into a frenzy. *The Cardiff and Merthyr Guardian* printed Barnett Lyons' complete letter in their issue of August 8th, 1868. The letter caused tremendous interest; dozens of letters, from both Jews and Gentiles, were received and printed by the newspaper. All as a body condemned the Thomas's actions. Comparisons were drawn with the Mortara case, and thousands of words week after week explored every point of view.

Reaction to Barnett Lyons' letter was swift. A letter was received from London dated August 15th, purporting to have come from Esther Lyons herself. In it she wrote, 'No one has ever made the slightest attempt, and still less coerced me to leave my father's house.... I declare I am quite ready to meet my father in the presence of some witnesses on his and my part, and to tell him what he already knows, that of my own accord I left his home, and that I have found in Jesus of Nazareth the saviour of my soul, and have been baptised in his name. As soon as my father accepts my proposal, and will kindly say so in your paper, I will let him know the time and place of meeting.'

From this time on all communication between father and daughter was carried on through the columns of the newspaper. On the 25th August Barnett Lyons wrote to the *Guardian*:

'Whoever reads this [Esther's] letter must, I think, concur with me in the impression that it does not appear, from its fluent style, to be the genuine language of a young Jewish girl who has just attained her eighteenth year: still, as my daughter is made to say that she is willing to meet me, I am too deeply interested.... I beg to say that I am ready and desirous to meet her in London (from whence she addresses me) at the offices of my solicitors.... She may be accompanied by any witnesses she pleases, but I desire to have the opportunity of conversing with her apart, to which she can have no possible reasonable objection.'

Three days later Barnett Lyons received a letter from his London solicitors stating that another firm of solicitors had communicated with them, arranging a meeting – 'Esther Lyons to go, accompanied by Mr. Joseph J. Allen (solicitor) with another gentleman and lady, to 36, Finsbury Circus, on Tuesday, 1st September, at 2p.m. or any more convenient time. Father and daughter to have a private interview. Afterwards Miss Lyons to return to the friends that bring her, and in the presence of Mr. Sampson Samuel – but not of the father

– to declare whether she will return with her father, or remain with those with whom she now is.'

He hardly had time to read this letter, however, before another arrived by the following post. It was from the Thomas's solicitors, Messrs. Norris & Allen. The uncertain hand of Mr. Thomas again showed itself: 'Sir, I regret to say that at present a difficulty as to the meeting proposed... has arisen... I doubt not that some other arrangement will be made... I propose seeing your solicitors on Monday morning.

Messrs. Sampson Samuel & Emanuel were well aware of the facts of the case. They knew of the continued heartbreaking delays which Mr. Lyons had suffered at the hands of the Rev. Nathaniel Thomas and his wife. When Mr. Allen did not call the following Monday as promised, and being Jewish themselves, all their seething contempt of the Thomas's momentarily came to the surface. It is more than likely that Barnett Lyons gave his authority to the letter they sent to Messrs. Norris & Allen. In any case, Mr. Lyons had by now returned to London post-haste on being informed of this turn of events. On arrival he found that a further letter had arrived from Messrs. Norris & Allen arranging a new meeting at 20, Bedford Row, W.C.

Messrs. Sampson Samuel & Emanuel wrote a letter to Norris & Allen, stating that 'they did not consider that they had acted in a manner consonant with that uprightness and straightforwardness which the dignity of their profession demanded. Still...as Mr. Lyons was in London, they wished this interview to take place without delay.'

It is not the chronicler's intention to record petty squabbles between those who should know better. Norris & Allen's reaction to this letter showed unwarranted bias, and their reply must be quoted since in it they threatened to bring about the complete collapse of negotiations. They replied that they 'did not like the tone of the letter, and that if it were shown to their clients the interview might not take place at all.' They demanded a retraction.

Sampson Samuel realised his mistake. He withdrew the letter, and substituted another, simply agreeing to the new arrangements. An interview was subsequently arranged for the following Thursday at 3p.m.

6

But what of Esther Lyons herself during these negotiations? Very little is known of the actual details of her movements. It has been established that she slept the night of March 23rd at 'Croome Villa,' Roath, in the company of Sarah Carver. The next day the girls were removed to the house of a Mrs. Keep, of No. 2, Brighton Terrace, Cardiff, who kept them there two days at least. It is certain beyond doubt that the Thomas's, during their first emphatic denials both to Barnett Lyons and the police, knew exactly where they were, and in their twisted minds glorified in the knowledge that they were fulfiling their religious calling by converting an adolescent, lonely Jewish girl, giving her fantastic luxuries which could not last, and filling her mind with the reflection of their own false glory.

As the pace of Mr. Lyons' search increased, the girls were sent to separate destinations; Esther Lyons, under first one, then another assumed name, to a Baptist institution near London, and Sarah Carver, of whom it was feared she might unwittingly implicate those concerned in the abduction, to 11, Dover Place, Clifton – also under another name – where she remained, impatiently, some considerable time. It was from this address that Sarah Carver forwarded Esther Lyons' letter to her father.

7

Barnett Lyons was a well-educated man, who loved letter-writing. His voluminous correspondence to the *Cardiff and Merthyr Guardian*, running into thousands of words, forms the basis of our narrative. Had it not been for this correspondence he might never have seen his daughter again.

Following a promise he had made to the *Guardian*, he wrote them an account of his interview with Esther that fateful Thursday. We here publish extract from his long letter:

'I went into the office at 20, Bedford Row, accompanied by my son, my brother-in-law, and my solicitor (Mr. Sampson Samuel). On our arrival my companions were requested to stay in the office down-stairs, and I was shown upstairs into a small back room at the rear of the house. After waiting nearly an hour by myself, my daughter Esther entered the room.

'And now let me endeavour to portray my emotions. When she left my house and protection she was in a robust state of health, happy and contented-looking. I found her now trembling and nervous, and oh! so fearfully emaciated and haggard that my heart ached for my poor misguided offspring.. She was clothed in very poor attire, not the same as she was accustomed to at home.

'I moved closer to her, and told her of the deep gloom and sorrow that had fallen upon our hearts and home, in consequence of her disappearance.

She said, 'I did not wish it to be so.'

'How could they have made you leave us – what did they say or do?' I asked.

Esther began to speak quickly, as if she were repeating a statement, saying, 'she had suffered a perfect martyrdom,' but she suddenly faltered, and, trembling all over became so terrified that she could not continue.

'I spoke to her quietly and reassuringly, 'Will you come home with me?'

"How can I, father ? I have taken – I have been baptised!"

"Never mind; I will forget and forgive all that.'

'Esther did not reply, but dropped her head and began to weep, as if she were bewildered. I begged and entreated her, tried to comfort her, but she was by now trembling as if torn by some violent emotion.

"I shall go mad! I shall go mad!' she cried, and fell sobbing into a chair.

'I waited a little while, then suggested that she take another week to make up her mind.

"I cannot do that,' she sobbed, the tears subsiding, "I must ask my friends whether I may do so.'

★

The whole of this interview was watched intently by Mr. Allen, through a glass aperture in the wall. He now came forward to end the interview. Mr. Lyons was then ushered downstairs, and Mr. Allen called up the others, Reuben Lyons, his uncle, and Mr. Samuel. Mr. Lyons remained below.

Reuben and his uncle embraced and kissed Esther, but were not allowed to question her.

Mr. Allen then became very formal. He asked Esther Lyons whether she would go with her father or remain with those friends with whom she had lately resided.

Esther Lyons had come to a decision in her adolescent mind:

'I will remain with my friends with whom I have been staying,' she replied.

Lyons' interview with his daughter served only to increase his determination to win back his child by any means. He wrote to the *Guardian*:

'...I do not consider myself bound by the original agreement, which I did not sign...I merely submitted to the interview to obtain a clue to my daughter's whereabouts. I trust you will, with your usual kindness, insert this correction, as it might tend otherwise to my prejudice when the case is brought before the Court of Chancery.'

The publication of these words sounded the knell of retribution to the Rev. Nathaniel Thomas, his wife, and their associates. It meant that a national scandal would bring their world tumbling down about them. As it was later brought to light at the trial, Esther Lyons was not the first innocent Jewish girl to have been 'converted.' (In most cases, it appeared, the 'conversion' had lasted only as long as there was something to be 'got out of it'!) Others had fallen prey to their promises – even Esther's younger sister Dinah had received a New Testament from them...

★

The public trial was held at the Town Hall, St. Mary's Street, Cardiff, during the week of the 26th July, 1869. It lasted four days, and caused a tremendous sensation in Cardiff. Newspapers devoted whole pages, gigantic sheets packed with massed columns of type, to their exhaustive reports. Jews and Christians of all denominations alike thronged St. Mary's Street the day the Trial opened. The papers called it a women's trial, and certainly the ladies took the opportunity of showing off their latest finery. In their hundreds they stormed the Town Hall on every day of the trial.

The chronicler would like to record the trial in detail, but space does not permit. Interested readers may like to read the voluminous reports in the Cardiff Reference Library, by referring to the details appended below.[3] Not one day passed without its sensation.

At the commencement of the first day's hearing, Mrs. Lyons, Esther's mother, fainted, and had to receive medical attention, when her daughter entered the courtroom. This was understandable, since it was the first time that she had seen her daughter since her abduction. At the conclusion of the hearing Barnett Lyons attempted to serve subpoenas upon several witnesses present on behalf of the Thomas's. As Mr. Lyons approached them a person of burly stature suddenly appeared and threatened Mr.Lyons with a loaded revolver!

For four days the trial was a wonder.' The whole story (with embellishments) was gone through again. And at the end of it the jury, which had contained neither Jews nor Baptists, returned a verdict against Mr. and Mrs. Thomas. After a long consultation they decided that there was sufficient evidence to prove that Esther Lyons left her father's home in consequence of the enticements of Mr. and Mrs. Thomas.

They therefore awarded the plaintiff £50 damages.

★

To the court, to the public, to the newspapers, this was the end of the story. But Esther Lyons did not return to her home and parents. The *Cardiff and Merthyr Guardian*, patient recorder of a past era, adds the last sad postscript to this chronicle, stating in its issue of August 7th, 1869, exactly one year after the publication of Barnett Lyons' first letter, 'she has returned to London, from whence she is to go to a religious institution in Germany.'

Barnett Lyons had failed: she was lost to him forever.

From *CAJEX*, Vol 2. No 3 July. 1952

O.M. EDWARDS (1858-1920)

Owen Morgan Edwards, from Llanuwchllyn in Meirionnydd, is one of the great figures of modern Welsh culture. He worked unflaggingly to promote the status of the Welsh language, to provide it with a popular literature, with popular magazines in Welsh and in English, and with children's material in particular. He set up the magazine *Cymru* (1891-1920), which was touched upon in the chapter on 'The Promised Land', as well as the much-loved children's journal *Cymru'r Plant*, 'Children's Wales', which ran from 1891 until O.M.'s death in harness in 1920. He was also a gifted Oxford academic, was briefly an MP for his native Meirioneth constituency, and, as the Chief Inspector of Schools in Wales, did a huge amount of pioneering work to secure a place for the native language in a school system which had until that time been exclusively English and inveterately hostile to Welsh. While aware that Edwards's view of Welsh history was naive and idealistic, and that his literary style was occasionally marred by effusiveness, I had no idea, when I began researching this book, that I would find him guilty of a serious case of racial prejudice. When a Welsh-speaking friend of mine who has some Jewish ancestry said I would find a passage on the Jews in O.M. Edwards's 1889 travelogue *O'r Bala i Genefa*, 'From Bala to Geneva', I had little doubt what I would find: a sentimental portrait of the Jews, almost certainly extending to them the same idealistic and pious portrayal which Edwards gave to the Welsh, and probably finding some homely comparisons between Jewish worship and that of the Welsh of Meirionnydd. I suppose it is in some ways a tribute to the gentle and appreciative nature, and the studied avoidance of controversy, displayed elsewhere in Edwards's work, that when I read the book I found the actual passage almost unbelievable. However, having read it and re-read it, it is all too real, and it must be recorded that such a great servant of Welsh culture as O.M. Edwards produced this shameful, credulous, extended endorsement of the age-old conspiracy theory about Jewish greed. The socialist critic Gareth Miles also confessed to surprise when he first read Edwards's comments: 'How could a Welshman so civilised, so intelligent, so humane, so humorous, so entertaining, so mischievous have cherished such abominable prejudices against a nation whose history and religion had influenced ours so strongly?'[4]

As a matter of interest, it is worth adding a few details to explain the real nature of the Joseph Brafman whose work is the source of Edwards's conspiracy theory which he reports uncritically in this passage. Brafman was a Russian Jew who had abandoned Judaism and had become a Christian. He was professor of Hebrew in a Minsk theological seminary and was also a keen collaborator with the Tsarist secret police, who were ever on the lookout for supposed Jewish conspiracies. It is a sad fact that oppressed minorities like the Jews can, under the pressure of the majority community's hostility, produce individuals who, in seeking to escape the persecution, join in enthusiastically with the condemnation of their own people, sometimes doing so with a dark creativity far excelling that of the non-Jewish persecutor. For its part, Wales too has produced its share of anti-Welsh Welshmen, the early twentieth century novelist, playwright and short-story writer Caradoc Evans (1878-1945) made a career out of calumniating his own people for the delectation of English prejudice in a way very similar to that in which Brafman exposed his fellow-Jews to Gentile hatred.[5] Brafman's books *The Book of Kahal* and *Local and Universal Jewish Brotherhood*, codified and sought to give academic credibility to some of the wilder Jewish world-conspiracy theories. They later became the basis for the notorious anti-semitic publication, the work of many hands, *The Protocols of the Elders of Zion*.[6] It was upon spoken accounts of Brafman's own two books that O.M. Edwards based the prejudices he expresses in the following passages. It is interesting to note that when Thomas Ellis edited O.M. Edwards's travel books for re-issue after his death, he tactfully left out this offensive material. Edwards's views in these passages admit of no excuse. It is, however, only fair to say that I can find no evidence of similar prejudice elsewhere in Edwards's work, and to add that in his devotional writings he was happy to use specifically Jewish – not merely Biblical – material for religious instruction; and that he was later happy to publish admiring material about the Jews such as that written by T. ap Simon and quoted in this book in the chapter 'The Promised Land'. The unworthy opinions in the following passage show how even an otherwise generous nature like O.M. Edwards's can prove vulnerable to the irrational virus of anti-semitism.

from FROM BALA TO GENEVA.

Yes, my curious friend, I have realised for a long while now, that the Jews, the old Israelites of the Bible, are still a living nation. I remember well the time when I felt this first. I was preaching, around five years ago, in a mountainous area in Cardiganshire, and as I went towards the chapel, on that cold November morning, I saw heaps of corn rotting on the hillside. I asked the kind farmer who was with me if they had had a bad harvest. 'No,' he said, referring to the corn, 'that there's the work of the Jews'. My sermon was weighing too much on my mind for me to ask more about them at the time; but I knew then that it was possible to see that what one sees every day on this Continent can also happen in Wales – a Jewish wolf falling on his prey in the darkest hour.

Around a month ago, I was walking in the evening along the banks of the river Neckar, in the town of Heidelberg, thinking of Wales, and feeling *hiraeth*. I heard a sweet sound, the sound of melancholy music, rising and falling with the breeze, and I thought for a moment that I was hearing the singing of Communion in Llanuwchllyn. I wandered around for a while, wondering from where the singing was coming, but in the end I found myself outside a plain building, like Cynllwyd Chapel, at the end of a narrow muddy street. As I drew nearer to it, I could hear the singing in all its sweet strength, and I knew well that the Germans could not sing like this. I looked up, and I could see the Hebrew writing on the wall, a verse of the Old Testament, saying that holiness becomes this place. Then I understood I was standing before a synagogue, and that I was hearing the old Psalms of Israel. That melancholy tune was not for the sufferings of the Saviour, but for the sufferings of the nation which refused him; the hymn was not

Remembering his groans in the garden

but was

> By the rivers of Babylon, where we sat down, and where we wept
> when we remembered Zion.

I pulled at the door for a long while, but I could not get in; and
when the singing had finished I started off for the river again,
humming –

> O Lord do thou give heed
> To those of Abraham's seed;
> Restore their state.

When I got to the house, I asked Frau Nebel, at suppertime, if there
were many Jews in Heidelberg. She looked at me in shock, and said
there were enough of them wherever there was blood to be sucked.
'Our students go to them,' she said, 'and ask to borrow a thousand
marks. "You may," the Jew says, "if you write that you are getting two
thousand." Then, when he sees his chance, the Jew comes to his
debtor to say he has to pay the debt, or write on it that it is three thousand. In the end, the Jew sucks everything the poor student has, and
many a one has broken his heart or has done away with himself'.

I asked if she would come with me to the synagogue the following
Saturday. Good heavens! She would not come. What would her
neighbours think of her? But I went. The service had started. I
removed my hat after going in, and the moment I removed it, the
finger of every Jew in the place was pointing to my head. I saw that
they were all wearing their hats and I put mine back on my head,
although it was not one of the better-looking ones, it had been in the
water of the Scheldt with that Fleming, and having seen that my hair
was covered, every Jew turned back towards Jerusalem again. The
priest was singing something I could not understand, while the
Levite was holding the scroll beside him, and all the congregation
answered in song. I began thinking. It was hard to realise that the
oldest nation on earth – a nation in comparison with whom the
Romans and Greeks are only infants – is still a living nation. And yet,
here they were before my eyes, – some old Haggai, some young
Jeremiah or Zechariah. The women were in the gallery, there was one
incomparably pretty girl there – some Rachel or Rebecca – I saw her
afterwards walking through the vegetable market.

> She walks in beauty like the night.

And they were singing old hymns, hymns that were sung before Homer told the grief of Troy and before Virgil praised Aeneas and his descendants. How long and how exciting their history! I think we should know more about them so that we can see how certain is the judgement of God. Do you remember us writing an essay together on the influence of the Jews in the history of England, and the great research that was done? Do you still sympathise so much with them? I thought at that time that you had just been reading Ivanhoe. Do you remember the way you insisted on making the essay too long by reciting their endless sufferings, instead of keeping to your subject, which was their influence on our history? Do you remember how hard it was to persuade you that it was of necessity, and perhaps of justice, that Edward I banished them from England? I do not know for sure if you would admit laughing in your anger when we came across the story of that sea captain who stranded the Jews in his ship on a sandbank in the middle of the sea, and told them as he raised the sails of his ship that they should pray for some Moses to come and guide them through the waters. But we must remember, although their treatment in England was so harsh, that this was the gentlest treatment they received. Amongst the other bad effects of the Crusades was the fact that they inflamed the passions against the Jews in England. But after that, they had a pretty fair treatment on the whole. They were looked on by everyone with a kind of scornful distaste. But this affected them in the same way it affected the Gypsies – their life withered, and their numbers reduced. In the lands where their houses were burned above their heads, where their women were ripped open alive, where their babies were thrown from bayonet to bayonet, they have thrived and multiplied. But in England, where they have had every fair play, there are fewer of them than anywhere. I can explain this strange fact. But before doing that, I must tell many other things I have learned about them – things that cast a great deal of light on lines in their character that we cannot explain. I have asked many people who deal with them in business, and I have had many a lengthy conversation with learned Jews. But I do not have time to start to tell my discoveries tonight, my train leaves in half an hour.

Hotel France, Strasbourg.
As I was wandering through Basle Museum this morning – one of the richest collections of Medieval items – I happened across a stone

which reminded me of the promise I made the day before yesterday, that I would tell you some interesting things I know about the Jews of these days. This stone had been part of the city wall, somewhere towards the base; but before that it had been on a Jew's grave, as the writing upon it tells; –

> This gravestone lies above the Rabbi Jacob, son of David, who was murdered, and who died honourably upon the Sabbath day, and who was buried on the Monday, the eleventh day of Elus, in the year 6090. May the garden of Eden be his resting place, with all the other righteous, for ever and ever, Amen.

There are thousands of stones like this in the earth of the Continent, stones recording mad attacks on the Jews by the mob, when it had been inflamed by something, by a sermon on the Crusades, or by a desire to possess the property of the circumcised. The history of many attacks like this can be seen, the heartbreaking scenes which followed them have been kept in mind since the earliest days up to the recent massacre in Southern Russia; but if it were not for this stone, the world would not know about the murderous attack of the Christians of Basle on the Jews in the month of *Elul 6090* – August 1030. When the behaviour of the nations towards one another is judged before the throne on the last day, will not God call some strange witnesses?

The Jews are hated for the things which make them useful in the world. In the Middle Ages, and indeed, in the Dark Ages before that, they were the doctors of the world, they knew about the qualities of herbs and minerals. Their reward for this was to be burnt and drowned as sorcerers. They were feared and hated because they were familiar with poison, and could play with death. Ages before banks were established, they were also the financiers of the world. They were usurers, undoubtedly, but one must remember that where there is great uncertainty, interest is high, and people were very glad to be able to borrow money when commerce had scarcely begun. Before condemning Shylock, consider how hard it would be to conduct commerce without credit at all, and remember that the Jews were the only moneylenders until very recently. But was there not more increase in commerce in England than anywhere in the last four hundred years, and why were there not Jews there also? Yes, there was an astonishing increase in commerce, and while commerce increased, the Jews, contrary to their practise in every other country, were impoverished and perishing. The reason for this is that they were not persecuted in England, and it is persecution which has given the Jews their ability to succeed. It was this which taught them the unyielding persistence, that stubborn flexibility, that makes success certain to those who possess it. At times their houses were burned, and their valuable merchandise was hauled into the street, their velvet and silks were spoiled, their gold and gems were thrown away and they were chased as though by a hunt from hiding place to hiding place – but they had learned to suffer in silence, they looked on the rage of the Christians as they looked on the devastation of a wave or a sudden flood, they did not think about revenge; but once the tempest had gone past, they applied themselves to recover their wealth, as though nothing had happened. Their genius is not more than that of other nations, none of them have reached the greatest goals of their professions except Spinoza. The secret of their success is their persistence, which they have learned through suffering. This can be seen in the history of at least one of them in England. When Benjamin Disraeli first stood up in the Parliament of Great Britain, he was forced to sit down by the laughing which his many-coloured dress and his strange manner of speech caused. He did not get angry, but persisted, until he won the highest place in that Parliament.

Can one justify the hatred of the nations of the Continent towards the Jews? I have thought a great deal before replying – yes, without a doubt. For one thing, their presence has been an obstacle on the road to developing commerce; although they have been, in one sense, of great value. Because they are Jews, and therefore open to heavy losses through the attacks of the unruly mob, they had to charge high prices for lending their money. At the same time, their presence made Christian banks unnecessary. The result is that only in England, where there are only a few Jews, did banking develop as it should, there alone can the businessman borrow dormant money for a reasonable price. By today, this has made the Bank of England the bank of all the nations; and has made a small crossroads in London, known as Lombard Street, the treasury of the world. But had the enemies of the Jews seen far enough to see this? No, certainly, they had not seen the distant results, but they had felt the effects which caused them, the usury and cruelty of the Jews.

A few years ago, a prophet rose amongst them to show them their untruth. A poor Jew by the name of Jacob Brafman. After researching their history for many years in poverty and need – because he was only a poor cobbler, and he had a large family to keep – he published a book in the bitter spirit of the old prophets. I searched for the book a great deal, and my bookseller in Heidelberg told me that it had only been published in Russian, and that it was not now available. That bookseller was a Jew, although I did not know that at the time. But I spoke to people who had read the book. Brafman shows that Jews are a separate government within the country in which they live. In Eastern Europe, their Council has the right to charge a tax on the meat they sell and the right to mediate between one Jew and another. These two things give them great power. Through the tax, the Council has enough money in hand to employ attorneys or to bribe officers of the law. Through the ability to settle matters between Jews, the Council can get the parties completely into its hands; because, before undertaking to reconcile them, it makes them sign their name under a fake bill, and they have to pay the money if ever they sin against the Council again. The Council makes use of the Christian law to force those who anger it to pay the unjust debt. But why do the Jews themselves allow themselves to suffer such oppression at the hands of their Council? Because they get great benefits from it. It is the Council which controls their operations, so that two Jews will not run after the same prey. They work as follows, – suppose that a man is living in his own house and smallholding, contented and debtless. A Jew comes by, he does not remember the Ten Commandments, and he goes to the Council to ask for that house for himself. After he has paid some money, the council transfers the house and smallholding into his possession, without the real owner knowing anything of what is going on. But how will the Jew be any the better off? He is certain he can cast his net without any other Jew disturbing him. He will go to the man, who thinks no ill, and will tempt him through offering him wines, and silk, and gems and splendid furniture on credit, and in the end drives him a pauper from his home. Are the Jews able to do this and sing the Psalms of David at the same time? Yes they are, because they look on the property of all the uncircumcised as lawful prey of the children of the promise; the gentile's property, says one of the writings of the Council, belongs to the Jew on the same condition that the fish of the sea belong to him – if he can get them. Remember that Brafman is talking most particularly about Eastern Europe, about Russia and Austria; I have not had the advantage of seeing for myself to what degree this is true of the Jews of Germany. We shall get proof yet, I know you will not believe it without it.

Their mutual understanding in commerce is a uniting bond between them. It is easy to see that the scorn of the world and having to live among foreigners makes the synagogue more of a home to them, makes their religion the more dear, and their hymns the sweeter. Consider the contempt of the Jews for the unfaithful one who deserts them. Have you heard of their excommunication ritual? There's Spinoza before the synagogue, on the charge of denying the traditions of the fathers. The synagogue is dressed in black; the black wax candles stand in vessels full of blood, and throw a weak light on eyes which are full of rage as they behold a traitor and a heretic. His own former teacher declares the long and terrible series of curses above his head; the candles fall down and are extinguished in the blood; and the last thing the excommunicated person hears as he leaves the darkened synagogue is the deep Amen to the curses from the depths of hearts filled with hatred and bitterness. No, it is not an easy thing for a Jew to leave his nation, the bonds of worldly welfare and love and fear are too strong.

What is the condition of the Jew today? He is everything which the prophets depicted. Listen to Ezekiel -

> Then I looked and behold a hand sent before me, and a book folded within it. And it unfolded before me; and it had been written over front and back, and there was written upon it, grief, lamentation and woe.

The whole writing, front and back, has been fulfiled. Despite everything, this nation is still stiff-necked; I thought as I saw it trying to give to God the worship he rejects, that they are still 'hard-hearted and hard-faced sons'. Read the first six chapters of Ezekiel, gaze at every sentence, and you will have a living picture of the condition of the Jews in these days.

What is the work of the Jews today? He is everything except what God intended at the beginning for him to be. Inscribing the holiness of the Lord on the bridles of the horse, sanctifying the world, teaching religion to the nations was their work; but their whole soul is directed towards making money. The Jew does not talk about holiness and religion – perhaps he does not understand what they are any more – but about gold jewellery and gems and fine clothes. He was sent to proclaim another world; he sold his soul for this world. Is their condition hopeless? Was it of the last day that the prophet spoke? –

> Their silver shall be cast into the streets, and their gold shall be
> put aside; their silver and their gold will not be able to save them
> in the day of the Lord's anger; their soul will not be satisfied and
> their bowels will not be filled, because of the iniquity of their
> transgression.

No; I think that they refer to this. I think that the Jew will also be saved. For one thing, God is very merciful. Did you notice the fifth verse of the tenth chapter of Ezekiel, –

> And the sound of the cherubs was heard in the courts without,
> like the sound of Almighty God when he speaks.

In the middle of the chapters of threats, when his wrath was greatest, his voice was as tender as the whisper of the wings of the cherubs. And the man of sorrows is easy to love; I know of a heart harder than that of the Jew, which was drawn to love him. The Jew's whole being is given to acquiring the gems, and jewellery and gold and silver treasures of this world at present, but I am quite certain that he shall find a better treasure, and that he will be heard singing, –

> There are more treasures in Your name,
> Than in all the Treasures of India.

Translation from *O'r Bala i Genefa*, 1889

SAUNDERS LEWIS (1893-1985)

With Saunders Lewis, we come to the most notorious example of anti-semitic prejudice in Welsh literature, although not the worst; I think the above article can claim that title. I summarised Lewis's career and the background to his attitudes towards the Jews in the opening chapter, so I will confine myself here to some additional remarks. There is no doubt at all that Lewis subscribed for a period from the late 1920s and up to the start of the 1940s to the conspiracy theory which saw international Jewish financiers as a class of rootless capitalist oppressors promoting their own financial interests above those of the nations in which they dwelt. This paranoia could be found both on the left and the right of the political spectrum, although Lewis had imbibed it from the neo-Catholic right. He was a great admirer of T.S. Eliot, and sought to imitate in Wales Eliot's status as an oracular and authoritative cultural commentator and as a literary champion of tradition, order and civilisation against the chaos of the modern world which he dreaded so much. He adopted many of Eliot's ideas and techniques, imitating his style of eclectic phantasmagoric poetry as a means of portraying what he saw as the nightmarish chaos of the collapse of modern civilisation, and later imitating Eliot's revived verse drama form to embody the possibility of a re-imposition of order and traditional values. However, he also adopted from Eliot – and from the anti-modern neo-Catholic milieu of which he was a part – the belief in a Jewish conspiracy, a belief which fed that milieu's need for a scapegoat.[7] In his 1939 poem 'Y Dilyw', 'The Deluge', based on his experience of the Depression in the south Wales Valleys, he referred to the supposed role of Jewish financiers in New York in bringing about the downturn:

> Then, on Olympus, in Wall Street, nineteen hundred and twenty
>   nine,
> Busy at their immortal scientific task of guiding the profits of fate,
> The gods, with their feet in the Aubusson carpets,
> And their Hebrew noses in the quarter's statistics,
> Decided that the time had come to make credit scarce
> throughout the universe of gold.

Lewis also expressed similar sentiments in several articles and speeches until, in due course, the Nazi persecution of the Jews became so apparent that it put an end to such comments. It does not absolve Lewis from the charge of prejudice, merely sets a limit on its extent, to point out that during the time that he subscribed to this conspiracy theory he maintained a clear distinction between Jews per se and supposed irresponsible Jewish capitalists. His clear and repeated condemnation of Nazism and anti-semitism from the 1940s onward, although it does not redeem his earlier prejudice, also needs to be noted. Turning to the text of his work, whereas the above quote was a passing reference in a long poem, the following poem, given in full, 'Golygfa Mewn Caffe', is more pervaded by suspicion of the Jews, and is a good example of the kind of mindset which had given a home to such suspicion. It is the only other example of anti-semitic imagery in Lewis's small body of poetry. Published early in 1940, it is set in Aberystwyth, the traditional Welsh cultural capital. The references to "Kosher vinegar" and to "Golder's Green" occur in an atmosphere – heavily indebted to the early Eliot for its style – which stresses the supposed dehumanising and deracinating effects of the modern world. Jewishness, seen as something super-national or un-national, is used as one more image to underline the perception that the old certainties of identity and culture are being dissolved in a corrosive mixture of modernity, internationalism and incipient totalitarianism – indicated by the images of masses and the military.[8]

A SCENE IN A CAFE.

From the haste of the uniformed garrison,
And their clamour in Great Darkgate Street,
Amidst the host poured from the mart and the college
And from the chapel schoolrooms and from the taverns,

Amidst the chequered crowd,
The sad crowd that had lost the virtue of the intellect,
The living dead, Amidst the mirthless sneer and the red talons
      of the women
With their lips, like wanton nightmares tearing
The sleep of their gorilla faces,
Amidst the fleeing crowd
Fleeing the death of air and the life from the bomb,
Amidst the speaking skeletons, the shambling ashes,
We had pushed through the doors of the cafe
Hiding our empty skulls behind our figleaves,
And grabbed a corner of a table against the army of Babel,
And shouted above the bones and the teacups
At a waitress nearby.

So swift was the service of the waitress –
She brought us oysters and Kosher vinegar and the burial
      service on toast.
The rain fell like a parachute on the street,
But the urban guards of the ash-cans stood
Like policemen in a row next to their houses.
And an old witch, with a cord around her neck, went
From can to can in the rain, and lifted each lid,
And found them, each coffin, empty.
And at the bottom of the road,
Next to the ashes eating over there in the cafe,
The ashes that had escaped from the cans,
The greasy females of Whitechapel, the Ethiopians of Golder's
      Green,
On a convenient lamppost, and with her cord, the witch
      hanged herself.
We saw her heels turning in the rain,
And we knew by her white gloves and their odour of camphor
That she hailed from the old land.
She was buried undenominationally by the BBC
on the wavelength of the empire.

                              28.2.40

Translation from Ed. Medwin Hughes, *Cerddi Saunders Lewis*, 1992

W.J. GRUFFYDD (1881-1954)

William John Gruffydd rose from humble origins in the quarrying communities of north west Wales to become professor of Welsh at Cardiff. He was a talented and effective poet, and a highly-influential editor, anthologist, and critic. He was a convinced Nonconformist, and was Liberal in his political sympathies, and, taking pride in his proletarian roots, he often found himself vigorously opposing Saunders Lewis's version of Welsh history and politics. He engaged in a lengthy public debate with Lewis in the 1920s through the pages of *Y Llenor*, 'The Writer', a magazine which Gruffydd edited from 1922 to 1951; Gruffydd championed a liberal Nonconformism against Lewis's more conservative neo-Catholicism. Although Gruffydd supported Lewis during the Penyberth arson affair in 1936 and 1937, he and Lewis stood against one another in a Parliamentary by-election for the University of Wales seat in 1943, Gruffydd for the Liberals and Lewis for Plaid Cymru. Gruffydd won by 3,098 votes to 1,330 after a quite bitter campaign in which he had accused Lewis of fascism, a charge which Lewis hotly denied. Knowing that, and knowing that Gruffydd had been Liberal Wales's most effective foil to Lewis's more conservative tendencies, it is all the more remarkable that Gruffydd could have written, and at such a late stage, an article like the following, taken from his editorial to *Y Llenor* in 1941 in which he displays anti-semitic prejudice. Gruffydd was a controversialist, given to disputes, outbursts, invective and contradictory opinions, so these comments are not as out-of-character as those we considered a little earlier from O.M. Edwards, who was Gruffydd's lifelong hero. However, they are entirely out of touch with the Welsh Nonconformity and liberalism for which Gruffydd was otherwise such an eloquent spokesman.

from EDITOR'S NOTES

Already the prospects in Wales are enough to break the heart of anyone who loves their country, – the men scattered the length and breadth of England, – and soon the women too will have gone, – the rural areas full of English people, the Welsh language facing dangers in her last strongholds, North Wales full of rich and crafty Jews who lap up all the resources of the country and leave the poor natives deprived and helpless. And by the way, is it not time for someone to protest openly against these Jews who have become a burden on Llandudno, Colwyn Bay, Abergele and the surrounding countryside?[9] Are the Jews completely unable to learn a lesson from the history of their nation in other countries? I had a conversation the other day with two or three of them, and I was shocked by their attitudes to the events around them. They do not yet realise that they have had any responsibiity at all for their afflicted state as a people in the Nazi countries. It appears that they have two main aims, and two alone, – escaping from every danger in every place whatever the danger to other people, and carrying forward their old traditional manner of enriching themselves on the weaknesses of the gentile. 'Antisemitism', you say. No, just trying to give a word of warning in time to a nation which deserves the best the world can give it, but which is in real danger in this country, as in every other country, if they continue to behave as they are. If they do not heed the warning, they will be a problem in Wales as well as in England, and when a nation becomes a problem it is vain for it to expect justice from the folk who suffer under the results of that problem. The sad thing is that an insignificant journal like *Y Llenor*, of which the world knows virtually nothing, is the only place a warning like this can appear. There is a simple reason for that – very few papers except the Welsh-language papers do not have the finger of the Jews in them, directly or otherwise.

From *Y Llenor*, Vol 20, 1941

GERAINT GOODWIN (1903-41)

This, thankfully, is the last example of anti-semitism in this section. It is from the work of the novelist from Newtown in Montgomeryshire, Geraint Goodwin. He made a successful career for himself as a Fleet Street journalist before becoming a full-time novelist, who became increasingly an advocate of Welsh identity and rural society in the face of the threats of the modern world. He died from consumption before reaching the age of 40. The following extract is from his most famous novel *The Heyday in the Blood*, published in 1936, and set in a Welsh border tavern. In this passage, the threat of the modern world to the values of the rural community is expressed via the intrusion of the character of Mr Birbaum, a caricature of a Jewish plutocrat, who has visited the area in order to secure a country girl as cheap domestic labour in his Golders Green home. It is a portrait based on age-old stereotypes of Jewish deceit and foreignness. However, in passing, it is worth noting that Goodwin's portrayal of the Welsh, particularly in the fantastic pidgin-English which he puts into their mouths, is possibly even more of a caricature than his portrayal of Mr Birbaum.

from THE HEYDAY IN THE BLOOD

'The Messiah...' Seth shouted again, getting worked up. 'I tell you! Wait till next Prelim. You beat us all right in 'Behold the Lamb', but, by Christ, we sing you to hell in 'Glory be to God'.'

'Sit down ... sit down. Haf be!' said Moses. This competitive spirit as between the villages always led to trouble.

'There's only one thing in music,' went on Seth. 'You must give a note its full value, like...doh, ray, me, soh...oh...oh...oh,' he warbled, waving his hand over his head like a hawk fluttering.

'Trumpeter, what are you sounding now,' said Twmi, reading from the label of the broken disc. 'Well, that's his last trump whatever.' He flung the disc into the fire, staving it into the ashes with his heel. He was enjoying the fun, breakages or no breakages, and his face was aglow. He was like that – a thing would have to go very deep before it rankled.

'Doh, ray, me, fa...fa...fa...' went on Seth, his head up like a hen drinking, his eyes closed in ecstasy.

'Like an old jay,' said Twmi, jerking a finger at him.

At this stage the company always said in loud whispers how Seth had a voice of rare quality, and how, if he only had it trained, he would be another Ben Davies; and Seth would pretend not to hear, but clear his throat in readiness.

'Let's haf penillion now,' said Moses. The penillion was a traditional tune for the harp with the words extemporized and most often topical, and often bawdy.

> I wass haf a sister Bella
> She wass haf a South Wales fella....

'Whist, whist,' broke in Dici in alarm. 'Remember the jentlemens.'

'Nice man, Mr. Birbaum,' said Moses unctuously.

'But what I can't see, now,' said Dici in his inquiring way, 'iss as how a Jew iss an Englishman.' He paused and scratched his head. 'For an Englishman can't be a Jew, now. Ysgyrn ... it hass me beat, it hass.'

'They arr the chosen race,' answered Moses. 'They can pick and choose, like.'

'Hush', said Wil, 'here he comes'.

Mr. Birbaum came in from the door leading on to the old wing, carrying a bottle of whisky which he and Mr. Shufflebotham split every night at dinner. He was a middle-aged man with a paunch which was as yet but a protuberance, a white creased faced and ringed eyes like an owl's. He nodded affably to the company, held out his hand in protest to an offer of a seat, and took a place on a bench alongside the wall.

'How do you do sirr?' said Dici, with a nod. He was given the still, self-conscious welcome of a people who could not but be polite. But the joy of the place had gone out like a fire damped.

'How hass things gone down the brook to-day?' went on Dici.

'Not bad; not bad. A few leetle ones. But they were taking a siesta I think.'

'Yess, yess,' said Dici looking wise. 'But I tell you, sirr, as how there's nothing to touch a coch-y-bondhu. Little black fly with a 'ackle as comes off the alders: Welsh fly, the *coch-y-bondhu*... gone all round the 'orrld it hass. The march brown iss goot but not azz goot. They eats a Welsh fly first like.'

'Vell, vell,' answered Mr Birbaum. 'It is all the same to me. The countryside is so beau-tiful.'

'Not pad,' said Dici modestly. He was upholding the conversation.

'Not bad!' answered Mr. Birbaum, coming alight. 'You vant to put it on the map, make it go, like the Sviss do. Nobody knows about it! Vales for the Velsh! I believe in Vales for the Velsh...but you can have too much Vales for the Velsh.'

'Yes: yes,' said Wili breaking in, in his best voice. 'Too insulated we arr... and that's straight.'

'Vhat is business vidout Nature... especially in the spring?' went on Mr. Birbaum.

He beckoned to Twmi in a confidential way and led the way back to his room. Twmi shuffled after him, swearing under his breath. Mr. Shufflebotham had gone to bed, having tired himself out thrashing the water. Twmi stood there, his face bemused. He guessed it was something important, or he would not have gone.

'Now Toome: – sit down, sit down,' Mr. Birbaum began, handing him a cigar. Twmi bit the end off and spat it into the fire and then lit up. He enjoyed a good cigar: his irritation eased off a bit.

'This is a leetle business chat,' the other said almost roguishly. 'No ... a little friendly chat.'

Twmi sat there, imperturbable, blowing the smoke in blue gusts around him. In awkward company he sat immovable, lifeless. He was giving nothing away.

'About Beti...' The father's eyes narrowed and a glint like a spark came in them. 'She is wasting her time.'

'What hass she done?' asked Twmi, his voice going strange.

'No, no, Twmi.' He patted him on the back affably. 'Beti is a good girl.'

'Humph,' said the father. But the grunt was more eloquent than speech.

'You think it over,' said Mr. Birbaum. He had come to the end before he had begun. The going was too hard for him. He would have liked to say what was on his mind and got it done with – that his sister in Golders Green had written him to find a country girl when he was next in Wales. Country girls were cheaper than town girls, were not so flighty, and were satisfied with half the time off. That was what there was to it.

'Service...?' said Twmi in the same voice and with just the lift of an eyebrow.

'Oh no, said Mr. Birbaum, relieved and affable. 'She would be quite one of the family. My sister in London has beeg house, beeg car, beeg garden. Golder's Green is right in the country with its own shops, tubes, buses...everyting.'

'Think it over, went on Mr. Birbaum with the same affable pat. He felt that he had gained ground, but was not sure.

'Me think it over?' said Twmi. 'It's Beti's think. It's her funeral.'

That brought Mr. Birbaum's affability up sharp, but perhaps it was only Twmi's way of putting it. 'There's no hurry,' he said at the door.

'Right you arr,' answered Twmi, in that give-away-nothing tone.

He said nothing at supper until he had finished. It was his custom to have a raw onion with cheese: afterwards he carefully rinsed out his mouth with a little vinegar and then chewed a sprig of parsley.

Beti kept her eyes on her plate. She had seen her father go to Mr. Birbaum and knew only too well that something was coming.

'Wants her to go to London,' he said casually. He nodded towards the 'jentlemens' wing. 'The Jew wan.'

The mother stopped dead in her stride, in the act of clearing away. 'Talk sense!' she said.

The old man was nettled.

'Chance as a skivvy. Now you understand?'

'You arr always putting things in the wrong,' went on the mother shrilly. 'What did he say?'

'What I said, answered Twmi stolidly. 'No more: no less.'

'He could have asked me,' said the mother, her face taut.

'So he could: so he will, I daresay,' replied her husband with fine contempt.

'It's a chance,' she said tentatively. She had caught firm hold of the idea but she could only stretch out a feeler as yet.

The old man pushed his chair back.

'What you think, Beti?' her mother asked condescendingly. It was the first time they had noticed her existence.

Beti looked down at her plate, her forehead wrinkled in a frown. Her heart, which had seemed to leap up at mention of it, had now steadied. she could hear it drumming.

'I don't want,' she answered.

'There's a wan!' shouted her mother in exasperation. 'A chance like this and what she say. 'I don't want.' There's ungrateful you arr.' She went on and on in her shrill high voice.

'Haf be,' roared the father, as he got up to go. 'Beti do as she want.'

The mother waited until he had gone out and then began again.

'Leave me alone, Mam,' said Beti, worn out with it all. 'I will think: I will indeed.' She was on the verge of tears.

★

Beti was in the yard having a 'look'. Having a 'look' meant that she was doing nothing and when her mother's shrill voice was raised as it would be all she could say was that she 'was having a look'.

But she did not like to be in the house these days. Her mother's frown, her forced silences, were always a reproach. She was made to think that she was letting them all down, was doing something terrible, by not jumping at Mr. Birbaum's offer. This thinking it over was far worse than saying no right out: it kept with her all day long like a guilty secret. The first thing when she woke up she remembered Mr. Birbaum, and then it all began to work in her mind like bread rising; all day long she tried to keep it away from herself, but it always came back. There was no joy for her now – not until she said no, and then her mother would always hold it over her. So there would really be no joy ever again. And it was all because of Mr. Birbaum, that nasty man.' Everything served to remind her of Mr. Birbaum: she had never really disliked anyone before.

His great blue limousine was backed in the coach-house with a plaid rug thrown over its shining snout, and the old brake had been moved out into the yard for the hens to roost in it. The old cord seats were rotting in the dew and it was in a fine mess. And this was their brake! Why did her father let things like this happen? It was so unlike him.

When the big blue car started up, sending out a cloud of oily smoke into the eaves, the swallows, as one, darted out with a screech. Perhaps it was the noise, perhaps it was the smoke, or perhaps, thought Beti, they too did not like Mr. Birbaum. But the little ones were left there with their naked necks and heads, like a handful of bone spoons, showing over the rim of the clay-crusted nest. If they were poisoned by the smoke, who would care? Mr. Birbaum and the other English 'jentlemens' were just like the smoke. They made the air smell. They took something away from it all. She stood there with a bitterness in her heart she had never known before.

From *The Heyday in the Blood*, 1936

PAUL MORRISON

Without a doubt, the worst example of anti-semitic activity in Wales was the rioting which took place in the Gwent valleys in August 1911. It was the sole example of an anti-semitic riot in Britain outside London in the period from the middle of the eighteenth century to the present day. The full story is given in Ursula Henriques' *The Jews of South Wales*[10], so what follows is a brief summary.

The riots started against a background of widespread and protracted industrial unrest which had brought the Gwent coalfield to a standstill. On the night of August 19, with no prior warning, a mob attacked and looted eighteen Jewish shops in Tredegar. Police halted the disorder, and, due to the threat of further trouble, the army was called in. But they could not stop the rioting flaring up in neighbouring Valley towns over the subsequent few days, when Jewish shops were attacked in Ebbw Vale, Rhymney, Victoria, Cwm, Waunllwyd, Abertyswg, Brynmawr, Bargoed and Senghennydd before the riots finally ended a week later. The authorities took the issue very seriously, and there was a flurry of official reports and investigations. The matter was also the subject of anxious debate in the Jewish and non-Jewish press as correspondents sought for an explanation for the shocking episode. Both Jewish and non-Jewish commentators could be found wondering whether the activities of a few allegedly unscrupulous Jewish landlords had brought vengeance on the whole community; others sought to play down the anti-semitic element of the incidents, pointing out that the shops of non-Jews had also been attacked. Many on both sides – the Welsh because they did not like to think their own people could be so prejudiced, the Jews because they did not want to risk further trouble – found it hard to admit that this was anti-semitism pure and simple. But no amount of wishful thinking can alter the fact that the rioting contained a large element of undeniable anti-semitism.[11]

Both Welsh and Jews subsequently have seen fit to largely ignore the incident, treating it, understandably enough, as an isolated outbreak in an otherwise happy relationship. I could find no literary treatment of the subject until the production of the 1999 feature film *Solomon and Gaenor*. The film, a love story between a Jew and a Welsh girl in the Gwent valleys, is set against the background of the riots. It is the work of Paul Morrison, who is himself Jewish. A practising psychotherapist, he has also had a career as a documentary film-maker. *Solomon and Gaenor*, which was filmed in a mixture of Welsh, English and Yiddish, was Morrison's first feature film and starred Ioan Gruffudd and Nia Roberts in the title roles. It was nominated for an Oscar for Best Foreign-Language Film. The following extract from the screenplay depicts the riots themselves. In the scenes leading up to this extract, Solomon Levinsky has been conducting a clandestine romance with a local chapel-going Gentile girl, Gaenor. As the riots approach, he is contemplating running away from his family in order to join her. Meanwhile Gaenor's thuggish brother, Crad, is one of the ringleaders of the riots.

from SOLOMON AND GAENOR

OUTSIDE THE SYNAGOGUE. DAY. EXT.[12]
Solomon, Isaac and Benjamin approach the synagogue for the morning service.

The rabbi and a couple of the senior members of the small community, together with Philip, come scurrying up the track to greet them. The rabbi is small, bearded, bespectacled and chubby with a bossy mien. They go into an agitated huddle.

Isaac leads the family on the track home with characteristic determination. Solomon is doing his best to pretend nothing is happening that might interfere with his own plans.

SOLOMON (E)
Surely you aren't taking this seriously. You are well-respected here. This isn't Poland.

Isaac's face remains set.

OUTSIDE THE SHOP. DAY. EXT.
Dusk. Isaac is boarding up the windows of his shop with old boards and timber. Solomon holds up the boards while Isaac slams in the nails with mighty blows of his hammer. A number of neighbours stand watching, their faces expressionless. Something is in the air.

THE BACK KITCHEN. NIGHT. INT.
Rezl reaches into the dresser and pulls out her jewellry box. She snatches out the most treasured items and stuffs them into a hidden pocket in the lining of her coat.

THE SHOP. NIGHT INT.

Solomon moves quickly through the shop, and behind the counter. He looks up to check that there is no-one else around. Across the road two men are watching the shop strangely. He stares out at them. They move away. Solomon with a knife prises out a loose brick close to the floor. He pulls out a small wad of notes, the family wealth, counts off a few, adds them to a few of his own in a small purse, and stuffs them in his pocket. He returns the rest. He mutters to himself.

SOLOMON (Y)

A dank Mamme, a dank Tatte.
(Thank you Mama. Thank you Papa)

THE CHAPEL. DAY. INT.

Gaenor is singing, joining the hymn with rapt attention. She seems very calm. Her mother and Bronwen stand with her.

Members of the congregation peer to look at her. Noah stands with another woman, bespectacled, shrewish. He steals a glance. She is very beautiful in the peace and fullness of her. Noah's partner looks at him disapprovingly and he drops his head.

REVEREND ROBERTS (W)

Ma'n pobl ni'n dioddef.
(Our people are suffering).

He looks around at the assembled crowd.

Teuluoedd Cristnogol da yn diodde'. Does ganddo ni ddim lla'th i'r plant, dim bwyd i'r anifeiliaid. Dim lluniaeth i'r cleifion ac hyd yn oed yma, yn nheyrnas y glo, allwn ni ddim twymo cartrefi'n hen bobl ni. Ein pobl ni sy'n gweithio i greu'r cyfoeth ac ein pobl ni sy'n diodde', tra bo' eraill yn pesgi ar ennillion ein cywilydd.
(Our good Christian people are suffering. We have no milk for the children, we have no feed for the animals. We cannot nourish the sick, we cannot even in this citadel of coal give warmth to our elders. Our working people who create the wealth are suffering, while others grow fat on the proceeds of our shame...)

THE SHOP. NIGHT. INT.

Rezl reaches behind the brick and pulls out the leather pouch with the money in it. She looks at it curiously, then stuffs it also into the pocket in her coat. She catches her husband's eye at the window. They understand one another. They have been here before. Old fears are being aroused, and old training utilised.

THE YARD. NIGHT. EXT.

Philip and Rezl are throwing food, bedding, and bags into a hand cart. Solomon furtively adds a trunk. Finally they help the old man to a sitting position, his legs dangling over the back. He is in a state of shock, his eyes staring out of his head.

A motley crowd watches the front of the shop.

Isaac and Solomon each with a handle of the cart pull it along a narrow track leading away from the shop. The family follows behind.

THE BARN. NIGHT. INT.

Darkness is falling, and the barn is lit by old lamps. Solomon anxiously helps to unload the bedding from the handcart. Rezl is making up temporary beds on the hay. The children are romping around, noisily oblivious.

ISAAC [Y]
Leman-ashem, bleib ruik. Zay mizzn nisht vissn as mir zennen doo. (For God's sake be quiet. They mustn't know we are here.)

The children, frightened by Isaac's vehemence, turn to wide-eyed silence. Isaac turns to their host, a local farmer who has agreed to help them out.

ISAAC [E]
Thank you. Thank you. It's very kind.

TREFOR LLOYD [E]
It's no trouble. I just hope it all passes off quietly.

REZL [E]
We pray for peace.

She sees the trunk.

Solomon, how long do you think we are staying?

Solomon shrugs his shoulders helplessly.

TREFOR [E]

My wife is praying too. And in case that doesn't work there are other ways of taking care of the shop.

He pats his shotgun.

Better not to show your face. Try to get some sleep.

He leaves. Isaac puts a wooden beam across the barn door to secure it. He turns off one of the lamps and leaves the other burning low.

The family settles down to sleep. The old man snores loudly. Faint cries and shouts can be heard in the far distance. Solomon pretends to shut his eyes, then opens them again. Rezl and Isaac are talking in low tones. Solomon watches them. His mother starts to weep softly. Isaac reaches out his arms to comfort her. They continue holding one another, talking in low tones. Solomon shifts his position impatiently. He clenches his fists. He is trapped. He closes his eyes.

GAENOR'S PARLOUR NIGHT. INT.

The Saturday night ritual. Gaenor is cleaning and blacking the fireplace. Her mother is polishing the ornaments and trinkets. Outside the street is alive with voices.

Wyn knocks at the scullery door. Crad sweeps up his jacket and runs to join him. Gaenor hears the muttered voices at the back door.

She works rhythmically, repetitively, inside her own world. She waits. A strangely excited Crad puts his head back round the door.

CRAD [W]

Hwyl bach. Wela i ti nes 'mlan.
(Bye, lass. See you later).

THE BARN. NIGHT. INT/EXT.

Solomon opens his eyes. His parents, the children, all seem to be asleep. The shouts and cries are closer now, more insistent. He creeps out of the blanket he shares with Philip.

Philip's eyes start into anxious awareness. Solomon grips him by the wrist.

SOLOMON [E]

(*whispering*) You don't know. You don't know anything. Don't set yourself up as God.

Solomon emerges onto the roof of the barn, a small bag over his shoulder. Out here in the night, the shouts are louder and much closer, and in the distance he can hear loud singing.

The distant lights of torches make their way along the valley.

OUTSIDE THE SHOP. NIGHT. EXT.

On the street, Solomon clings to the shadows, cautiously approaching the shop. The odd individual runs down the street excitedly. Some people seem to be waiting at the far end of the street. He passes the shop and heads on in the direction of the hillside.

Suddenly he hears loud shouts and running boots. Torches approach from the far end of the street. The waiting group has been swept up by a large crowd on the loose. Solomon scuttles back and slips quickly into an alley opposite the shop. He steps into the shadows as the crowd surges in his direction.

The crowd is clear about its purpose. Stones are thrown through the upper-floor windows of the shop, and the boards are prised off the lower windows. Crad, bearing aloft a torch and his face fit garishly by the flame, is one of the ringleaders.

CRAD (W)

Dewch 'mlan bois.
(Come on boys).

Someone arrives with a jemmy, and Crad soon busts the lock and levers open the door. Men and women begin to swarm into the shop, shouting and laughing. Solomon watches in desperate impotent rage.

INSIDE THE SHOP. NIGHT. INT.

Crad is at the till. Disappointed to find nothing there he flings it to the ground. His eye alights on a bolt of cloth that another looter has pulled out and is draping round him. Crad roughly seizes it. It's the cloth from Gaenor's dress. In the back room among the prayerbooks he finds a felt bag. It looks like a purse. He unbuttons it and pulls out the old man's tallit – his prayer shawl. From behind the house comes the sound of breaking glass. A figure in Isaac's shed is wildly swinging at his stock with a club. The house is a macabre nightmare of torches and looters, some grim-faced and purposeful, some laughing hysterically and dancing, some squabbling over their finds, yet none looking into his neighbour's eye, all released into a lust for all they have been denied.

OUTSIDE THE SHOP. NIGHT. EXT.
Soon the looters begin to emerge, laden with goods – boots, jewellry, cloths. They display their spoils gleefully.
   Solomon gives a snort of fury, and makes to charge at the crowd. He is knocked to the wall and his arms pinned from behind.

                     ISAAC [Y]
Zei kein nar, villsti derharget verrn?
(Don't be a fool, do you want to be killed?)

Solomon struggles to get away, while his father continues to drag him back.

                    SOLOMON [Y]
Loz mikh avek, leman-ashem. Di konst nisht zen vooss zay makhn?
Mir velln alts farloyren.
(Let me go, for God's sake. Can't you see what they are doing? We will lose everything.)

Before long they are wrestling, fighting one another in earnest. Some other agenda has taken over between them.

                      SOLOMON
Loz mikh avek, mamzer di.
(Let me go, you bastard.)

Isaac's grip is like iron. He hisses into his son's face.

                     ISAAC [Y]
Di zest vi zay zet oys. (You see what they are like.)

                    SOLOMON [Y]
Nein, di bist toye – Zog es nisht.
(No. You are wrong. Don't say that)

ISAAC [Y]

Di trakhst az kh'veiss nisht voos gesht?
(Do you think I don't know what's going on?)

Solomon momentarily ceases in his struggle.

Ikh ken a jeddn hoyz in dem tol, in kh'veiss voos zay reddn. Zog mir
as es iz nisht emess.
(I know every house in this valley, and I know what they are saying.
Tell me it isn't true.)

Solomon attacks the old man in a frenzy, but is no match for the older
man, who maintains his grip.

SOLOMON [Y]

Loz mikh avek. S'iz mein eign lebn. Di konst mikh nisht kontrolliren.
(Get off me. It's my own life. You can't control me.)

Isaac spits in his son's face.

ISAAC [Y]

Oyb di gayst mit der maydl, far ins bisti toyt. Mir velln zoggn kaddish
far dir.
(If you go with this girl, you will be dead to us. We will say Kaddish
over you.)

Solomon is in a wild fury of rage and tears. His struggles have begun to
draw the two of them into the street, and into the lights of the torches. Some
people are beginning to look at them curiously, one or two are pointing.
  Suddenly a cry goes up.

LOOTER [E]

Police!

The crowd begins to disperse, as quickly as it arrived. The clatter of an
approaching horse can be heard. Some people run down the side street past
Solomon and Isaac, who gradually cease their struggle and turn to look.
Others disperse into the darkness and shadows behind the houses. In a few
seconds, all have disappeared.
  A mounted officer clatters into the village, accompanied by Trefor Lloyd

and followed by a troop of footsoldiers. It's too late. House and shop have been all but emptied.

THE BARN. NIGHT. INT.

Solomon stands in the barn, his father close behind him. He looks dazed, shocked into obedience. All the fight gone out of him.

Rezl and Philip are awake, expectant, wide-eyed with fear. The old man is praying in the corner. Philip prays under his breath. Mrs. Lloyd and her eldest son and daughter sit with them. Mrs Lloyd holds Rezl's hand.

Rezl rises to greet her son. He embraces her. No words are spoken. She holds him in her arms.

GAENOR'S BACK PATCH. NIGHT. EXT.

Gaenor waits at the end of the garden near the privy. She scans the fields behind. It's a dark night. She carries a small bundle on her shoulder. The last pig has gone from the sty. All is silent, apart from the occasional distant shout, and the barking of far-off dogs.

A figure approaches from the dark. She calls out softly.

GAENOR

Solomon!

The figure begins to climb the gate into the garden. She runs towards him.

GAENOR: [W]

Solomon. Ti 'ma.
(Solomon. You're here.

The figure eases himself over the fence, and turns to face her. It's Crad.

Gaenor gasps in flight. Crad looks a strange sight. His eyes are wild and bright. He is laden with goods and cheap jewellry. He reaches over the fence and picks up a bundle of cloths.

CRAD [W]

Helpa fi 'da rhain 'nei di.
(Help me with this lot, will you.)

Gaenor stays rooted to the spot.

CRAD [W]

(*Tyrannically*) Helpa fi nei di ferch? Fi 'di laru. Rhaid cwato nhw.
(Help me woman, will you? I'm bushed. Got to hide it.)

Mechanically, she reaches for the bundle. Among them she recognises the roll of cloth from which her dress was made. She drops the bundle.

She looks, frightened, into Crad's eyes.

He holds her gaze and reaches into his upper shirt pocket. He pulls something out and proffers it to her. He sinks on his knees grinning mockingly, still holding out his gift. It glints in the faint moonlight.

It's a ring.

THE SHOP. MORNING. INT.

Early morning. The Levinsky family stand in the debris of their home. Mr. Cohen stands with them, taking notes. Philip is in shock. Tears fill his eyes. Solomon holds Benjamin in his arms. Philip turns to Solomon.

PHILIP [E]

It was you. You sinned against God. It was you.

Windows have been broken. The door swings on broken hinges. The place has been all but picked clean.

Isaac stands in the doorway like a statue, looking out onto the street, arms folded, grim retribution in his eyes. People walk past with their heads down.

Rezl wails pitifully. Solomon can't bear to hear it. It's as if his heart has been cut out. He wanders into the empty kitchen. The old man sits among his books on the floor. He sits thumbing the pages. He talks more to himself than to Solomon.

EPHRAIM [Y]

Zay hobn nisht geshtert di sforim. Zest. Zay hobm nisht geshedikt di sforim.
(They didn't touch the books. See. God is good. They didn't harm the books.)

Benjamin calls out. The back door is off its hinges. Solomon goes to look. On the step are a bundle of things that have been left for them by compassionate

but anonymous neighbours. Pots and pans. Blankets. Bread, eggs, milk.
Solomon surveys them, his face expressionless.

From *Solomon and Gaenor,* 1999

GWENALLT (1899-1968)

Like the above item, this is not an anti-semitic piece, but a depiction of anti-semitism. In this, the third and last extract in this book from the work of David James Jones ('Gwenallt'), we find him attributing to the main character in a novel some uncomplimentary opinions about the Jews. As was mentioned in the first chapter, Gwenallt was imprisoned in the First World War for being a conscientious objector. It was on this experience of imprisonment that he based this novel, entitled, with deliberate irony, Plasau'r Brenin, 'Mansions of the King'. One should certainly not identify Gwenallt too closely with the main character in the book, Myrddin Tomos; Gwenallt at the start of the novel stresses that all the characters are imaginary, and the negative attitude towards the Jewish prisoner Kleinski is attributed specifically to the main character – who is also given other failings – and is nowhere endorsed by the authorial voice. The novel seeks to present the dehumanising aspects of life in a military detention camp and later in prison: the innocent evangelical character Bili Mainwaring loses his mind in captivity, and Myrddin Tomos finds it hard to retain his sanity and his humanity. Gwenallt himself was radical in his politics, as his conscientious objection showed, and his subsequent work, while consistent with the traditional Christian position that the Jews need to recognise Christ as their Saviour (as was shown in the poem quoted in the chapter 'Jerusalem Destroyed') does not indicate any prejudice. In fact, his last book, *Y Coed,* 'The Trees', takes its title from Gwenallt's last poem, composed in his final illness, which was one of a long sequence based on the Holy Land and which deplores the persecution of the Jews. The 'trees' are those planted in memory of the Holocaust victims:

> Six million trees in Jerusalem, they were planted here
> A tree for every corpse cremated in the furnaces of fire...
> ...And when they have, in the course of years, grown to their
> fullest height,
> That generation will see that we were not exactly saints of light.

The sequence also contains an admiring poem entitled 'Yr Iddewon', 'The Jews', with seven stanzas in the following vein:

> She is a nation which has kept her history,
> Her religion and traditions are one;
> Her land is as it has been for centuries,
> And historical are her lightning, wind and sun.

In another poem with the same title, 'Yr Iddewon', published in 1942 in the collection *Cnoi Cil*, he shows similar admiration, although in the context of the fascist persecution of the Jews during the Second World War. In it, he gives five stanzas of the most vitriolic anti-semitic invective, attributing to the 'greasy, lousy Jews' all the evils of which anti-semites throughout history have accused them: murdering Christ; fomenting revolution; worshipping idols; amassing wealth. Having involved the reader in this offensive material, he then switches suddenly to three stanzas of praise for the Jews which show that the first five stanzas were shock-tactics designed to challenge people's prejudices. In those last three stanzas, he pleads for mercy for the Jewish people, says our own society is making them scapegoats for its own materialism, and concludes by describing them as follows:

> Pilgrims of the spirit,
>   Witnesses of the eternal,
> God's children in our midst
>   To damn our love of the material.

The poem as a whole, with its jolting switch from aggression to compassion, is clearly an attempt to subvert the rhetoric of anti-semitism and expose its coarseness of spirit and logic. However, it is not entirely successful in that aim, largely because the invective is allowed to dominate, and the praise – intended as a coup at the end of the poem – lacks the same vigour.[13] As Milton found in creating the character of Satan in *Paradise Lost*, evil can often be easier for an artist to display than good.

A similar aim of exposing anti-semitic attitudes is at work in the following passage from *Plasau'r Brenin*, published in 1934, but set during the First World War. Using the same kind of accusations against the Jews as employed in the poem quoted above, the passage shows Gwenallt deliberately displaying, via his character of Myrddin Tomos, how even socialists could participate in the widespread anti-semitic prejudice of the period. The prejudice is shown to be exacerbated by the fact that the brutal prison regime forced prisoners to search for at least one other category of people whom they could despise more than they were themselves despised.

from MANSIONS OF THE KING

Within three days, another prisoner came to the guardroom. A Jew from Russia. Isador Kleinski by name. He was a middle-aged man. He had curly, shiny black hair, prominent white eyes, a row of teeth as white as ivory and a long, patriarchal, fragrant beard. He had a dry coarse voice as though he was used to eating ashes.

When he was in Russia, he had been a member of a secret Communist society, one of whose aims was to kill the Tsar. The Jew told Myrddin Tomos of the oppression and violence of the Tsar, the corruption and the immorality of his court, and how the ignorant workers and peasants were mistreated by the greedy officers of the government. Isador Kleinski and others were appointed to kill the Tsar. One day, they were told by spies that the Tsar was planning to travel by train, and that that train would be crossing a particular bridge on the railway at a particular time. The King would be in the last carriage. Isador Kleinski and his party went to lay gunpowder under the bridge. When the train came over the bridge, the last carriage was blown to smithereens, but the Tsar was in the first carriage. Some of the members of the secret society were caught by the government officers and executed; others were imprisoned and the remainder were hunted like mountain partridges. Kleinski himself had been in St Petersburg prison, in the Schlusselberg ostrog, suffering his penance in the katorga in the saltmines of Ust-kut, the ironworks of Pertrovsk and the gold mines of Siberia. But he succeeded in escaping from Holy Russia, having to leave everything behind, except the fleas. He wandered from Russia to Geneva, to Paris and to London, where he met Lenin and Leon Trotsky. Kleinski prophesied great things about them. They were the hope of salvation for Russia's people. Kleinski came, in due course, to Cardiff, and kept a pawnshop in the Docks community when he was taken into custody for refusing to join the army.

Myrddin Tomos imagined seeing the Jew standing behind his pawnshop in Cardiff, receiving watches, jewellery and clothes as hostages; lending sixpence to the Docks workers on Monday night, and getting back sixpence and a farthing on Friday night, and selling second-hand false teeth to dentists.

The Welshman's work in the camp was to bring food from the cookhouse to the guardroom prisoners. When he took dinner to Isador Kleinski the first time, the Jew refused to eat it because the thumb of a Gentile was on the edge of the plate. Myrddin Tomos learned the lesson. He had to carry every plate and saucer on the palm of his hand and keep every finger under the vessel. The fingers of the Goyim were unclean things to the Jew. The Welshman was not fond of the Jew, or of the other Jews he met. To him, Jews were greasy creatures.

★

The prisoners were lucky to have one another's company, and to stay in the same room, even though their ideas and thoughts were so different. The captivity made them close friends. Myrddin Tomos, Bili Mainwairing and Jac Niclas were three Welshmen, and spoke Welsh, and that bound them closer. There was not much communication between them and Isador Kleinski. One might have expected that Jac Niclas would have been friendly with the Jew because they were two Communists, but there was a distance between the Welsh Communist and the Jewish Communist. Bili Mainwairing, sometimes, conversed with the Jew about the state of his soul, and Bili believed it would be a fine thing to save a Jew, one of the men of the nation which crucified his Saviour.

Isador Kleinski sat apart, in the corner of the guardroom, reading Russian and Yiddish newspapers, and writing on long sheets of paper. They were articles which were published in the Communist newspapers of Russia to fan the flames of revolution there. He got his Communist newspapers and magazines into the guardroom, and he sent his inflammatory articles out from there, through bribing the guards, because a soldier could be bought with a packet of Woodbines. Watching the Jew writing his epistles, Myrddin Tomos looked on him and his nation as the enemies of the civilisation of Western Europe, the greasy creatures who fanned the flames of rebellion in the nations, and sowed the seeds of materialism, attaining their debased goals through their miserly wealth and their persistence. They should all, every one, be swept away towards Zion, to create there the kind of world they desired...

(Later the prisoners are separated and taken to prisons)

Now and again between the industrious scrubbing, Myrddin Tomos would cast a guarded look towards his fellow-washers, and to his great surprise, he knew one of them, the Jew Isador Kleinski. when he caught his eye, he smiled at him, and the Jew acknowledged him. He was glad to see the Russian, and all the memories of the camp came alive in his mind. The following day, and every subsequent day, the two would wash next to one another and when the guard turned his back, they tried to carry on a hushed conversation. Isador Kleinski had been taken straight to Hall C, and there he had been the whole time. He had not been near Hall A. As he was long acquainted with the prisons of Russia the captivity of an English prison was just child's play to him. He taught Myrddin Tomos many of the tricks and dodges of prison, amongst them the way to hold a conversation with the prisoner in the next cell without language by banging the wall; the prison code.... Myrddin Tomos did not use the prison code much as it was such a clumsy and slow way of holding a conversation, and, more than anything, a prisoner would be punished heavily if he was caught using it. It was not worth the trouble.

One oppressively hot afternoon in June when Myrddin Tomos was scrubbing tiredly above his washtub he looked at the face of Isador Kleinski and saw he was about to faint. Just then the warder came up to the Jew and told him harshly: – 'Get on with your work.' In a flash, the Russian had grabbed a bucket of boiling water which was nearby, and he was about to throw it over the warder when Myrddin Tomos rushed forward and kicked the bucket from his hands. The warder jumped at the Jew, hit him to the floor, put the handcuffs on his wrists and took him away to the punishment cells. Myrddin Tomos never saw the Jew again

Translation from *Plasau'r Brenin*, 1934

J. EIRIAN DAVIES (1918-1998)

It is a relief to turn from the vexed question of prejudice to the safer subject of sympathy. However, even sympathy can be a fraught with difficulty, as this poem by the Carmarthenshire-born poet James Eirian Davies shows. He was a Calvinistic Methodist minister and an influential modern poet, particularly on religious subjects, where he was a liberal thinker. This 1944 poem about a Jewish refugee from Nazi persecution tending an allotment in Wales, although well-intentioned, nonetheless does contain an unfortunate reference to Jewish facial characteristics, which spoils the intended effect somewhat.

A REFUGEE.

Fearful and rather hasty was your going,
You stocky, stooped, rotund one, hooked of nose,
The gold a crust upon your fingers glowing,
Your gentle eyes in mourning for their woes.
Tonight on this allotted patch of soil

That slopes up from the Bryn to Pen-y-Cae
You think of old Vienna as you toil,
And all the wealth you knew in times gone by.
And here once more you're outcast, hunger-ridden,
Like all the sad forefathers of your race,
Like them, by Herod swept upon the midden,
A little orphan leaf torn from its place.
But search the waste, and all its stinking mire,
And you'll discover, somewhere, the Messiah.

1944

Translation from *Awen y Wawr*, 1948

LORD ELWYN JONES (1909-)

Llanelli-born, and Welsh-speaking, Elwyn Jones is the most distinguished lawyer Wales has produced. He became Lord Chancellor and before that, he was one of the British prosecutors of the Nazi war criminals at the Nuremburg trials from 1945-1946. As these passages show, he was well-qualified to comment on the significance of the trial as a means of exorcising the demons of anti-semitism: he had been brought up with Jewish friends, had adopted a Jewish refugee from the Nazi persecution before the war, and had met and become an admirer of the Zionist Chaim Weizmann in the early days of the conflict, an admiration which later led him to visit Israel. The following passages, from his autobiography *In My Time*, illustrate these episodes.

from IN MY TIME

Most of the families who lived in the terraced houses of Old Castle Road were Welsh. There were a few English like our nextdoor neighbours, the Pedleys and the Bodmans. The Irish O'Sheas lived two houses away. A pious Jewish family lived at the other end of the road. One Friday evening when I was walking home from school an elderly Jew asked me to come into his house to light the gas lamp in his kitchen. It puzzled me greatly. I had no knowledge then that on their Sabbath pious Jews forswore all such activities.

I never sensed any racial animosity in Llanelli. I do not recollect any anti-semitic feelings in either of the two schools to which I went. Harold Benjamin was one of my friends at school. His older brother

Isaac had been a friend of my older brother Gwyn. Harold won a scholarship to Oxford and took a brilliant First there. He became a solicitor and sent me some briefs when I started at the Bar, when briefs were most welcomed, as did R.I. Lewis, another Jewish school-mate. Like the Welsh, the Jews believed in education and, however poor, made sacrifices to give their children this start in life.

There were marked class differences in the town, though no one asked you who your father was. The assumption that every person is as good as another was at the heart of our social behaviour. In moments of exaltation in Wales, I have felt that Thomas Traherne in the seventeenth century expressed its essence when he wrote: 'You never enjoy the world aright, till the sea itself floweth in your veins, till you are clothed with the heavens, and crowned with the stars: and perceive yourself to be the sole heir of the whole world, and more than so, because men are in it who are every one sole heirs as well as you.'

★

I shared the evening lectures at King's with Richard Latham, a friend who had won brilliant Firsts at Melbourne and Oxford. He had a Jewish business friend, Wilfrid Israel, who owned a department store in Berlin. Just before the war, when the persecution of the Jews became increasingly violent, Mr Israel tried to get as many Jewish children as he could out of Berlin to England. Richard organized the English end, Polly and I, – we were married by this time – chose Margit from a sheet of photographs. She was only fifteen. We agreed to be her guardians and learned her story later. Her father was a graphic designer, a Christian who refused to divorce his Jewish wife and renounce his children in compliance with Nazi decrees. When in 1939 his studio in Cologne was looted and burned and he was beaten up by the Nazis, he decided to take his wife, son and daughter to Berlin in the hope of being able to establish a new home there.

In 1938 all Jewish children were forbidden to attend German schools. Margit's parents found a place for her in a Jewish art college in Berlin where she studied design and textiles. Part of the course involved visits to Israel's store to study materials. On 10 November 1938 came the terrible *kristalnacht* (crystal night). The Nazis looted and burned all Jewish business premises. Margit was in the Israel store at the time. I have asked her what she remembers of those events. She told me that she had tried in vain to obliterate them from her memory. She wrote: 'I escaped down a rear staircase during the fire. I ran home and looked for the all clear signal from my mother. A prearranged handkerchief "code" on the balcony was put up by my mother if the Nazis were in the flats. When the handkerchiefs were out we just kept on walking.' By such devices Margit survived. She wrote:

> In May 1939 I left for England. A letter came from Polly and Elwyn in April to welcome me. It was my passport to life. [Margit still has the letter.] I left on what was to be the last Jewish children's 'transport' out of Berlin and Le Havre. I remember my parents were not allowed to come to the station to see me leave and that I was permitted to take very little with me. Little else remains in my mind of the sad and miserable journey. I was met by Polly at Waterloo Station in London. Later I discovered that shortly after my departure my parents and my brother were arrested by the Nazis and disappeared into concentration camps. Afterwards I learned that my brother had been gassed in Theresienstadt Camp.

Polly remembers vividly going to meet Margit and bring her home. The arrival platform was crowded with German Jewish children. Some were extremely young, some were clutching shabby toys. All were pale, thin and exhausted. Each child bore a placard bearing identification details in large letters and the name of the sponsor. Polly spotted Margit. She bore the description 'Margit "Sara" Reiter'. The Nazis added the name 'Sara. to every Jewish girl's name, while 'Israel' was added to boys' names.' They were compelled to wear a yellow star. None of the children spoke English. Margit, when she arrived at Harwich, was asked where she was born. She replied 'Köln'. The immigration officer said: 'No, not Köln. child. Cologne.' She burst into tears. Beautiful, steady and intelligent, Margit became one of our family and helped to bring up our first two children, Josephine and Dan.

She married Brian, a Catholic whom she met in the Lake District, where Polly had been sent in October 1940 to have our second baby. Brian was in the navy during the war and served in the north and south Atlantic. In due course he became headmaster of a notable English school. Margit's father and mother survived the war although her mother had been subjected to inhuman medical experiments in a concentration camp. Margit's marriage has been a happy one. She and her husband respect each other's religion as Margit's parents did.

They are now grandparents, and Margit named her first child Josephine, after our eldest.

★

The Nuremberg Trial

Julius Streicher, coarse and depraved, was despised by the other prisoners in the dock, who treated him like an outcast. From 1925 to 1940 he was Gauleiter of Franconia. He published the obscene newspaper *Der Stürmer*, which had a circulation of 600,000. Week after week in his articles and speeches he spread the virus of anti-semitism. He had the Nuremberg synagogue destroyed and he publicly supported the Jewish pogrom of 1938. He called for extermination of the Jews and continued his propaganda of death when the 'final solution' was being murderously carried out.

Walther Funk, a miserable, crumpled figure, pleaded not guilty almost tearfully. He had been the key link between the Nazi Party and the German industrialists and financiers who backed Hitler and was in Goebbels' Propaganda Ministry. From 1938 on he was Minister of Economics, president of the Reichsbank and 'Chief Plenipotentiary for War Economics'. He agreed with Himmler that the Reichsbank should receive gold and jewels and currency from the SS and instructed his subordinates not to ask too many questions. The SS loot came mainly from the dead victims of the concentration camps: their gold teeth and fillings, spectacle frames, wedding rings, jewellery, watches, brooches and necklaces. He presented himself at the tribunal however as a small man with no power in the Nazi state – 'often at the door, but never let in'. After listening to his evidence I wrote in my notebook:

> Dead men's bodies tell no lies
> Nor the relics and rings of a mother who dies.
> The blood that was shed was red.
> Seek not now to mock the dead
> With faint denial, lame apology.
> You trod that road of shame. No eulogy
> Of Strauss, no tears for martyred Jew
> Can save you now. You knew
> The sin your creed engendered
> The tears of blood when your minions tendered

192

Gas vans, death vans as red flames burned.
You cast your bitter bread. It has returned
On tides of justice and deep waters of compassion.

★

Missions Abroad

I had hoped to visit Israel ever since my meetings early in the war with Dr Chaim Weizmann, who had played such a great part in its foundation. Polly and I were happy to accept an invitation to accompany George Thomas MP to Israel in 1957. We stayed in Jerusalem and Tel Aviv, Haifa and Beer-sheba, We met the Mayor of Beer-sheba, a former student of philosophy in Vienna, in his modest home set in a lovely garden in the Negev Desert.

They called Beer-sheba 'the pressure cooker'. Not only was a green oasis being created in the arid desert but also a fusion was being attempted of immigrants from different levels of civilization with different social patterns of behaviour, Ringleted Jews from the Yemen mingled with university-trained professional people from the troubled heart of central Europe. Settlements such as Boker, where the then Prime Minister David Ben-Gurion made his home, thrived in the desert. Revivim, Mash-abbe-Sade and Eilat itself were further advances on the road to making the Negev bloom as it did centuries ago when the Nabateans ruled it from 'rose-red Petra'.

We drove long distances over sandy tracks: there were fewer roads then. Black goat-hair Bedouin tents like crumpled umbrellas were scattered about, Water was the over-riding concern. Hydrologists were working out ways of bringing water to the Negev and learned historians were studying how the armies of ancient Rome had survived there. It did sometimes rain in a sudden deluge and the problem, they told us, was how to retain and save this precious life-giving water and how to cultivate plants which could survive on little of it. Great advances have been made since then. If Israel and her neighbours could only live in peace together, the experience and skill of the Israelis in making the desert bloom could transform vast desert areas of the Middle East and enrich the lives of all its peoples, Arab and Jew alike, I remember Golda Meir, then Israel's Foreign Minister, asking when I met her in Jerusalem, 'Must our children continue to be brought up in our frontier areas in trenches and under the shadows of guns?' Golda Meir, direct and unpretentious, gave us the impression of a wise grandmother determined to hold her family together in difficult circumstances. She was one of the most impressive women I have met.

Jerusalem stirs emotions unlike any other ancient city: the holy places, the olive garden at Gethsemane, the steep cobbled alleys between ancient stone walls, the crowing of a cock on Easter morning. The past is alive there and will not release you.

During my visit I addressed a gathering of lawyers in Tel Aviv, I described how deeply moved I had been looking out from my bedroom window in the St David Hotel in Jerusalem at the holy places I had learned about as a child in Tabernacle Chapel, Llanelli. When I sat down the Chairman of the meeting said genially that they knew. King David was a great king but until I spoke they had not realised that he had been canonized by the Church of England.

From *In My Time*, 1983

W.G. SEBALD (1944-2001)

The following extract shows the experience of a kindertransport child in Wales from a different perspective, in which the Welsh hosts are less sympathetic to the adopted child's cultural inheritance than were Lord Elwyn Jones and his wife. It is the work of the German-language author Winfried Georg Sebald, who was born to a Catholic family in Wertach im Allgau, Bavaria. He left his native country at twenty to study in Switzerland, and spent most of the rest of his life in a voluntary exile in England, lecturing in Manchester, and, from 1970, at the University of East Anglia in Norwich, where he became professor of European Literature. He began writing novels in his forties, in his native German, using a dreamlike and non-linear unparagraphed style, mixing elements of history, travelogue and memoir. His first three major works, *Die Ausgewanderten*, 1992, translated as *The Emigrants* in 1996, *Die Ringe des Saturn: Eine Englische Wallfahrt* in 1995, translated as *The Rings of Saturn* in 1999, and *Schwindel, Gefuehle* in 1999, translated as *Vertigo* in 2000, won numerous prestigious literary awards in both the English and German-speaking worlds. Sadly, Sebald died shortly before the publication of this anthology. Although he was not himself Jewish, the Jewish experience is a frequent feature in his work. Much of his writing deals with the experience of exile and of memory, and he explored particularly the relationship of his own post-World War Two generation with the Germany of his parents' era. He has been praised for his expression of the dislocation many Germans of the post-Holocaust era felt as they grew up in a country which was afraid to discuss its painful recent history; in many cases, it was only in middle life that they began to ask questions, recover memories and adjust perceptions. The subject of an expunged past is explored in this extract, taken from *Austerlitz* (2001) in which the narrator recounts the story of Jacques Austerlitz, a Prague Jew brought to Wales on a kindertransport just before the outbreak of war to escape the Nazi persecution. He was brought up in Bala in north Wales by a Welsh Calvinistic Methodist minister and his wife, who erased his memory of his previous life and of his native language, and who brought him up with the name Dafydd Elias. When his foster mother dies and his father is taken to Denbigh mental hospital, 'Dafydd Elias' is given a hint of his real identity, and in later life he starts to unravel the troubled relationship with his past. The story is based partly on that of a former kindertransport child, Susie Bechhofer, as recounted in a Channel 4 documentary; she was brought up by Welsh nonconformist parents and only recovered her Jewish identity in later life. In the following passage, the images of the drowned valley and the Welsh supernatural otherworld act as metaphors for the young 'Dafydd Elias's' presentiments of otherness and of estrangement from his true identity, together with the first stirrings of identification with the Jewish experience.

from AUSTERLITZ

In this way a kind of Old Testament mythology of retribution gradually built up inside my head, and I always saw its supreme expression in the submersion of the village of Llanwddyn beneath the waters of the Vyrnwy reservoir. As far as I can remember it was on the way back from one of his journeys to preach away from home, at either Abertridwr or Pont Llogel, that Elias stopped the pony-trap on the banks of this lake and walked out with rue to the middle of the dam, where he told me about his family home lying down there at a depth of about a hundred feet under the dark water, and not just his own family home but at least forty other houses and farms, together with the church of St. John of Jerusalem, three chapels, and three pubs, all of them drowned when the dam was finished in the autumn of 1888 In the years before its submersion, so Elias had told him, said Austerlitz, Llanwddyn had been particularly famous for its games of football on the village green when the full moon shone in summer, often lasting all night and played by over ten dozen youths and men of almost every age, some of them from neighbouring villages. The story of the football games of Llanwddyn occupied my imagination for a long time, said Austerlitz, first and foremost, I am sure, because Elias never told me anything else about his own life either before or afterwards. At this one moment on the Vyrnwy dam when, intentionally or unintentionally, he allowed me a glimpse into his clerical heart, I felt for him so much that he, the righteous man, seemed to me like the only survivor of the deluge which had destroyed Llanwddyn, while I imagined all the others, his parents, his brothers and sisters, his relations, their neighbours, all the other villagers still down in the depths, sitting in their houses and walking along the road, but unable to speak and with their eyes opened far too wide. This notion of mine about the subaquatic existence of the people of Llanwddyn also had something to do with the album which Ebas first showed me on our return home that evening, containing several photographs of his birthplace, now sunk beneath the water. As there were no other pictures of any kind in the manse, I leafed again and again though these few photographs, which came into my own possession only much later along with the Calvinist calendar, until the people looking out of them, the blacksmith in his leather apron, Elias's father the sub-postmaster, the shepherd walking along the village street with his sheep, and most of all the girl sitting in a chair in the garden with her little dog on her lap, became as familiar to me as if I were living with them down at the bottom of the lake. At night, before I fell asleep in my cold room, I often felt as if I too had been submerged in that dark water, and like the poor souls of Vyrnwy must keep my eyes wide open to catch a faint glimmer of light far above me, and see the reflection, broken by ripples, of the stone tower standing in such fearsome isolation on the wooded bank. Sometimes I even imagined that I had seen one or other of the people from the photographs in the album walking down the road in Bala, or out in the fields, particularly around noon on hot summer days, when there was no one else about and the air flickered hazily. Elias said I was not to speak of such things, so instead I spent every free moment I could with Evan the cobbler, whose work-shop was not far from the manse and who had a reputation for seeing ghosts. I also learned Welsh from Evan, picking it up very quickly, because I liked his stories much better than the endless psalms and biblical verses I had to learn by heart for Sunday school. Unlike Elias, who always connected illness and death with tribulations, just punish-ment, and guilt, Evan told tales of the dead who had been struck down by fate untimely, who knew they had been cheated of what was due to them and tried to return to life. If you had an eye for them they were to be seen quite often, said Evan. At first glance they seemed to be normal people, but when you looked more closely their faces would blur or flicker slightly at the edges. And they were usually a little shorter than they had been in life, for the experience of death, said

Evan, diminishes us, just as a piece of linen shrinks when you first wash it. The dead almost always walked alone, but they did sometimes go around in small troops; they had been seen wearing brightly coloured uniforms or wrapped in grey cloaks, marching up the hill above the town to the soft beat of a drum, and only a little taller than the walls round the fields through which they went. Evan told me the story of how his grandfather once had to step aside on the road from Frongastell to Pyrsau to let one of these ghostly processions pass by when it caught up with him. It had consisted entirely of beings of dwarfish stature who strode on at a fast pace, leaning forward slightly and talking to each other in reedy voices. Hanging from a hook on the wall above Evan's low workbench, said Austerlitz, was the black veil that his grandfather had taken from the bier when the small figures muffled in their cloaks carried it past him, and it was certainly Evan, said Austerlitz, who once told me that nothing but a piece of silk like that separates us from the next world. It is a fact that through all the years I spent at the manse in Bala I never shook off the feeling that something very obvious, very manifest in itself was hidden from me. Sometimes it was as if I were in a dream and trying to perceive reality; then again I felt as if an invisible twin brother were walking beside me, the reverse of a shadow, so to speak. And I suspected that some meaning relating to myself lay behind the Bible stories I was given to read in Sunday school from my sixth year onwards, a meaning quite different from the sense of the printed words as I ran my index finger along the lines. I can still see myself, said Austerlitz, muttering intently and spelling out the story of Moses again and again from the large-print children's edition of the Bible Miss Parry had given me when I had been set to learn by heart the chapter about the confounding of the languages of the earth, and succeeded in reciting it correctly and with good expression. I have only to turn a couple of pages of that book, said Austerlitz, to remember how anxious I felt at the time when I read the tale of the daughter of Levi, who made an ark of bulrushes and daubed it with slime and with pitch, placed the child in the ark and laid it among the reeds by the side of the water, yn yr hesg ar fin yr afon, I think that was how it ran. Further on in the story of Moses, said Austerlitz, I particularly liked the episode where the children of Israel cross a terrible wilderness, many days' journey long and wide, with nothing in sight but sky and sand as far as the eye can see. I tried to picture the pillar of cloud going before the people on their wanderings 'to lead them the way,' as the Bible puts it, and I immersed myself, forgetting all around me, in a full-page illustration showing the desert of Sinai looking just like the part of Wales where I grew up, with bare mountains crowding close together and a grey-hatched background, which I took sometimes for the sea and sometimes for the air above it. And indeed, said Austerlitz on a later occasion when he showed me his Welsh children's Bible, I knew that my proper place was among the tiny figures populating the camp. I examined every square inch of the illustration, which seemed to me uncannily familiar. I thought I could make out a stone quarry in a rather lighter patch on the steep slope of the mountain over to the right, and I seemed to see a railway track in the regular curve of the lines below it. But my mind dwelt chiefly on the fenced square in the middle and the tent-like building at the far end, with a cloud of white smoke above it. Whatever may have been going on inside me at the time, the children of Israel's camp in the wilderness was closer to me than life in Bala, which I found more incomprehensible every day, or at least, said Austerlitz, that is how it strikes me now.

From *Austerlitz*, 2001

DEWI STEPHEN JONES (b. 1940)

This powerful poem by Dewi Stephen Jones, from the Rhosllannerchrugog area near Wrexham, shows how an experience of the historic subjection suffered by the Welsh opens the gate to sympathy with the far greater sufferings of the Jews. *Kristallnacht* is the name given to the night of November 10, 1938, when Nazi-organised gangs unleashed a pogrom against German and Austrian Jews, killing 36, imprisoning 20,000, and burning and looting 195 synagogues and thousands of shops and homes. The Welsh Not mentioned here was a shaming device used in some Welsh schools in the nineteenth century when official policy was hostile to the use of Welsh in schools. It was a sign which was hung around the necks of schoolchildren caught speaking Welsh; children could transfer it to the neck of the next child to use Welsh; the one left wearing it at the end of the day was beaten. The poem uses the identification with oppression engendered by the Welsh Not as a means of interpreting the far more terrible Jewish experience.

THE NIGHT OF CRYSTAL

Go,
the bruise does not mend,
and come to the water's edge
and its layer of ice in Bryn yr Ywen,
the overflow on the colliery's hayfield,
a patch of ground like still waters.

One of a crew on a shrivelled earth,
bending above the water like a peasant to his furrow
and a film of black water
widening as the one hand
clamps
and the other
sinks in the mud
to raise part of its cover, ice
that is scarcely of any thickness;
and the thrill of its elevation
is like guiding a mirror out of its hovel,
the panes without history,
new-minted with no yesterday to their world,
of the lineage of some lost planet
that had never yielded to a fall,
and the polish of their lens
with no speck of dust
to hang like death's insect
a reminder of the blood-red sperm
intent on wounding the egg...

The windscreen withers
like the face of the rose when the insect causes havoc...

In our lust for the proverbial purity
our soles had joined in the bloody dance.
The brick went through the window
the night of *Kristallnacht.*

The fate of a man the fate of a folk -
the violence like I had seen in a picture by Chagall:

a nameless one
  his wound
like a lame wing –
always the yoke,
lower than the Welsh Not,
awkward
  this collar.
part of a coffin lid,
the orange-box carpenter's effort –
  '*Ich bin Jude*'
by the coldness and the bite of the iron –
the wooden window without polish,
the black cover over the light, a board
from the dirt of our coal shed.
Fear
  with a broad hand
had coloured his breast.
He wears the heaviest winter coat
the night of the yellow star from the ancient dirt.

Shall there come
from the bow and sun of his violin
the empty sound
  or the cry
as from the womb of the synagogues?

And to their assignation
like the peat heathers, they arise
from the ashes of the charcoaled amens.

Translation from Eds. Gwynn ap Gwilym,
Alan Llwyd, *Blodeugerdd o Farddoniaeth Gymraeg yr Ugeinfed Ganrif*, 1987

TIM SAUNDERS (b. 1952)

A Cornishman who has learned Welsh – among other minority languages – and made it the language of much of his literary output, Tim Saunders is attuned to the role of language in forming identity. In this poem, he reflects on the way the Yiddish language and culture was largely destroyed during the Holocaust.

LANGUAGE

I'm turning the pages
   from right to rectangular left,
   with the dust of the libraries
     lashing
       my fingertips
with a voice,
with meaninglessness,
with a scream,
   a language which seethes
      in the ashes,
that howls
      in clouds of smoke.

This is a language which
     has been stifled,
     has been suffocated,
     has been burned to embers
over the level acres,
   across the marshes,
   through the pines,
      under the piles of waste
   and in the skulls.

Here she is now
   silent.
     In the trains
      in the shops
    on the buses
      in the taverns
   on the dirty streets
      in the broad squares
   on the patched fields
      in the dark workshops
   on the barbed wire
      in the gas chambers.

Here she is, a corpse

on the velvety boards
of the cigaretted linguists,
raw
to be sliced
by the plastic knives
of the dialectologists,
a sweet prey
for the clutches of keen-to-publish lecturers,
for the jaws of etymologists,
for the bottomless pits
of the lexicologists,
full to their slick gorge:
and here am I
staining my fingers
(from right to screaming left)
in the language's blood.

Translation from *Teithiau*, 1977

BOBI JONES (b. 1929)

Cardiff-born Robert Maynard ('Bobi') Jones is another writer who learned Welsh as a second language. As an academic and eventually Professor of Welsh at Aberystwyth, he has made an immense contribution not only to Welsh scholarship in his extensive critical publications, but also to poetry, in which he has displayed an adventurous style, a wide variety of technique and tone, and a consistent concern with issues of identity, spirituality and justice. The first of the two poems given here shows Jones identifying with persecuted Jews whose world was expressed through the Yiddish language. A Welsh-language writer is bound to feel a natural affinity with a people whose experience is mediated through a language which is itself under threat. The second, entitled, with deliberate irony, 'Antisemitic Song', seeks to explore the mentality of Gentile prejudice, again making passing reference to a similar prejudice against the Welsh.

THE SPEAKERS OF YIDDISH

Rats, according to the Medes
and the Persians, are we too;
and in cellars we are familiar
with meeting other rats
from Slovenia, from Latvia, from Brittany,
the unremarkable districts of the city.

But we dare (we Yiddishers)
to have longer noses
than the other rats,
and the lord and lady of the palace
noticed this. For shame the two denied that WE
were there at all. 'John! did you hear
what the gentleman said?

Rats! In our house!' But somehow Fritz next door
realised – thanks to his operatic ears
and his recitative eyebrows –
we were there. We were not performing rats
perhaps; but they had to call
The Pest Control Officer all the same.

'From the show, four million were destroyed,
they squeaked Yiddish
sewer-brown.
As for us, we will never do much
in their place, hopefully,
except roll over and die
with socialistic tidiness.

'But from their words
neat naked tails are created:
if you kept them in a cage
they would spread bubonic plague in no time.
Their syllables were familiar with sewers,
and very fertile. To control them
it was necessary to put down – As2, O3
or Zn3 P2 or coca-cola.

'And why? What difference was there
between them and us,
say? There was only gas to answer.
Did these, I wonder, find
more dirt? Did they carry
more infections – like music, antiques, varied protests
and individuality of hat? Scarcely.
'They were us. Perhaps they had pretended
that they had teeth. Whatever, rats
are rats – just like us
and the race which ran after the pied
coat from a dream back through the dungeons of language
on white camels to the same place in the end...
        to their Egypt'.

Translation from *Canu Arnaf,* 1995

ANTISEMITIC SONG

We should not be like this
Afraid to open our mouths
The slightest degree, to say that Jews
Commit the odd transgression.
There's no reason why we should be unable
To curse them from time to time.

We should not be like this:
We can insult the Welshman
Without worrying for a moment that the popular press
Would consider us anti-
This-that-or-the-other all the time. It should be
An honour for them to be treated
Like any impartial nation. But
Somehow, if we whisper one
Surly syllable about Jews, then what
We did in Germany
Drops on our shoulders like a bakestone:
We should not be like this.

Conflict and *Shoah*

And there are pieces of flesh soullessly
in our thought, while the jackals
Howl their drifts through our dreams. This
Is stupid. Still, the sun is wild
Like fright, and there's nothing
A father can do to shelter his child,
Or myself from a tear,
Except let the planet
Commit suicide:

This is completely stupid.
And every time a policeman
Touches his hat to consent
Good morning we expect a thrashing:
Never again to cut the hair in silence
With the easy unracial scissors,
Never again to rest the palm
On the velvet darkness in a balcony.
We should not be like this,
The whole thing's completely stupid.

Still, we can't criticise them any more
Confidently. When they shoot Arabs, it is we
Who feel the shame. In the sight of their
Power we discover the scream
Of the barbed wire, the expulsion
Of the smoke drifting through the brambles.
We have found our bed in their flesh;
There's no organ within us
Where we can hide ourselves from them.

We should not be like this.
We are scattered across their fear,
And across the failure to understand them. Undoubtedly
We therefore now must live their death
And they are now strange witnesses to every Arab
how they go to answer for themselves.

Translated from *Canu Arnaf*, 1995

TONY CURTIS (b. 1946)

Carmarthen-born Tony Curtis is one of the most prominent Welsh poets currently writing in English. He has also had an influential career as an editor, critic and lecturer. His 1995 book, *War Voices*, dealt with the experience of armed conflict, and included the following poem set in a concentration camp, an impressive imaginative identification with the power of Jewish identity in adversity.

SOUP

One night our block leader set a competition:
two bowls of soup to the best teller of a tale.
That whole evening the hut filled with words –
tales from the old countries
of wolves and children
potions and love-sick herders
stupid woodsmen and crafty villagers.
Apple-blossom snowed from blue skies,
orphans discovered themselves royal.
Tales of greed and heroes and cunning survivors,
soldiers of the Empires, the Church, the Reich.

And when they turned to me
I could not speak,
sunk in the horror of that place,
my throat a corridor of bones, my eyes
and nostrils clogged with self-pity.
'Speak,' they said, 'everyone has a story to tell.'
And so I closed my eyes and said:
I have no hunger for your bowls of soup, you see
I have just risen from the Shabbat meal –
my father has filled our glasses with wine,
bread has been broken, the maid has served fish.
Grandfather has sung, tears in his eyes, the old songs.
My mother holds her glass by the stem, lifts
it to her mouth, the red glow reflecting on her throat.
I go to her side and she kisses me for bed.
My grandfather's kiss is rough and soft like an apricot.
The sheets on my bed are crisp and flat
like the leaves of a book ...

I carried my prizes back to my bunk: one bowl
I hid, the other I stirred
and smelt a long time, so long
that it filled the cauldron of my head,
Drowning a family of memories.

From *War Voices*, 1995

DONALD EVANS (b. 1940)

Cardiganshire-born Donald Evans is one of only three Welsh poets to have won the National Eisteddfod crown and chair double twice. He is a master of the Welsh strict metres, as shown in the first of the two poems about refugee Jewesses given here. The second, on the same subject and with the same title, is an example of his equal facility in free metres.

A JEWESS

Here on this sombre sea's land – this place
  By the church and the strand;
The vale with fitting headland
Above, Belsen is at hand.

The chambers are no distance – nor the gas,
  Nor the flames' incandescence;
The charnel and the violence,
In your wax their fires dance.

Within your breast is their Hades – madness,
  Not lying in history's
Cold lap. Far closer are these:
Their hatred a neighbour breathes.

In your aspect of serenity – the caress
  Of your smile and the charity
Of your looks, the generosity
Of your hearth, there is terror to me.

The terror of the night camps comes: – opens a world
  Of shattered skeletons;
The knives in hands of demons,
The blood flowing from the wounds.

In you, the starved accents – of the best of men
  Of women and infants
Of the children of your race, their descendants,
Cry out in the butchers' hands.

And the voice of the furnace – rages
  For more of your race
As fuel for its malice
At the dust that's in your place.

And though the water is clear – in the sun
  There's no thoughtless cheer
To the bay now. Dachau's fear,
Its nightmare lust – it is here.

Translation from *Iasau*, 1988

A JEWESS

(who lived on a farm at Llanrhystud at this time)

So incomparably blue and smooth
the bay below me, and her life itself
foaming pure from the darkness of the wood;
its pitch coming green from the enormity of winter,
she herself pushing out suddenly from a shed door,
all encumbered with buckets
as she smiles across the yard...
But there was a train behind the smile thundering
in terrifying muteness
through the sun of the beach, a spectre of a steamtrain
roaring across a prairie of snow
with relish across its nightmare railway,
wheeling past our thousand faces
and the destination of the howling
materialised, gaping,
from the steel bounds of the breast
a terror hammered through the heat
with its seagulls, the same colour
as the station and the camp
nearby... so far away.

But her shining greeting waved
from the bay to the yard
one thickness of arrant consonants
joining regularly with the savour
of the violet sea and the jingle of buckets.
But through the gaps of the green words
a squad of corpses stared
into the dazzling region, cold weaklings
somehow dragging themselves bound through the jaws
of their doors, the embrace of endless death.

She approached from her labour to begin a conversation
of praise for the yellow weather;
the leaves of the ash tree;
the blueness of the sea and the light
of the earth, a Jewess's spirit
smashing white through the gloom of her hell
to this home by the shores to praise the light.

Translation from *Barddas*, 231-232, July/August, 1996

NOTES

1. The author was born in Cardiff, educated at Cardiff High School for Boys, served throughout the Second World War and was a founder member of the editorial board of the Cardiff Jewish Ex-Servicemen's magazine, *CAJEX*. Although untrained, he was also a talented artist.

2. 'Lyons versus Thomas: The Jewess Abduction Case 1867-68', *The Jews of South Wales, op cit*, 131.

3. References: *The Cardiff and Merthyr Guardian* August 8th, 1868; August 15th, 1868; August 22nd, 1868; August 29th, 1868; September 5th, 1868; September 12th, 1868; September 19th, 1868; September 26th, 1868; July 24th, 1869; July 31st, 1869; August 7th, 1869.

4. 'O'r Bala i Belsen', *Barn*, No 383/384, December 1994/January 1995. See also Hazel Davies, 'The Early Books and Travel Documents of O.M. Edwards' in Ed. Hywel Teifi Edwards, *A Guide to Welsh Literature 1800-1900*, (Cardiff, University of Wales Press 2000).

5. Evans, in seeking for accusations with which to attack the Welsh, invoked anti-semitism in reviving the supposed connection between the Welsh and the Jews, this time in order to bring anti-semitic prejudice to bear on his own people. In the *Daily Express*, he wrote: 'The trouble with the Welsh is that they are not Welsh, Our place of origin is somewhere on the Red Sea. I believe that our ways were so abominable – leading astray the loose women of Egypt and tricking the House of Israel – that Egyptian and Jew combined to rid the land of us. We wandered hither and thither and found ourselves in Wales. But our mentality is Oriental, hence our friendliness with the Jews. This is a byword; wherever two or three Welshmen are gathered together, there is also a Jew.' That was in 1923, and is quoted by Hywel Teifi Edwards in 'O'r Pentre Gwyn i Llaregyb' in Ed. M. Wynn Thomas *Diffinio Dwy Lenyddiaeth Cymru*, (Cardiff, University of Wales Press, 1995), 26. Caradoc Evans, nursing a lifelong hatred for Wales and cursed with a relentlessly negative view of human motives, made a late attempt to write, as he put it, 'without anger'. One of the short stories which resulted, published posthumously in 1946 as *The Earth Gives All and Takes All*, had a Jew as its main character. However, its expression is so obscure, and its narrative – deprived of the directing energy of Evans's malice – is so confused, that it does not merit inclusion.

6. See Barnet Litvinoff, *The Burning Bush, Antisemitism and World History*, (Glasgow, Fontana, 1989), 267.

7. For a more extended treatment of the relationship between Lewis, Eliot and the anti-modern tendency of the inter-war period, see *Sefyll yn y Bwlch*, by the present author, (Cardiff, University of Wales Press, 1999).

8. Totalitarianism, whether of the left or the right, was indeed Lewis's greatest fear. This needs to be borne in mind when considering the occasional accusation against Lewis that he was a fascist sympathiser. He certainly aired the anti-semitic opinions detailed here, he was certainly instinctively more conservative than radical, he certainly backed Franco above the Republicans in the Spanish Civil War, and he was certainly tardy – along with many British politicians who subsequently opposed Hitler – in waking up to the dangers of Nazism. But the truth is not served by exaggerating Lewis's faults. A study of his work, particularly the extensive weekly columns on world affairs, 'Cwrs y Byd', which he wrote right through the Second World War, does not support the

conclusion that he was a crypto-fascist. He condemned fascism regularly, seeing it, along with Communism, as the fullest expression of the barbarism that he most feared in the modern world. What the critic Dafydd Glyn Jones described as the 'oddly academic' nature of Lewis's criticism of fascism is better understood when one bears in mind Lewis's mistaken belief that the Allies were themselves on the way to becoming totalitarian states and that a universal scepticism as to the motives of all the great powers was therefore the best attitude with which to confront the world conflict. It should also be pointed out that the remarks Lewis made during his anti-semitic period were not supported or endorsed by other members of the nationalist movement, either at the time or afterwards. The next nearest parallel in the nationalist movement of the period would have been the Francophile Ambrose Bebb, who, as Gareth Miles has pointed out, in communicating to the Welsh people his enthusiasm for the French right-wing leader Charles Maurras (a hero of T.S. Eliot also) saw fit to make no mention of the Frenchman's virulent and undisguised anti-semitism. Although Lewis gave an all-important lead to Welsh nationalism in the 20th Century, many of Lewis's attitudes – such as his predilection for social hierarchy, his political conservatism, his cultural Francophilia, and his neo-Catholicism – were uncongenial to the Welsh. They have tended to adopt those of Lewis's arguments that suited their needs, such as his passionate advocacy of the Welsh language, and have quietly ignored those attitudes such as those outlined above – and including anti-semitism – which did not.

9. There had been small Jewish communities, mainly of Sephardi Jews, in Llandudno and Rhyl since the end of the First World War, when they had fled the collapsing Ottoman empire. However, it would seem that Gruffydd was referring in this article to Jewish refugees who had moved from London, Liverpool and Manchester to avoid German bombing. Most of these returned home after the Allied invasion of Europe.

10. 'The Tredegar Riots of August 1911', *op cit*, 151.

11. For a balanced treatment of the subject see Dr William D. Rubinstein's article on the subject in the *Welsh History Review*, December 1997.

12. In this screenplay format, Int and Ext denote that the scenes are 'Interior' or 'Exterior'. 'E', 'W' and 'Y' in brackets after the character's name denote the language of the next lines as English, Welsh or Yiddish; English translations are given after the Welsh and Yiddish dialogue.

13. It is perhaps true to say that Gwenallt's talent for invective generally was often more highly-charged than his talent for praise, and that his aggressive polemic, even when used ironically, has a vigour that his rather dutiful eulogistic passages often lack. This fact weakens the intended effect of a poem employing both modes, like the above.

WELSH AND JEWISH

This chapter is devoted to experiences of Wales as seen through the eyes of writers of Jewish background. As a Gentile, I am conscious of the need for caution in seeking to interpret the Jewish experience, so I will confine my introductions, as far as possible, to factual material.

Considering the small size of the Welsh Jewish community – as mentioned in the introduction to this book, its high point was probably around 5,000 people in 1914 – it has produced some important writers, most notably Dannie Abse and Bernice Rubens, but also Lily Tobias, and, by adoption, Judith Maro. This collection, concerned as it is with the relationship of the Welsh to the Jews, is confined to material which deals in some way with Wales. The pieces are largely self-explanatory, although in nearly all of them, the respective claims of Welshness and Jewishness – sometimes conflicting, more often complementary – are explored.

BERNICE RUBENS (b.1927)

A member of a Cardiff Jewish family, Bernice Rubens is the author of a number of novels, although Wales only figures prominently in a small minority.[1] Most noteworthy of these, for the present purpose, is *Brothers*, published in 1983, which tells the story of Jewish immigrants fleeing the Russian Empire and finding a home in Wales. I have chosen the following three extracts to begin this chapter, as the process they portray was shared by many of the emigrants who swelled the ranks of Welsh Jewry in the late nineteenth and early twentieth centuries.

from BROTHERS

'There are many or our people over there,' Khasina answered, 'They will welcome you.' He paused and drank from his glass, 'You must leave,' he said, and there was no mistaking the urgency in his voice, He spoke like a prophet-messenger, 'You have learned a hard lesson in Odessa,' he said, 'There are harder lessons to come.' He reached into his pocket for a pencil and note-book and, tearing out a sheet, he wrote down an address. He took his time with it, concerned with its neatness and legibility, familiarising himself, for his own sake, with the strange letters and shapes, so alien to his Russian hand. He handed the paper to Zelda. 'Look after it,' he said, 'You will find me there and I shall help you,' He downed his glass. 'I take the train at midnight.' He took each of their hands in farewell, then he turned quickly, and left with no formal leave-taking, and the three Bindels stared at the space he had so recently occupied and all or them wondered whether he had been a fleeting vision in their fearful eyes. Yet they heard the echo of his warning words and saw on the counter the undeniable proof or his recent presence. They read the address without understanding it. Wales, he had said. A place in England, they surmised, which was where his train and his boat were taking him. Wales, they said to each other, laughing at its strange sound, realising that that laughter was the very first they had given voice to since the epidemic of death in their families. And in that laughter there was hope, as if the visitor had, with his calling-card, sanctioned them to have faith once more. That it was not enough to chant 'We must survive', without finding the wherewithal to do so. That it was permissible to leave the graves of husband, parents, grandparents, that their memory lay not in tomb-stones, memorial candles or flowers, but in the consummate impertinent act of their own survival, Zelda folded the piece of paper and put it in her blouse.

'He's right,' she said softly, 'Aaron has two years before he is called. In that time we must try and sell the tavern,' She looked at her sons with little confidence, 'Well, we must try,' she said. 'But who will buy it, Mama?' Aaron asked. 'We must try,' she insisted, though she knew that the possibility of a sale was very remote. Tavern-keeping was a Jewish trade, and no Jew in Odessa would stake a future in that town of his mourning. But she must try'. 'We shall make our future in England.' she said. 'In Wales,' Leon laughed. She hugged them both. Their long mourning was over.

★

It was in the spring of 1887 that Aaron finally took Rachel for his bride, roughly at the same age as his father had taken his mother. The long years of their patient courtship had in no way dimmed their love for each other. Barak was not well enough to travel to the wedding, so the honeymoon was spent in Leipzig. Barak's fur business prospered with many employees, though Barak himself, in his failing health, took little part in it – Zelda cared for him with a loving tenderness. When she asked after Leon, hungry for his news, her question was private, for Aaron's ear alone, for she feared the tears that would greet his answers. Aaron was filled with a deep hatred for his brother for the hurt he caused with his neglect, and he resolved to confront him on his return. But Leon grew more and more distant. When Aaron moved into the Ruboff house after the honeymoon, he invited Leon to lodge with them, and Rachel too did her best to persuade him. But Leon declined their offer and kept to his own strange quarters, and the *landsleit* community looked with some bewilderment on this arrangement and wondered yet again, what would become of that younger Bindel who shunned their society and was not like a *landsleit* at all. Their doubts were confirmed when Leon finally moved his person into the valley. With his savings, and his share of the tavern inheritance, he bought a small miner's cottage in Senghenydd, far from Jew or synagogue, with only Pavel to keep a weekly eye on him and hold his tongue when Aaron asked for news of his brother's welfare. For such news was untellable.

Leon had fallen in love with one Margaret Davies, not the red-headed one or Leon's first exile dreams, but one very much of her kind. A coal-miner's daughter, a million miles from Odessa, close to Eisteddfod and chapel, and to whom the word pogrom was meaningless and would remain so all her life. Leon kept Margaret a closely guarded secret, except from Pavel in whom he confided. But though Pavel was sympathetic he was deeply appalled by Leon's treachery. Leon too was aware of the monumental sin he was committing but he rationalised it as part of his personal method of survival. Even so, he feared Aaron's reaction, and at Pavel's suggestion he resolved to see more of his brother and repair those bonds of fraternity that were so frayed. So thenceforth, every Tuesday when he travelled to Cardiff to collect his goods for sale, he called at his brother's house. On one such visit, he was given news of Rachel's pregnancy. He rejoiced with them both, but he was fighting envy in his heart. After each visit to his brother's house, he was gnawed by feelings of jealousy. For he too wanted a home and a family, and he wanted to make that home with Margaret. Now that his brother would become a father, the need to make a decision regarding his own future was paramount, and he resolved that whatever consequences might ensue, and he knew that they would be catastrophic, he would propose to Margaret at their very next meeting, and hope that she would accept him. He knew it as his only way to happiness. Suddenly he thought of his mother, and with that thought, he understood for the first time, the magnitude of his transgression. Such an act that he had in mind would be for ever beyond her forgiveness, and perhaps would, finally, sever the bond between them, that bond that he had for so long teased and imperilled. He would keep his marriage a secret from her, for if the truth were told, she would mourn him as though dead, and she herself would possibly die of imagined sorrow. He loved her enough to keep that secret, and Aaron, out of the same love and within that same mourning, would do the same.

The years passed and quietly the century turned. It was Easter Sunday in the spring of 1903, and the bells tolled all over the world in cathedral, church and chapel, In the town of Kishinev in the province of Bessarabia, they were tolling too, and were a signal to the onset of the most bloody pogrom of all. In his cottage in Senghenydd on that day, Leon Bindel was as yet unaware of the events which decimated the tribe he had foresworn. Later he was to hear of them and their awesome facts would exacerbate the guilt that had soured his heart and had been so doing for many years. That day he was aware of another event, for it was the barmitzvah birthday of his son. They had called him David as something of a compromise. Margaret had drawn the line at Benjamin, insisting that it was no name for a son of Wales, so they had settled on David, which conveniently doubled for the country's patron saint and the King of Israel. They had had no more children, which Leon considered was a blessing; for the marriage had begun to sour shortly after David's birth. Leon's fractured English which had so attracted Margaret when they had first met now irritated her profoundly. Every aspect of his foreignness was a source of her displeasure. The sharp differences between them, the tribal and cultural barriers, seemed more and more insurmountable as the initial passion waned. Leon had never sought to tutor her in his history, and had not insisted on the boy's Jewish upbringing. But he had drawn the line at baptism. Margaret had grudgingly acquiesced. Leon, for his part, had done his best to become part of the life of the valley for he warmed to the mining community who, for the most part, accepted him. As his domestic strife became more and more acute, he often thought of leaving his marriage but it was the mining community that kept him there. That and David, from whom he would not be parted. Besides, his pride forbade a separation from his wife even though legally he would have had grounds. For Margaret was still a beautiful woman and was much sought after by bachelor miners. He could hardly blame her for her pursuit of pleasure since her life at home was miserable and silent. Leon's mood was unusually gloomy. She did her very best to enliven him, but she couldn't understand his guilts and his sorrows. He would laugh only with David, and in the Working Men's Club in the High Street, she was told. But at home he was disposed to melancholy, He went to Cardiff twice a week to collect his goods and always returned in sullen mood. He longed to see Aaron but he was too proud to call. Four years before, Mr Ruboff had died, and Pavel had brought message that Rachel would be especially pleased if he would attend the funeral. He had gone and stood by the graveside, trembling in the echoes of his childhood tongue. Nobody spoke to him. Aaron had shaken his hand. That was the last time he had seen his brother. His brother's daughter he had never seen. He longed for a meeting; between Chaya and David, but he was too proud and too wary of refusal to drop hint of it in Pavel's ear. That same kind ear was privy to news from Leipzig too and Leon learned that his mother was well and sending him her thoughts. That Barak still lived and that his condition was stable. Leon knew that, at this stage, only he could make the move to return to his family, but that return had to be alone, and though he longed for it, his pride would allow no move in that direction.

From *Brothers*, 1983

LILY TOBIAS (1897-1984)

Born Lily Shepherd to a Jewish family in Ystalyfera in the Swansea Valley, Lily Tobias, a novelist, broadcaster and playwright, was an aunt of Dannie Abse.[2] She published her first short story at the age of 12, in the Swansea weekly *Llais Llafur*. Her first book, *The Nationalists*,[3] published in 1921, was a collection of short stories, most of them published first in the *Zionist Review*, and all of them drawing heavily on her Welsh background. The book's cover showed a red dragon within a Star of David. She later published several novels: *My Mother's House, Tube, The Samaritan*, and *Eunice Fleet*. She and her husband Philip Valentine Tobias, whose family had founded the *Jewish Chronicle*, settled in Palestine in 1935, but he was killed shortly afterwards in an Arab riot against the Jews. She continued to live in Israel, on Mount Carmel, where she was an important representative of Welsh, and indeed British, Jews. A lifelong Zionist, she was a leading member of the movement in Wales before she emigrated, and worked tirelessly for Zionist causes in Israel too until her death in Haifa in 1984.

The Nationalists is a fascinating work, not so much for its literary merit (which it must be admitted is not great) as for its subject matter and for the insight which it gives into the experience of a Jew who had been brought up within a Welsh-speaking community and who identified strongly with nascent Welsh national aspirations. At the same time it gives what I believe must be a unique literary record of Zionism in Wales before the Balfour Declaration – the bulk of the material was published before the First World War. The introduction by the former editor of the *Zionist Review*, Leon Simon, while recognising that the stories are propagandist, says that their literary qualities transcend that category. In truth, while the stories certainly do have literary qualities, albeit of the rather over-decorous style of the period, those qualities, whether characterisation, dialogue or narrative, are completely subordinated to the requirements of the Zionist message. Characters are only of interest to the degree to which they conform to or deviate from the Zionist ideal, dialogue is almost always about the Jewish national question, and the narratives are subjected to alarming leaps of perspective as dictated by the necessities of the Zionist focus.

The stories are almost exclusively set in Wales, in rural villages, mining communities or cities, and the characters portray a variety of responses to both Welshness and Jewishness. Welsh nationalists are invariably portrayed very sympathetically, and Welsh people who Anglicise themselves and who scorn their language and culture are put in a critical light. Several Welsh characters, particularly those of a religious background, are shown to display a greater sensitivity to Jewish identity and to Zionist aspirations than some of the Jews themselves. It is interesting, in these portraits, to see the evangelical sympathy with Zionism being portrayed from the receiving end. In the following extract, a young Jewish woman who has distanced herself from her Jewish background meets a Welsh friend's elderly uncle:

> 'Merch anwyl,' he exclaimed in his broad, emphatic accents, 'and proud I am to meet you, for sure. Why, I do love the Jews, indeed I do. You are the people of the Book, and the Lord will show his wonders through you yet. You have got a big job in front of you, my gell.'
> 'And what is that, Mr Jones?', asked Sarah politely as she recovered her breath.
> 'The return to Zion, my gell,' said the old man solemnly. 'Oh, that I could live to see the day!'[4]

As for the Jewish characters, not surprisingly, those who seek to assimilate and disguise their Jewish identity are implicitly criticised, while those who avow their Jewishness, and even more so those who embrace Zionism, are approved. Reading these stories is like opening a window onto a world which would have been hidden from the attention of most Gentiles in Wales. Here, in the years before and during the First World War, is a community of Jews, many rooted in Wales and identifying with its people, others more recently arrived and still carrying the accents and attitudes of the ghetto; some poor, others flourishing, some devout, others secular, some playing down their Jewishness, others proudly owning it. A world of *shabbas* meals in mining villages, of the web of patronage and social competition in the Jewish relief societies and the synagogue, of Jewish shopgirls begging the Saturday off work, of uneasy friendships with Goyim, of uncomfortable relations with embarrassing 'foreign' relatives, of the tension between assimilation and affirmation. And running through this complex world is the disturbing, inspiring ideal of Zionism, which was still, in those days, an aspiration, an act of faith. Many of the stories compare the Welsh and Jews as two small peoples with proud religious and cultural histories, both seeking a political settlement that would affirm and safeguard their identities. The following story, 'The Outcasts', also shows fellow-feeling between Welshman and Jew, although in this case, the Welshman is one whose socialism and pacifism has isolated him within his own community, and who is shown to be able to identify even more readily with the outcast Jew as a result.

THE OUTCASTS

The schoolmaster saw him first at a bend in the winding valley road – an unkempt toiling figure, wearily humped under the burden of a pedlar's basket – or was it not rather the age-old wanderer's pack of sorrows? The image came aptly to mind at sight of the characteristic face, with its dark poignant eyes, hooked nose and reddish beard: features that carried their own tale to the schoolmaster, still fresh in memories of student days in Germany.

'Poor old chap' he muttered, and forgot him as he stepped aside into an exuberant lane to cull botanic specimens for next day's lessons.

But a little later the sound of raucous cries brought him back into the high road, to see the pedlar crouching against a hedge, his arms crooked upwards to shield his head from a shower of stones that hurtled past. Beyond him pranced a number of small boys, yelling excitedly: 'Jew! ol' Jew! Le's pull his basket, Gwilym! Ar hen Jew! Jew!'

'Stop it, you rascals!' shouted the schoolmaster, striding forward and waving his stick in the air. With one accord the tormentors fled in retreat, while their victim lowered his arm and gazed dumbly at his rescuer. The latter felt an unreasonable resentment at the terror that strained those haunting eyes.

'Why, what a coward!' he thought. Aloud he only said 'Are you hurt?' noticing a thin streak of blood run down the man's fingers.

Apparently the question was not understood. The man merely fumbled with his basket, stepped awkwardly forward and muttered unintelligibly, his eyes averted.

The schoolmaster repeated the question in German. The other looked up eagerly, thrust out his bleeding hand, then rubbed it on his coat with a faint smile. 'Ach, das is garnisht,' he said, and began to pour forth a stream of Yiddish. As they walked along the schoolmaster gathered with difficulty the recent outlines of Israel Goodman's history. He had not long arrived from Russian Poland, and was living in the town at the head of the valley with *landsleit*, who had generously fitted him out with a pedlar's basket and licence. Thus equipped, he set forth to earn his daily bread, in a strange land among strangers whose language he could not speak. The prospect of so precarious an enterprise did not seem to appal him. 'A coward?' thought the schoolmaster, modifying his view. Was he married? A closer look discerned unexpected youthfulness behind the stoop, the haggard lines, the unruly beard. He was barely thirty, had a wife and two children.

At this point a cottage came into view. The schoolmaster paused at the gate, and asked his companion to enter, that he might rest and bathe his wounded hand. A slight fair woman, with a little boy at her skirts, emerged from the open door to greet them.

'What, Will?' she said to her husband, half vexed, half smiling. 'Another tramp?'

'One of the oldest species in the world,' he answered whimsically, lifting up his little son into the air. 'I found him being stoned by my disciples, who failed to see his resemblance to your dear Lord. Will you set tea in the garden, Mary dear, while I take him to the shed for a wash – there's some lint in the toolbox, I believe?'

The child followed him and his guest round the flower-edged path, the mother standing a moment to gaze after them with tender eyes. This was the man whom the village covertly abused for his abstention from chapel – dark had been the comments and predictions when she, 'the good girl,' had married him. 'A better Christian than any of them,' she told herself fiercely for the thousandth time. And this conviction seemed to penetrate even the alien mind of the Jew, who, with clean and bandaged limb, prepared gratefully to depart, was bewildered at being further detained, led to a shady corner of the garden, and told to sit at a table laden with fresh tea, new-laid eggs, and currant jam in a bright-blue dish. Instinctively he put his hand into his pocket and glanced anxiously about. His host broke into a reassuring smile.

'Sit down, there's no payment. You are a man and a brother –' He turned away abruptly at the strange moist look in the Jew's eyes. Then seizing up his little boy on his knees, he added, 'Besides, I've got to make up for my pupils' behaviour. I hope that sort of thing doesn't happen often.'

'Why not?' said Israel, recovering confidence and beginning to eat. 'You make me think this is Paradise. One need surely go no further – not even to Jerusalem, where my father fled, saying that there alone could the Jewish soul be safe, Yet just now when those young Christians attacked me, I lost hope and thought, 'Surely, this is but as Russia after all, and I need not have escaped with such toil and anguish from the horrors there."

'Was it so dreadful – what happened to you in Russia?'

Israel shrugged one shoulder vehemently and lifted both his hands. His tale was full of vivid detail but was briefly told, Returning from the perils of the Russo-Japanese War, he had found his town in turmoil and despair, A pogrom of marked ferocity had just taken place, and the smoking trail of ruin, pillage, and murder lay red over the whole Jewish community. His own home had been sacked and destroyed, his parents cruelly beaten, his sister ravished and killed before their eyes, while his wife and children had fortunately escaped to relatives in another town where they lay seriously ill for months afterwards. He himself was suffering at the time from a fever contracted at the front, and inadequately nursed, and maddened at the havoc wrought by the mob connived at by the ruling power that had used him relentlessly in its service, he had gone shouting his protest to the local authority, only to be thrown into prison for such blatant audacity. By the efforts of friends he managed to escape, and after untold hardships arrived in England, tramped his way penniless to P...., and was now endeavouring to earn enough money to send for his wife and children.

'Your little boy, he said, looking wistfully at the plump, rosy child – how old is he – four? My little son is about the same. I have never seen him – he was born soon after I went into the army. But they tell me he is very thin and pale.

'When he comes, he shall be made fit,' cried the schoolmaster, getting up and pacing the grass.

'Things are better here, my friend. There is much that is wrong – but not so bad as that. It is not Jerusalem your people need. These narrow religions and nationalisms cannot cure the world's evils of hate and ignorance and tyranny. Socialism, my friend – enlightenment of the people and abolition of economic slavery – internationalism and the brotherhood of man –'

The Jew got up too and cast a hasty glance around; something of the earlier look of alarm and terror sprang into his eyes.

'It's all right,' laughed the schoolmaster. 'No spies here – nor, policemen. And if there were, it wouldn't matter. This isn't Russia, you know. It's a free country!'

'God be thanked,' said the Jew fervently. 'But I tell you, for such talk by the young men all the miseries have come. And alas, it was the old and the innocent who were the victims. What did we wish for but to be left in peace? It was the same when I was born. At that time too there was a pogrom in my father's town. The Christians were made to believe that an epidemic which raged was caused by the Jews – even though the Jews suffered from it also – and the Virgin would not be appeased until the Jews were punished. So there was robbery and murder. My father escaped with his young wife across the border into Germany, where I was born. But there too it was difficult to live in peace, and after a time my parents returned. That is why my father always looked to Jerusalem as the true refuge of the Jew.'

*

In fifteen years the fortune of Israel Goodman underwent a change. It would have been hard to recognise 'the tramp' in the prosperous merchant of P....'; whose eldest son seemed every inch a British soldier in his proudly donned uniform.

'Good-bye, dad and mam,' he said gaily at the leave-taking. 'Don't worry over me – you know I feel I owe England something for the freedom she's given us. Be sports, both of you!' At that moment Israel thought, curiously enough, of his old father who had died peacefully in Jerusalem – while his wife strove with her tears in remembrance of her baby boy, the little life that had flickered out before she had reached these merciful shores, And afterwards both talked of the Christian schoolmaster, who had been such a good friend to them in those early struggling years.

Fate, however, had not dealt too kindly with him. His disregard of chapel, together with his unconcealed Socialism, had gradually proved too much for the decorous Welsh villagers, and he was eventually obliged to leave his post and the pleasant cottage in the valley. After an unsatisfactory existence in a Midland town, he came back to the neighbourhood of P...' but the Goodmans had seen little of him and his family. It was soon after the passing of the Military Service Acts that he paid them a welcome visit, and found the amiable merchant in gloomy mood.

'So your son thought it his duty to join up – I wonder if he still thinks this is a war for freedom. Of course, I haven't believed in it at all.'

'Ah, you're a Socialist,' said Israel with a faint smile.

'An Internationalist,' said the schoolmaster, the old enthusiasm lighting his fine haggard face. What's the sense of killing brotherslaves? My son thinks the same, only he's really more of a Christian, – and can't reconcile killing with God's love. But the Tribunal says he's too young to have opinions, though ripe for bayonet practice, so he's awaiting arrest any day. But there's something wrong – have you had bad news?'

'No – no-' said Israel nervously. Only the police have been here several times lately, inquiring – you know I was born in Germany, and I never troubled to get naturalised here. Of course, I am well known, still, one fears.'

★

It was about eighteen months later that the schoolmaster again visited Israel Goodman. He had not long left the grim prison where his son was serving his third sentence, for persisting in his belief that war was a crime against God. The dreary structure in which Israel Goodman was interned seemed therefore in congruous setting.

'Mary saw your wife yesterday,' he hastened to assure the anxious man. 'She is well and cheerful, and hopes you will both soon be released. ('God forgive us,' he muttered, recalling Mary's picture of the forlorn desolate woman). When your son knows all – you have not yet heard?'

'No, it is a long time since he wrote. Did I tell you of his last letter – from Palestine, you know? He had visited his grandfather's grave, and 'seemed to have had a vision. I cannot quite understand – something about an end of graves, no more dying in Palestine, but living there – and a future home. Would we could go to him there! Our business is ruined – even a speedy release – but *your* son?'

The schoolmaster described the visit without embellishment. He added that his own position had now become untenable in consequence of the support he had openly given his son. He had not only been asked to resign his post – he and his wife had received notice to leave the house they occupied. So they were giving up everything and going once more into the wilderness.

The Jew and the Christian gazed at each other in silence – outcasts in a world that was a negation of the ideals of both.

From *The Nationalists*, 1921

MAURICE EDELMAN (1911-1975)

Maurice Edelman was born to a Jewish family in Cardiff and was educated there and in Trinity College, Cambridge. After a spell as a reporter in France and North Africa during the Second World War, he became the Labour MP for Coventry West in 1945 and then for Coventry North West from 1950 until his death. He wrote 11 novels, nearly all with a Parliamentary background. His interest in Jewish matters can be seen by the choice of subject of his final novel *Disraeli in Love* (1972), and by his authorship of a biography of David Ben-Gurion. As for Welsh affairs, they can best be seen in his second novel *Who Goes Home*, from 1953, in which the main character, John Vaughan, is the son of a Welsh statesman, Geraint Vaughan, who is a thinly-disguised portrayal of David Lloyd George. The Leader of the Opposition, George Morgan, is also a Welshman, and the action of the book centres on John Vaughan making a reluctant political comeback by fighting a by-election in the fictional mining town of Cwmbrau. In the novel, the by-election is being fought as a kind of referendum on a controversial 'American Bill', proposed by the Minister for Economic Co-Operation, Erskine, which would allow America the right to build military installations in Britain and to run them according to American laws. The first such base has been opened in Cwmbrau, amid great controversy, and Vaughan is urged to make the by-election a fight for British independence. The choice of this issue as a *cause célèbre* seems to owe something to the real-life controversies surrounding the building of the Penyberth bombing school in the 1930s and the eviction of the people of the Epynt mountains during the Second World War to make way for a military training ground. This is how George Morgan describes the Americans' arrival in *Who Goes Home*:

'Imagine the scene,' he went on. 'A column of Americans arrives at Cwmbrau. They evict three hundred of the lads. And their women. And their children. Evict? No. fair play. There's compensation. They settle down with the squalid paraphernalia of their washing-machine civilisation. Their G.I.s make themselves comfortable with their whisky standard of pay. And then, on top of all this, Erskine wants them to have the right to be judged by their own courts, the right to have rights over and above our own rights in our own country. He wants to start them doing to us what the Egyptians stopped us doing to them thirty years ago...

'Its going to be the debate of the people. They're going to say whether they want high wages as base-constructors for the Americans – or their liberties. They're going to say whether they want to be hewers of wood and drawers of water in their own mountains.'

Vaughan is persuaded to stand for the by-election, relying on the power of his father's name to swing the issue. The following passage shows him electioneering in Cwmbrau:

THE RETURN FROM CWMBRAU

From the square outside the hotel the sound of singing bloomed, and then faded when Vaughan pulled down the heavy sash. The miners who had carried him over a mile on their shoulders from the large Congregational hall all the way through the main streets of Cwmbrau, past the Committee Rooms of their opponents, where they had halted for brief abuse, to his very door, were reluctant to go home although it was already late, the buses had stopped running, and only a train's whistle or the clatter of shunting in the valley accompanied the singers in the deep silence.

Vaughan was happy. For the first few days he had been pushed from one meeting to another by Davies, his agent, introduced to leading members of the Miners' Lodges, and taken for long walks with a claque of canvassers over the curves of packed, back-to-back houses, where he was welcomed, surprisingly to himself, by his own portrait grinning back at him from almost every window; and, in the afternoons, by miners' wives who brought him cups of hot, dark tea that he had to drink as an act of ceremonial courtesy, whether he liked it or not.

Walking alongside his agent's car, accompanied by the bullying demand from the loudspeaker to 'Vote for Vaughan, Peace and

Independence' – an instruction that brought faces to every window and door – Vaughan soon found himself agreeably involved in a multitude of new intimacies. Everyone called him Johnny. The old miners, squatting and coughing in the sunlight on their porches, would stop him and say, I knew your dad. We went to classes together, or would clasp his hand and detain him while they told him an anecdote of Geraint and Cwmbrau.

He had little need for active campaigning. On the platform he was normally a diffident and inadequate speaker. But in Cwmbrau, though in all appearance he seemed a stranger, tall and stooping among the square, upright miners, tweed-jacketed among the blue-suited men with their caps and white mufflers, he felt an atavistic ease that brought him together with them in comfortable conversation. They loved him on trust. He was 'Geraint's Boy'. The power of his father's name that had brought great glory to Cwmbrau had passed, as if by a laying-on of hands, to his son. Even the children, his faithful attendants, who followed him in squads sucking lollipops and picking noses, watched him with awe when he began to speak from the car.

Once he had become accustomed to the daily routine of canvass and meeting, Vaughan became stimulated by the enthusiasm of his supporters. No sooner did he arrive at a Working Men's Club under the guidance of Davies, who seemed to know every elector by name, than he was greeted with a handshake all round, and countless offers of drinks. He had no need of speech. All that was necessary was that he should stand with a glass of beer in his hand, a smile of general approval on his face, and listen contentedly to the assurances of his supporters.

'You're in,' they would say. 'The other lot? They'll get a few up there' – a wave towards Cyn Garth, where the managers and shopkeepers lived – but down here, man, we're solid.'

Davies wasn't so optimistic. 'You're not in till the votes are counted,' he told Vaughan when he left him at the hotel entrance. I've been in elections with great mass meetings – pulled the roof down – like Morgan's on Tuesday. And then – when the day comes – the quiet ones come out. The ones who don't go to meetings. And you add them up, and they've won.'

'Yes,' said Vaughan, thoughtfully.

He sat in his arm-chair listening to the grave chorus of Cwm Rhondda, muted though it was by the closed window, rising like a consecration into the night. He felt with it a desire to triumph in the election so that he might dedicate his life from now on to those who had given him their affection and faith, and had reposed in him their hopes.

From *Who Goes Home*, 1953

MIMI JOSEPHSON (1911-1998)

Like the previous entry, this poem is taken from the pages of *CAJEX*, this time from 1955. It illustrates the painful dilemma facing a Jewish woman from Wales who is acutely conscious of the claims of the small country in which she has been brought up, but equally conscious of the claims of Israel, the small country to which so many diaspora Jews were emigrating during this period. Mimi Josephson was born in Swansea but lived most of her life in Cardiff, moving to Cambridge in the 1980s. She married Abraham Josephson, a schoolteacher in French, in 1935, and Brian Josephson, their only child, became a brilliant scientist and the only Nobel prize-winner Wales has so far produced. She taught in a school for a time herself, and also privately, and was interested in the teaching of gifted children and later of dyslexics. Her literary activities included writing poetry and short stories, and she also had published a number of 'profiles', some based on interviews with prominent figures such as Dylan Thomas.

WHICH LITTLE LAND?

Child of Israel –
Child of Wales.
Torn between two loyalties,
Two duties, two demanding loves.
Which one shall I serve –
Which little land?

For Israel needs another voice,
A singer bold to tell the world
Of ancient hopes but now fulfiled;
Of mighty strivings to be born anew
And how, triumphant now, she stands –
A home where all the exiled ones
May rest and praise their God.
By race I count myself thy child
Must I not sing, O Israel then, for thee?

And yet this Wales – this kindly land
That gave me birth and nurtured me;
Where God has taught my thoughts to sing.
A country worthy of all praise
And seeking, too, her newer bards.

To show the peoples of the earth
How she has borne her heritage,
And still maintains her ancient pride.
Is it not meet, O Cambria, then,
That I should raise my voice for thee?

Then which one shall I serve –
Since love for each tears at my heart?
For which land sing –
Which little land?

From *CAJEX*, Vol 5, No. 2, June 1955

JOSEPH DANOVITCH (1906-1983)

This brief but rather moving article, again from *CAJEX*, this time from 1967, shares with the previous items a deep feeling for the south Wales Valleys, where the author had spent his youth and where his father had been a pedlar. The Jews were not alone in leaving the Valleys following the Depression – half a million Welsh people did likewise. Joe Danovitch was born in Cardiff and married Gertie (*neé* Grunfeld) in 1933 by which time he had become a very ardent Zionist, following Jabotinsky's philosophy of a National Jewish Home in Israel. He was a very active Revisionist and was a delegate to the first World Zionist Congress after World War II in Basle in 1946. He was at one time also chairman of the Revisionist party in the UK. His dream was to live in Israel and he brought up his children that way. In 1949 he went to Israel for a short time to see if he could live there and returned after a few months determined to settle there after he retired, which he did in 1965. His widow still lives in Israel. The following article, written less than two years after his emigration, shows how a former Jewish son of the Valleys, now living in Israel, feels a hiraeth for his native land indistinguishable from that of any other exiled Welshman.

REFLECTIONS OF AN EXPATRIATE WELSHMAN

Eighteen months after leaving Wales for Israel I am at last able to attempt to collate and reconcile my impressions of Israel and my recollections of Wales. Eighteen years after the establishment of the Jewish State, the initial momentum which brought in nearly a million and a half refugees appears to have slowed down, and the crying need of the country both for security and economic reasons, is for a further great influx of immigration. The comparative situation of world Jewry having improved, no-one in his right senses would like to see this immigration resumed as a result of crisis, but the appalling loss of a third of the Jewish people in the Nazi holocaust, depriving the nation of the greater part of its intelligentsia, and pioneering potential, has now become very much apparent. While the complete integration, here in Israel, of Jews who have come here from all over the world, into a homogenous whole may only be a matter of decades, this progressive and outward looking country badly needs the know-how of Western immigration. Without intending for one moment to denigrate the quality of Jews from other areas of the world, the plain fact is that only Jews from the Western hemispheres have the technological know-how, and until the great reservoir of Jews in Soviet Russia accomplishes the elementary right of every citizen to emigrate, the void will be felt.

While the American emigrant to Israel usually brings a greater-capital and energy, the British immigrant generally connotes a sense of courtesy, highly esteemed, but not always emulated by the local population, and the absence of which, while deplorable, can be partially attributed to the tragic background of so many of the country's inhabitants. Integrity and a high standard of ethics are also ascribed to the British and in the academic world the British pronun-ciation of the English language is considered to be superior to that of the American, to the extent that a British teacher of English will usually be preferred to his or her American counterpart. There is a great admiration here for the efficiency of British offices and institu-tions and in particular, for the blessings of the British Welfare State and its Social services. What else, then, brings a British emigrant or for that matter, any emigrant coming here of his own free will? Primarily, I consider, to take his part in the preservation of the freedom of the State, so dearly won, and to feel extroverted here in a completely Jewish life, free from inhibitions and complexes, safe from the possibility of any sort of discrimination, and the necessity for a feeling of gratitude for even the mildest form of toleration. The simply marvellous climate and the beauty of the land are only secondary considerations to these factors. One aspect of life which is immediately apparent to the newcomer and which makes the most favourable of impressions is the youth of both sexes of the Israeli Armed forces, and the civilian youth, disdaining the Beatnik look and extremes in dress, gives one the feeling that there is no fear of demoralisation here and the hope and expectation that this will be a normal nation and not a Levantine State.

Israel holds in affection and esteem the memory of Lloyd George, and there is a Balfour Street in every town and village in Israel, for the authors of the Balfour Declaration are held in honour here. Men like Colonel Josiah Wedgwood, and Lord Strabolgi, doughty champions of freedom and the right to fight for it, are the embodiment of everything noble in the British character. There is in existence a British Israel Commonwealth Association and recently, with the visit of Dr. Horace King, Speaker of the House of Commons and incidentally a Welshman, to attend the inauguration of the new Israel Parliament building, crowds came to hear him speak at the reception held by the Association which followed. The spirit of the late Josiah Wedgwood's Seventh Dominion League, which would have made pre-State Israel a Seventh Dominion of the British Empire, is not altogether extinguished here. There is little on the Israel landscape to remind one of Wales, unless it be the eroded hills around Jerusalem bringing to mind forcibly the barren coal tips of my native land. The Welsh love of the Bible being traditional, in Wales one comes across everywhere place and chapel names like Tabor and Moriah, Sion and Ebenezer. The hymn and the psalm are synonymous in Wales as in Israel. David the King, and Dewi Sant had a common ancestor. Another great affinity is the mutual love of the Welshman and the Israeli for song, and my friend, Maurice Rosette, Secretary to the Israeli Parliament, and an ex Cardiffian, is striving mightily to raise the funds to be able to bring to Israel a Welsh choir to compete in the national Zimria. the Song Festival of Israel.

The nostalgia for the Welsh lilt and the Welsh hwyl is as strong in him as it is in me. There are residential areas in Israel as in Herzlia which bring strongly to mind Dinas Powis with its leafy lanes and well tended front gardens, but the denizens of the sea coast between Penarth and Porthcawl might well envy the golden sands, the blue green seas of the Israeli littoral, and the seven month Israeli summer when one wakes automatically each morning to the golden warming sun. This then brings this Welsh Jew (lay down, Richard Burton) to Israel. Never having suffered in Britain under the slightest disability, never having experienced anything but friendship and kindness. I can only compare myself, and here I am unwilling to provoke any controversy, to the Nationalist Welshman in his desire to throw in his lot with a people whose urge for national freedom transcends all material considerations, in the case of the Welsh Nationalist, the material benefits of the association with England, and in my case the fleshpots of a western way of life.

Penygraig, Tonypandy, Clydach Vale, Tonyrefail and Gilfach Goch and the whole Rhondda Valley, familiar to me and beloved since my dear father trudged round its hills carrying the pedlar's pack, these Welsh names evoke a nostalgia in me which I would not be without, and I eagerly tune my radio to the BBC programmes, and on Saturday nights at 7.45 p.m. to Sports News and sadly to another Cardiff City defeat. The whole of Israel cheered England home in its World Cup final against Germany, and when I hear English being spoken in the streets here I lose my inhibitions and my shyness and address myself to the speaker in the hope of finding a Welsh compatriot. There are vistas, breathtaking in their beauty in Galilee, and a spirit of holiness in Jerusalem. I am awed by the barren majesty of the eerie Negev, and I hope that my future is with these, but I still, one day, want to make a sentimental journey and retrace my steps in the Welsh valleys and see again the Welsh people I love and respect. There is too; a hallowed piece of ground forever dear to me, near Roath Park in Cardiff, where lie my dear father and mother. The transition from the Land of my Fathers to the Land of my Father's Fathers is not difficult for a Welsh Jew.

From *CAJEX*, Vol 17, No 1, March 1967

KATE BOSSE-GRIFFITHS (1910-1998)

Kate Bosse-Griffiths was another refugee from the Nazi persecution. She was Jewish on her mother's side, and was born and brought up in Luther's town,

Wittenberg, where her Lutheran father was a surgeon in charge of the local hospital. He came to prominence for his work in treating victims of an explosion and was visited personally by Hitler in 1935 to congratulate him. However, only a year later, the young Kate had to flee to Britain after she was dismissed from her new job in Berlin State Museum due to her Jewish ancestry. Her family later suffered persecution and her mother died in Ravensbruck concentration camp. In Britain, as an archaeologist specialising in Egyptology, she found work in Oxford, where she met J. Gwyn Griffiths, a Welshman from the Rhondda. They married and made their home in the Rhondda valley, where Kate Bosse-Griffiths learned Welsh and became active in Welsh literary circles, and in due course in Plaid Cymru and the Welsh language movement. On one occasion she was fined for refusing to pay a parking fine notice which had been presented in English only. The family later moved to Swansea where she was instrumental in establishing the Egyptian Museum in the city. She published a wide range of work in Welsh, including volumes on travels in Egypt, Russia and Germany, and some collections of short stories. Although a Lutheran by upbringing and choice, she retained a great interest in her Jewish ancestry and in Jewish subjects. The following article, written during the Second World War, shows her taking a characteristically honest and rigorous look to the work of the Nazis' favourite philosopher, Nietzsche.[5]

NIETZSCHE AND NAZISM

NIETZSCHE: Forty years after his death this name cannot be mentioned without fierce arguments. Nietzsche, the man who demanded the right to treat Darwin's theory of evolution as the basis to believe in the Superman; Nietzsche, the bosom friend of Wagner, and later his deadly enemy; Nietzsche, the mocker of Christianity; Nietzsche, who composed the rhapsodic songs of 'Zarathustra', the only modern philosopher who knows that the way to enlighten men is not merely through reason, but also through the feelings and passions; Nietzsche, who counted the body to be as valuable as the spirit.

The politicians of the Third Reich in Germany have claimed Nietzsche many times as their philosopher. It appears there is some basis for their claim. Nietzsche declared time after time that his great wish was to shape the Europe of the future, and to show the way to the generations that would come afterwards. Certainly, he was not understood in his own age.

But look closer at the Nazis' claims. It is known that the Germans never had from within their own people a harsher critic than Nietzsche. Listen to his words about the German race which is such a subject of pride for the Nazis

> As a nation that is characterised, from a racial standpoint, by incredible confusion and mixture, with a particular place, perhaps, for the pre-Aryan element, as the Central Nation in every sense, the Germans are more incomprehensible to their own mind, more comprehensive, more inconsistent, more unconscious, more difficult to prophesy about, yes, more terrifying than any other nation.
>
> (*Beyond Good and Evil*, paragraph 244)

Here, to be sure, he is playing with the idea of race. The dreaded word 'Aryan' comes to light here, even though it is used now against the Germans. Or listen to what he says about the Jews:

> The Jews without any doubt are the strongest and purest race which currently lives in Europe. (*Op. cit.*, 251).

He goes on to say that that, all the same, the Jews of his time are desirous of assimilating into the population of Europe. Contrary to the Nazi dogma, he says:

> Attention should be given to the desire (which in itself involves weakening the Jewish instinct) of assimilating into other peoples, and it should be assisted in every way; to this end it would be good if every anti-Semite was driven out of the country.

Further, he suggests mixing the race of the aristocratic Prussian officers with the Jews!

> It would be interesting to see if it would be possible to add to the hereditary art of commanding and obeying – the aforesaid land (Prussia) is a classic for both – or grafting on to it the genius in money and patience (and above all, some spirituality, which is very lacking in this area).

It is indeed ironic how there appears here also the Nazi idea of deliberately breeding a special race of men, such as has been done hitherto with animals; but here in the same way this idea is used in a way that is completely contrary to the ideology of the schools of the Third Reich.

However there is another side to the matter, and a much more dangerous side. The clothing of words in which the dogmas of Nazism are often wrapped comes directly from Nietzsche. For example, look at the formation of the idea about the difference between the priestly values and the standpoint of the warlike and loyal nobleman. The nobleman's standpoint, according to Nietzsche, is that good corresponds to aristocratic, and so on. 'Goodness = aristocratic

= able = beautiful = content = dear unto God'. And the opposite (the priestly standpoint):

> Only the afflicted are good; the poor, the helpless, only the low are good; the suffering, the needy, the afflicted, the ugly also are the only righteous ones, the only blessed ones; to these alone content-ment is given.

The idea of the Superman has also been followed by the Nazis. Everyone else in the world is no more than a path towards him. In dealing with this idea, Nietzsche was led to utter prophetic words. He saw a time coming when the small states of Europe would be destroyed as entities, when the development of democracy would have led to a social condition which will only know two kinds of men: the workers, obeying easily, easily directed, easily influenced, and a few dictators, the lords of men who lead the workers. It is easy to imagine that Hitler was intoxicated with ideas like these:

> 'The spread of democracy across the face of Europe is an unin-tentional means of creating dictators – using the word dictator in every sense.'

Nietzsche, the lonely, friendless man who came from the middle class, despised the workers completely in the same way. Here, perhaps, he lost his vision; on this point he is too much of a child of his age and his environment. He learned, by means of his classical studies, espe-cially through his study of Greek history, that a class of slaves was necessary in order to give a class of masters enough leisure to develop culture. He could not grasp that the place of slaves would now be taken by machines – or at least that this would be possible under worker-friendly direction. But his conviction was that the ordinary people, the mass – the 'far too numerous' are his words – should take the place of the slaves of the ancient world. Do we not here see before the eyes of our spirit the factory workers of the nineteenth century? It appears that Hitler, and everyone he stands for, has understood this philosopher in an extremely literal way. No, Nietzsche saw that a ruling class also needed a broad, wide and substantial basis. It appears that his ideas on politics and the Superman changed with time, and that he was badly disappointed with the Second Reich created by Bismark. At least, he could not follow to their conclusion his final ideas about the masterly amoral leadership.

Again, there is the question of woman in society. It is known that the Nazi principles only allow a subordinate status to the wife, as the helper of her husband and the mother of his children. This is a tradition which is deeply rooted in the mind of Germany. But it can be justified by Nietzsche's writings. I do not think that the philosopher anywhere else colours his theories so much with the colour of his personal experience. It is so dangerous for an educator to set as general truths the fruit of his own disappointments, and to draw from them laws for everyone! I also feel that in nothing else was Nietzsche so truly German. There was a time, certainly, when Nietzsche went to Rome hoping to win a girl as his disciple. We know he was disappointed in this case. Writing to a friend, he confesses that he spent very little time searching for a suitable wife. Unlike Socrates, he did not find the Diotima who could show him the true nature of love better than all the wise men of Athens in Plato's Symposium. In the form of Zarathustra, he prides himself that he knows virtually nothing of the female sex, except that he was never wrong in his opinion of them. And how wrong he was! He knew something about coquettish girls, educated wrongly, the middle-class girls of the Victorian age. He also knew Russian girls (to name a nation which promised great things, according to Nietzsche) belonging to the old nobility, who can teach the philosopher in a better manner.

'If you are going to the woman, take the whip with you!' That was the advice given to Zarathustra by a little old woman. I remember a day, when I was eighteen years old, when I went to my eldest sister and showed this sentence to her as a striking one that I had found in Zarathustra. It appeared to me like a penetrating symbol of the deep wish of maidenhood to have a masterful man, and of an Amazonian wish to fight and lose the day. I was very disappointed in my sister. She explained that this was a well-known half-truth from Nietzsche's lips, one that was much appreciated by young people growing up to be men; they often whispered it to one another. Apart from many intoxicating fruits, Nietzsche also has many of the half-ripe apples of wisdom. Perhaps it is precisely in this adolescent psychology that the Nazis saw their own image.

Translation from *Heddiw* 24, Vol 6, No 5, November/December 1940

JOSEF HERMAN (1911-2000)

Born to a Jewish family in Warsaw, the artist Josef Herman fled Poland in 1938 in anticipation of the Nazi persecution in which his entire family were later to die. Arriving in Britain, he lived first in Glasgow before coming to south Wales in 1944. He settled in Welsh-speaking Ystradgynlais which was to be his home for eleven years, during which time his portraits of the mining community of the Valleys earned him widespread recognition. The following two extracts telling of his experiences in Wales are taken first from an article published in the *Welsh Review* in June 1946 and then from his 1975 book *Related Twilights*.

A WELSH MINING VILLAGE

This mining village differs from others I know first of all in its colour.

The collieries are in the outskirts of the village, and the air is therefore clear.

A friend of mine who knows the French landscapes by heart compares the place when bright lighted with Brittany.

Violet roofs at the foot of green hills. Pyramids of black tips surrounded by cloudlike trees the colour of a dark bottle.

When the sun appears and gilds the air, the streets, otherwise uniform grey, become copper brown. This happens usually in the evenings, for the days are mostly behind a screen of slow rains, cold and blue like steel dust; the kind of rains which never promise to stop, and awake in you a feeling as hopeless as do many roads on a lost track. For the sake of truth I must add that only at the beginning did they awake in me a feeling of impatient anger. Afterwards I discovered to my own surprise that the rains here are more than a part of the general atmosphere. It is they that weave the strange tapestry of mood in which life here finds its order.

While the air becomes oily, the roofs and roads glossy, the river fuller and noisier, men bite their pipes, and finding cover in the entrance of the shops, enjoy, as always, a talk for talk's sake. Only dogs disappear from the streets, for the heavy doors of street philosophy are closed to them.

On the square of the village blue and red buses appear and disappear.

A little colourful cart with the standing figure of the milkman inside; in the twittering noise of the rain are the tapping steps of the tiny brown pony.

A woman walking over the bridge at the end of the street, the wind blowing against her; the white shawl rises from her shoulders and spreads like two huge wings.

A brown bus with miners returning from work.

Single short silhouettes with logs of wood under their arms, or groups of two or three fill up the square. The black statue of the policeman gleams like silk.

'Shwmai, Wyn!' 'Shwmai, Sid!' 'Shwmai, shwmai!'

Some turn left, others turn right.

Some remain and talk awhile under the awning with red and gold letters – 'Fish and Chips Restaurant', others walk forwards to the bridge.

But even glossy rainy hours are numbered.

A sunlighted evening glazes the village.

The river Tawe which has always two colours more than the sky – blackness of coal and yellow of clay – is now red.

White stones in the river.

Gilded cows walk over the stones.

Children in pink shorts hang on the trees near the bridge.

The hills are bright blue.

Over them lie brass yellow clouds.

'There you are,' said to me a man with a soft voice of secrecy, 'such is life here; mostly grey, but there is also a drop of gold in it.'

For weeks I wandered here on the hills, in the little streets, looking at the landscape, looking at walls and at men, at pits from far and near, sketching and talking to miners on the surface and underground, at work and at rest, studying their movements and their appearance.

This is a way of getting my faculties of concentration exercised, my intellect clarified; a way of getting myself through the thick cloud of insignificant incidents in which is enclosed before us every new reality.

There is a tradition among artists, particularly among writers, when they come to small places, to look for the so-called 'characters', and to represent them and their acts as the colour of the village. Yet a not easily satisfied observer will soon find out that the so-called 'characters' are lamentably alike everywhere. They are in Wales the same as in Poland, as in Scotland, among the Jews or Flemish peasantry. They rather remind of exotic spots in a landscape which may awake curiosity but do not satisfy a longer interest. There is no real depth in them; and therefore they surely do not typify any place. They only have connected anecdotes, and this does not possess a big enough form to embrace a full-blooded living man, nourished by tradition, formed by labour and moved by aspiration.

The miner is the man of Ystradgynlais.

Already in his appearance, although at first sight alike to other workers, the miner is more impressive and singular.

Sometimes I thought of old Egyptian carvings walking between sky and earth, or dark rocks fashioned into glorious human shapes, or heavy logs in which a primitive hand has tried to synthesize the pride of human labour and the calm force which promise to guard its dignity.

It would be true to say that the miner is the walking monument of labour.

By this singularity of appearance, amid the clean figures of the shopkeepers, the thin and tall figures of the town councillors, the robust figures of the insurance agents, the respectable figures of the ministers, and the fatigued figures of the schoolmasters, the miners form, like trees among vegetables, a solid group.

But what makes a group so singular outside is but the strong similarity within the group.

Like the houses with doors smaller than men, like the two china dogs on the mantlepieces, like the taste of the blackberry tart, they are similar in each house.

The kind of mauve scarf and the way they wear it; the manner of nodding their heads sideways in greeting, the feeling of relief and comfort they express as they stride in the middle of the road, the way of sitting near a wall and supporting their bodies with the heel of the foot.

Similar are also the troubles and joys.

What happens today to one happens tomorrow to another. Therefore there is sincere concern in each other's lives, and duties become habits.

Men must give each other a hand.

Familiarity breaks the ice of strangeness.

'You're no stranger here,' I was told the very day I arrived. A day later I was addressed as Joe, and now I am nicknamed Joe-bach.

If someone more individualistically-tempered does not like the familiarity, people here will easily find this out, and even the dogs won't bark after him.

Men need each other if only to talk to – or just to make the heart easier.

Thus men listen with heavy concentration, and share feelings, laughter, tears.

Birth or death are faced as a matter of fact, the first without too much fuss, the other without too much gloom. But the unexpected is encountered with gravity.

One afternoon a little street was empty but for a few dogs walking here and there. The two rows of houses and the black road between them were in a peaceful light.

An old man, bent like a walking stick with his head hanging down on his chest, was knocking at a door, then at another door, and so door after door, door after door. At every door he spent but a moment.

A woman or a man or the two together come to the open door, listen to the old man, some take the apron to their eyes, others just nod sadly.

When he came nearer to me, I thought that evening that Welsh must be the only language of music, of sorrow.

He had lost his son in the Far East. Then on the Teddy Bear Bridge I met three pregnant women. Their shapes were enormous and of unearthly beauty. Near them all Venuses would look but pale girls. Walt Whitman looking at them would repeat his psalm-sounding phrase: 'And I say there is nothing greater than mother of man.' The three mothers of man talked of death.

The whole village talked of death.

As in most small places, time and energy don't find their expression in movement, but rather in density.

In passionate calm rather, that brings out not so much the vivid as the heroic, not so much the ornamental as the dignifying simplicity.

This fashions primarily the form of speech.

Emotion replaces sentimentality, the quality of voice replaces the choice of smart words.

Not all music is expressed in the songs or instrumental compositions of a people.

Music lives first of all in the everyday modelling of the language, in the way of pressing our feeling into sounds for which words are but natural tails.

Here the tradition gives its lead.

The most admired is the man able to speak in the tradition of the old Welsh preacher.

How speaks an old Welsh preacher?

His voice knows only two colours: the bright yellow of a peaceful sun, and the threatening red of hell.

Only two sounds: the whisper of a branch moved by the wind, and the thundering of an empty barrel falling downstairs.

His hands know only two movements: the gentle movement of reaching for a flower, and of the whirling of mill-wings in a storm.

Only two expressions on his face – eyebrows, eyes, nostrils and mouth working it up simultaneously; first that of comfort from looking into a garden, and the sudden surprise of facing the dark mysteries of a forest.

When his voice goes higher, his body lifts up in the air.

With his voice coming lower his body falls across the pulpit rail, and to make sure that now he means no fun, that he is now on the earth, he hammers a closed fist on the open palm of his hand.

Even underground I saw men falling naturally into oratory.

Even fireside conversations are seldom 'clever' or dispassionate, although there are quite a few who have learnt the art of working out a case and swiftly proving a point; but the will to carry us closer to the object at the end of their vision keeps passion alive. It is this passion that brings even to the loud unordered life of the local pubs a nostalgic atmosphere half dreamy and half joyful. It is this passion which lights up the aspiration, and makes some of them read through heavy volumes of economics, sociology and philosophy, and prepare themselves for the task of leaders.

It is this passion which makes others sing, or write.

It is this traditional passion, this monumental appearance, that broadens the local and incidental, and the once individual becomes typical and symbolic.

But there are others who have no more passion left.

They are waiting for death.

Victims of silica dust.

You can pick them out with your finger.

They will say with a sad smile: 'A bit short of breath.'

This is Ystradgynlais, a Welsh mining village.

From *Welsh Review*, 1946, reprinted in
Josef Herman, *The Early Years in Scotland and Wales*, 1984

THE YEARS OF THE WAR: YSTRADGYNLAIS 1944-55

My wife and I set out in exuberant spirits (I had married Catriona McLeod in Glasgow in 1942) and we were overwhelmed by our first sight of Ystradgynlais, the Welsh mining village we came to through a chance meeting with Dai Alexander Williams, a carpenter who worked in the mines and who was also a gifted short-story writer.

Elsewhere in this book I have described in detail the quality of life in Ystradgynlais. Here I will set down my first impressions and the images which were crucial to my decision to remain there.

It was in 1944, either a June or July day, I can no longer remember, but vividly I recall the heat of that afternoon and how deeply I was struck by the quiet of the village around me. There was hardly a soul to be seen. In the distance, low hills like sleeping dogs and above the hills a copper-coloured sky – how often I later returned to the colour and mood of that sky! Its light reddened the stone walls of the cottages and the outlines of the stark trees. The railings and the cement blocks of the bridge had golden contours. Under the bridge, out of a cold shadow, trickled a pool of water which got thinner and thinner as it ran on amidst the dry stones and glittering pebbles. Then, unexpectedly, as though from nowhere, a group of miners stepped onto the bridge. For a split second their heads appeared against the full body of the sun, as against a yellow disc – the whole image was not unlike an icon depicting the saints with their haloes. With the light around them, the silhouettes of the miners were almost black. With rapid steps they crossed the bridge, and like frightened cats tore themselves away from one another, each going his own way. The magnificence of this scene overwhelmed me.

Every artist knows when he experiences something new, something he has never experienced before. What he may not know is the effect the experience may have on his whole life, or how it may shape the course of his destiny.

This image of the miners on the bridge against that glowing sky mystified me for years with its mixture of sadness and grandeur, and it became the source of my work for years to come.

The image filled me, too, with certainty that this village was the right place for me. I felt my inner emptiness filling.

Here I began working from scratch, as though I had never drawn or painted before. I worked on the spot, assimilating those experiences which struck me not so much by their actuality as by their symbolism, by the idealism which they represented. In computer terms, reality fed memory and memory fed imagination. I also made large charcoal drawings, studies of single heads; with these I once again began with reality, but aimed at a wider synthesis, both of form and of expression. I thrilled to a medium I had never used before: pastels – probably because pastels are the most direct medium of drawing with colour. With these pastels as well as with the pen and ink drawings of that time, I got nearer to the sculptor's approach to form than at any time before, to such a degree, indeed, that even today I am asked whether I am doing a sculpture.

★

In 1948 we bought a derelict pop factory and converted it into a studio with living quarters (until then we had lived at the Pen-y-Bont Inn). In 1951, having finished the mural 'Miners' for the Festival of Britain, I fell ill and for the next two years travelled extensively in sunnier lands. From about 1953 I spent more time abroad and in London than in Wales, but even in 1955 I was still thinking of returning to the incredible mining village which had become my home. I never did.

During my years in Wales I noticed a gradual awakening of interest in painting and sculpture. This was particularly noticeable in the immediate post-war years. A younger generation grew up, eager to take up painting, not in the hitherto amateurish way, but with the idea of becoming professionals, Many a beginner came to my workroom to 'talk things over.' Of course, the improved economic situation in the Welsh valleys had much to do with it, but credit must also go to two institutions – The Contemporary Art Society for Wales and the Welsh Arts Council – which did much to make painting and sculpture popular.

If I had to name one single individual who did most of the post-war pioneering work, it would be David Bell. When I first met him he was the Assistant Director of the Welsh Arts Council, Some years later he became keeper of the Glyn Vivian Art Gallery in Swansea. David was a sick man. Though his ill health was immediately visible, it was also what one least associated with him. He was a gifted poet and painter, but perhaps even more than this he was an administrator of great vision. He was clear-headed about the difficulties, but he was all enthusiasm and hope. 'The Welsh,' he used to say, 'are naturally gifted and drawn to music and literature, but I am sure that they also have a talent for painting, only, they don't know it yet.' And until his untimely death he made it his job to make his countrymen aware of this dormant gift.

There were other things that marked the changed situation. Large-scale exhibitions from the Arts Council of Great Britain were taken to Wales and shown in remote places where hitherto no works of art had been seen at all. The standard of the paintings and sculpture submitted to the National Eisteddfod went up, A new class of collectors appeared, and some years later two commercial galleries established themselves. The two main public galleries, the National Museum in Cardiff and the Glyn Vivian in Swansea, underwent a great change. In short, where at the end of the Second World War there had been literally nothing, something was now beginning to germinate.

In August 1967, in his introduction to the Gold Medallist Exhibition, Dr Roger Webster paid me the compliment of saying that I had had something to do with the creation of a universal symbolism out of the Welsh theme, and that this was of some significance to the Welsh. I hope that this is true, even if only in some small degree. It would please me to think that I was not only a taker but that I had also given something in return.

In 1955 Catriona and I parted and divorced. Two years later I married a women I had met at the time of my divorce, with whom I fell in love. We have two children – David, aged sixteen and Rebekah, aged six. For the first four years after our marriage we lived in London, then in 1961 we moved to Suffolk. This move was characteristic of my new situation: it no longer mattered to my work where I lived. I continued in the mood which had obsessed me since my years in Wales. From the beginning I always thought of painting as an unhurried, life-long discipline. True creativeness calls for repetition, in technique as well as in style; thus we achieve the intuitive familiarity with our restricted imagery, our inner world.

Realism has always irritated me; it is so much less than reality. It lacks what nature has in abundance: the power to move our feelings to such a degree that we rush to our brushes for relief! Realistic painting never does this to me. There is more to a miner or a peasant standing and doing nothing than meets the eye. Many, many years ago, an old Scottish fisherman from Stornoway said to me: 'I am more afraid of living than of dying', and these words made me resolve to look only at paintings purged of all trivia and inessentials. I told myself: the pain of living must never be too far from artistic expression.

I am never satisfied with putting nature or social life on record. When I look at things I see them like everyone else does; but when I close my eyes and try to recall them from memory, a great change occurs. Nature is so many fragments. What I see with my closed eyes is a simplified image, deep, synthetic, and in form it has the grandeur of a symbol; in that final symbol I also recognise the unity of my direction. This is why I make only notes from nature, and draw and paint from memory; the subject is then a lost world that I recover. In this way one call get an approximation of reality without becoming realistic.

Reading poetry I found stimulating and helpful to my work, but at no time more so than during my years in Wales. Here I must mention Walt Whitman, whose *Leaves of Grass* I read over and over again. Also, folk epics such as the Welsh saga *Mabinogion* or the Scandinavian epic *Fritiof* interested me.

At that time music also played a part, and I frequently listened to Beethoven's 'Ninth' and Wagner's 'Ring.' Wales is renowned for its singing and I found the rehearsals of some of the male choirs of the district most absorbing.

My love for African primitives and icon painting comes from these days, too.

All this defines my attitude to painting both before I went to live in Suffolk and during; the time I spent there. Although my life in Suffolk was the nearest to bliss I ever came, in another place and under different conditions I know that I would have carried on in the same way and painted the same things as I still do now, in my sixty-second year and back once again in London.

From *Related Twilights*, 1975

DANNIE ABSE (b. 1923)

Even if it had not been possible to find work by Jewish authors other than Dannie
Abse, then this chapter, if confined to his output alone, would still display a rich
variety of material depicting the Jewish experience of Wales. The quality and
range of Abse's work in this field would make him a one-man genre even if the
Welsh Jewish community had produced no other writers. A poet, playwright,
editor, essayist and autobiographical author, he is one of three distinguished
brothers of a Cardiff Jewish family. His brother Wilfred became a psychiatrist,
and his brother Leo became a politician and MP for Pontypool, and is also a
successful and provocative author, although his work is mainly political which is
why it does not appear in this primarily literary anthology. Lily Tobias, whose
work we saw in the previous item, was their maternal aunt. Dannie Abse himself
became a doctor, working in London, although retaining close links with Wales.
His poetry, capable of humour, humanity and profundity, and gifted with an
assured lyricism, has made him one of the leading English-language Welsh poets
of the century. His 1998 book, *Welsh Retrospective*, which brought together most
of his poems about Wales, displays the scope and depth of his engagement with
his homeland, dealing not only with autobiographical subjects but with the stuff
of ancient Welsh literature and history. The following extracts from his work are
only a small selection from a wealth of material which could have been included,
so I have concentrated mainly on those items which deal with the encounter
between Welshness and Jewishness. They begin with several passages from his
popular autobiography of his youth, *Ash on a Young Man's Sleeve*, published first
in 1954, and move on to several of his poems on Welsh subjects, before concluding with extracts from a later autobiographical work, *A Poet in the Family*.

from ASH ON A YOUNG MAN'S SLEEVE

It was Friday night and we were Jewish. The two candles burning
symbolized for me holiness and family unity. My mother could speak
Welsh and Yiddish and English, and Dad knew swear words as well.
One of my big brothers would say the prayer and we would eat. My
brothers' names were Wilfred and Leo. The meat was kosher. 'Wash
your hands, wash your hands, wash your hands. Comb your hair.' I
loved my brothers best.

In the schoolyard, too, they would dance around me:

> 'Dan, Dan, the dirty old man,
> Washed his face in a frying pan;
> Combed his hair with a leg of the chair,
> Dan, Dan, the dirty old man.'

'I'll do you in, Keith Thomas,' I said furiously. That settled it. Keith and I would lead a procession of whooping boys into the lane and we would threaten each other, Spit at each other, and finally swing our fists against the air until, by chance, one of us would get our face in the way and the fight would end. Fierce it was. Afterwards I would go into our garage so that I could weep alone and not show the shame of my tears to the other boys.

I loved my brothers best. Leo was a revolutionary. I already knew the Red Flag and the Alphabet.

> A stands for Armaments, the Capitalists' pride,
> B stands for Bolshie, the thorn in their side...

Oh, election day was a holiday. I would go over the town looking for a Labour car. I couldn't find any, so I chased the Liberals instead, and insulted the big slick cars that wore the blue colours.

> Vote, vote, vote for Johnny Williams,
> Kick old Whitey in the pants.

'What are you shouting for?' said my enemy Keith Thomas, his eyes, poison blue, leering at me. 'Vote, vote, vote,' I shouted. Keith pulled a penknife out of his pocket, unclasped it and tested the edge with his thumb. 'It's sharp,' he said casually. 'You broke my finger-nail,' I said. An election car passed by. 'Vote, vote, vote,' I shouted. 'Quiet,' ordered Keith, and he once more tested the edge of his knife ominously. 'You coward,' I said, 'fight like a Great Britain.' The street was empty. A cat slept on the sunlit doorway.

'Shut up, you podgy Jewboy,' said Keith.

'Podgy son of a whisky man,' I said.

'I'll slit your throat,' said Keith.

'I'll bash you on the nose,' I retaliated.

'I'll cut you into pieces,' said Keith.

'I'll split your lip,' I answered.

'I'll cut your ears off,' Keith said.

'I'll put your eyes out,' I said.

'Shut up, you podgy Jewboy,' said Keith.

'Podgy son of a whisky man,' I said.

Keith slowly came towards me with his penknife ready.

'Fight like a Great Britain,' I said.

Round the far corner ambled Dirty-face, pushing a pram, his dog following behind.

'Gosh,' I said, 'there's Dirty-face.'

We both hesitated. Then we ran away. We were both afraid of Dirty-face. In the Park I heard Keith shouting: 'Podgy Jewboy. Podgy Jewboy. Podgy Jewboy.' I walked home quickly to ask Wilfred to buy me a penknife. This was all a long time ago. I was ten years high and I lived in South Wales. I was not to play with Dirty-face, or go down the Docks, or make noises in my belly when visitors came. I was to tie up my shoe-laces, be kind to the cat and wash. But there were more 'don'ts' than 'dos'. And throughout all this my mother kissed me.

*

When breakfast was over, I had to go to the synagogue, rain or shine, for it was Saturday morning, I used to sit next to Bernard and Simon. We would wear our skull caps and whisper to each other beneath the chant of the Hebrew prayer. A man with a spade-shape beard would stutter and mutter at us now and then and again. Shush, shush, his eyes said. Such and these times, we would stare at the prayer book and giggle. It seemed natural that the prayer book wasn't in English but written and told in some strange language one read from right to left, some mystical language one couldn't understand. Obviously, one couldn't speak to God in everyday English. We stood up when the congregation stood up and sat down when they sat down. The men were segregated from the women lest they should be deviated from their spiritual commerce with God, The women prayed upstairs nearer to heaven; the men downstairs nearer to hell. The sermon would begin and I would stare at the red globe that burned the never-failing oil. The Rev. Aaronovich, a man with an enormous face, gave the sermon. Usually his tone was melancholy. Every New Year, Rosh Hashana, he would begin his speech, raising his hands, eyes round, mournfully direct, 'Another year has passed... another nail... in the coffin.' The congregation knew this preface to his sermon by heart. They could have joined in, if they so wished, in some sorrowful chant; instead (except for the elders who nodded their heads slowly as if watching vertical tennis) each would nudge and pinch his neighbour.

However, this Saturday morning in 1934, the Rev. Aaronowich was almost gay. I stopped staring at the red globe and ignored the scrubbings and scratching of Simon and Bernard. He spoke in English; with a Russian and Welsh accent, throwing in a bit of Yiddish when his vocabulary failed him. I think I could understand what he was saying. I believe he proclaimed that it was an honour to be alive, good to breathe fresh air, miraculous to be able to see the blue sky and the green grass; that health was our most important benediction and that one should never say 'no' to the earth. (Also, that the congregation should as Jews avoid ostentatiousness.) Never to despair, for when one felt dirty inside, or soiled, or dissatisfied, one only had to gaze at the grandeur of the windswept skies or at the pure wonder of landscapes – one only had to remember the beauty of human relationships, the gentleness and humour of the family, the love and tenderness when a young man looks upon his betrothed – all things of the earth, of the whole of Life, its comedy, its tragedy, its lovely endeavour and its profound consummation – and I understood this for only that morning my brother Leo had read me from a little blue book words that sounded like 'Glory be to God for dappled things' – though, then, I didn't know what 'dappled' meant. And the Rev. Aaronowich spoke such beautiful things in such a broken accent that his voice became sweet and sonorous and his huge mask-like face rich, ruffled, handsome.

Afterwards, there was nothing to do but to stare at the red globe again, as the congregation offered thanks to God. In that red globe the oil of Jewish history burned, steadily, devotedly. Or was it blood? Blood of the ghettoes of Eastern Europe. My brother Wilfred said a world flickered in that globe: the red wounds of Abel, the ginger hair on the back of the hands of Esau, the crimson threaded coat of Joseph, the scarlet strings of David's harp, the blood-stained sword of Judas Maccabeus – David, Samson, Solomon, Job, Karl Marx, Sigmund Freud, my brother said lived in that globe. Gosh.

The service seemed interminable, the swaying men, the blue and white *tallisim* around their shoulders, the little black *yamakels*, the musty smelling prayer books, the wailing cry of the Rev. Aaronowich, the fusty smell of Sabbaths centuries old. Thousands of years of faith leaned with the men as they leaned – these exiled Jews whose roots were in the dangerous ghetto and in dismayed beauty. Their naked faces showed history plainly, it mixed in their faces like ancient paint to make a curious synthesis of over-refinement and paradoxical coarseness. One received a hint, even as they prayed, a hint of that unbearable core of sensual suffering. As they murmured their long incantations, I saw in their large dark eyes that infinite, that mute animal sadness, as in the liquid eyes of fugitives everywhere. I was eleven years old then: I could not have named all of this but I knew it ... I knew it all.

How different seemed the synagogue when empty. With people in it I felt safe – as if God were far away. I was wrong, of course, but that was how I felt. Once I entered the synagogue on a weekday, when no one was about. It was almost dark inside: the light glimmered through the stained windows, the red globe burnt outside the Ark in which were kept the scrolls of the Torah. The darkness had weight but the weight had stillness. It was so silent that I tiptoed. I was an intruder in the House of God. I was afraid. I wanted to run out, escape. Supposing God rose out from one of the corners, from the stillness, from the silence, from the dark, I thought I heard a motion from the other side of the synagogue. My heart turned over beating fast. Were there not footsteps coming towards me? I held my breath that I might listen better. Surely I could hear someone breathing nearby. He was behind me, I knew it, I was afraid. I ran out from the silence, from the dark, into the glittering sunshine and the loud street, not even daring to glance over my shoulder. I didn't want to see the face of God. It would have been a face of space and silence.

When the service was over, we walked the three of us into the late morning rain of a Saturday in 1934 and sabbath or no sabbath we boarded a tram. We held our pennies tight and tried to look away when the conductor shouted, 'any more fares, please'. It was to no purpose: we bought the yellow penny tickets and looked at their numbers. 'I've got a seven on my ticket,' I said. That was lucky. And the tram lurched down St. Mary's Street. 'There he is, there he is,' shouted Simon. We poked our heads through the window and the wind and rain blessed our faces. Sure enough there he stood, as usual, opposite the Castle, selling papers.

'Paper Sir? ...Thank you Sir.'
'Paper Lady? ...Thank you Lady.'
'Paper Sir? ...Thank you Sir.'
'Paper Lady? ...Thank you Lady.'
'Paper Sir? Paper Sir? ... PAPER SIR? ... Bastard!'
'Bastard, bastard,' we yelled.
He smiled back at us. 'You little bastards,' he grinned.

In Queen Street, an ex-miner played an accordion, a tombstone in one of his lungs. The music soared plaintively, insistently, across the rainy street: give, give, give, give, give. The traffic lights changed to green – the orange reflection rubbed off the wet surface of the road and a blue-green smudge usurped its blurred place. And the traffic passed on, passed on. The rain, thin and delicate, lost from the damp sky, sullenly fell forever. A car backfired. Still, as the tram blindly hurled its way towards Newport Road, in the distance like a frail echo, I imagined the accordion music, its sad dark melodies of give and give and give and give.

'Bastard.' I liked that word. I used it on my brother Wilfred. 'You big bastard,' I said affectionately. Astonished, he made me promise not to speak it again. So I looked it up in a dictionary.

We sat down to eat: Leo reading the *News Chronicle*, and Wilfred and my mother chatting. The meal was good. Cold Meat and Pickled Onions and Chips. A meal with shape to it, see. Very tidy mun. 1934. Saturday. Cardiff. Rain. Glory be to God for dappled things.

★

'You don't believe in Christmas, do you?' Sidney said to me.

'What's it like to be Jewish?' asked Philip.

'S all right,' I said.

'What's the difference?' demanded Philip.

'They puts 'ats on when they pray, we takes them off,' Sidney said.

'It's more than that, their blood's different,' said Philip, 'makes their noses grow.'

'Megan's coming round our house this evening,' I interrupted, making a face. Sidney and I didn't like girls because they wore knickers and Megan was especially silly. Lots of things were silly. Girls were silly, Miss Morgan our schoolmistress was silly, washing behind the ears was silly, going to bed early was silly. Now Philip was silly, because he didn't know what it was like to be Jewish. It wasn't anything really, except on Saturdays. We walked down the street wishing for snow and letting our breath fly from our mouths like ectoplasm. Soon it would be Christmas holidays, and presents and parties. The shops were crowded with voices. We pressed our noses against the window-panes, breathed, and wrote our names with our fingers on the misted glass. 'Leo loves Megan,' I wrote. It was all cotton wool in the windows, and the smell of tangerine peel, and a man with a long white beard.

'There's daft, i'n'it?' said Philip.

'Look, Father Xmas!'

'Where do flies go in the winter-time?' asked Sidney suddenly, and we all laughed sharing a secret.

When I arrived home, my brother Leo was squeezing a blackhead from his forehead; then he combed his hair.

'Megan Davies,' I shouted at him. 'Megan Davies.'

'Do your homework,' he said.

'Who loves Megan Davies?' I cried.

He hit me harder than he meant for I fell against the wall and a bruise come up like an egg on my head.

'Put some butter on it,' my brother said, 'and stop crying.'

'Bloody, bloody, bloody,' I screamed at him.

'Now then, enough of that,' he thundered. But the front door bell rang and he thought it was Megan, so I was given a penny to shut up.

It was only Uncle Isidore ...I don't think I've told you about him. I'd like to tell you. Of course, he's dead now, but I remember him quite well. He's become a sort of symbol really. You know, my parents still live in Wales, but we children have grown up and left home – as much, that is, as anybody can ever leave home. Anyway, when old Dafydd Morgan comes round the house at Cardiff these days, he and my parents get to talk about the kids.

'And what about Wilfred, your eldest son?' Old Morgan asks.

'All right,' says my father, 'not just an ordinary doctor but a psychiatrist.'

'Fancy,' says Morgan, 'Wilfred not just an ordinary doctor! Now my son Ianto 'e 'ad the gift do you know, just like his mother before she caught pneumonia, before she was... exterminated, God rest her soul.'

'And Leo, my second son,' interrupts my father. 'Ah yes, Leo, Leo, there's a boy for you,' smiled Morgan. 'A boy in a million. Very spiritual. And a credit to you; goes to chapel, I mean synagogue, regular, I understand.'

'A solicitor, Mr. Morgan, very clever.'

'Yes, very clever. Fancy, a solicitor! A very spiritual solicitor, I should think. Pays, I always think, to go to chapel – I mean synagogue. The connections do you know? Apart, of course, as a remedy for the spirit. But what about your third son, the youngest?'

'Our third son, Dafydd Morgan,' says my mother, 'is no good. Won't do any work.' 'Just like Uncle Isidore,' exclaim my father and mother, in unison, lifting up their hands hopelessly.

'Fancy,' says Morgan. 'Now my son Ianto...'

Uncle Isidore wasn't exactly an Uncle. Nobody knew his exact relationship to the family; but my parents called him 'Uncle', and my cousins called him 'Uncle', and my uncles called him 'Uncle'. He used to visit our home regularly, once a week, to collect his half a crown and eat a bit of supper. He went around all my relations' houses to receive a silver coin and grumble. It wasn't even as if he were a religious man. He just lived that way and the rest of the time he would read at Cardiff Central Library, or return to his dingy bed sitting-room and play his violin. Not that he was a competent musician. On the contrary, he would scrape the easy bits and whistle the difficult phrases. That was his philosophy and his life. He always looked as if he needed a good wash, a shave, and a haircut. Uncle Isidore would pick me up and rub his face against my cheek. 'Like a baby's bottom,' he used to say to me. He smelt of dirt and tobacco. Eventually he died of kidney trouble. That's all I know about him. It doesn't seem very much. Uncle Isidore was just an oldish, untidy man, a sort of amateur beggar, who wouldn't work but read in the Reference Library and forever played his violin. It used to disturb people that he didn't have a reason for living. Dafydd Morgan would lecture him beginning with the inevitable sentence, 'The purpose of life is...' and end up his discourse hopelessly, saying, 'The Jews, bach, are generally an industrious people.' Now if Uncle Isidore had played his violin, say, like Yehudi Menuhin, my parents would no longer say, 'Our third son is like Uncle Isidore, what are we to do?' – but, rather, they'd exclaim, 'If only, oh if only our third son was like Uncle Isidore.' For I know that Uncle Isidore was an artist, a real artist – except that he just didn't have the necessary accident of talent. Yehudi Menuhin plays the violin and millions listen. Menuhin, thus, has a purpose in life; But when Uncle Isidore played, even the cat would rush for the door. Nobody listened. So, we say, he had no purpose in life. He was contemptible, a rogue, an outlaw. I never cried when Uncle Isidore died. Nobody did. There was a small funeral and my father and my uncles gave some conscience money for his burial. That's all.

When the front door bell rang, Leo gave me a penny to shut up. He thought that it was Megan Davies, but it was only Uncle Isidore.

'Workers of the world unite', grinned my uncle at my brother.

'You should talk,' Leo said.

'Leo hit me,' I said.

'What?' cried Uncle. 'That is coercion. 'We can't allow coercion.'

'But he gave me a penny,' I said.

'Then you're a rich lad,' he exclaimed, and looked so dismal that I offered him the coin.

'That's all right, lad,' he said to me. 'I'll live without it.'

'Go on,' I insisted. 'Mama says you need it. Take it.'

'Ah,' said Uncle, 'your Mama is so right. She's a gentlewoman she is, and do you know, lad, she used to be the prettiest girl in South Wales – Jewess or Goy.'

'She still is,' I said, big-eyed. 'No, no,' said Uncle. 'Now she's the most beautiful.' Yes, Uncle Isidore had the soul of a gentleman.

The front door bell rang again.

'Megan Davies, Megan Davies,' I screamed.

Leo rushed to the door and I heard their voices together; and then the door slammed. I was left in the house alone with Uncle Isidore. He kicked the fire and the flames spat out of the coal, curling round his black boot. Mother would return soon and cook the dinner. Philip was silly asking me what it was like to be Jewish. Uncle Isidore stared into the fire with tremendous sadness. I wasn't sure whether he was awake or asleep. It was silent in the room but for the loud ticking of the mantelpiece clock. Suddenly he turned his head towards the window.

'You could stand there,' he said vehemently, 'all your life and look out.' And then he stared into the fire again. I walked over to the window, almost on tiptoe, afraid to disturb him. I gazed out. Down the road I could see snow falling under the lamp-post, and above, between the clouds, a few stars in the cold sky. 'Uncle?' I asked. 'Well?'

'Uncle, what's it like to be Jewish all your life?' I asked.

'S all right,' he said, and for a moment we smiled at each other.

From *Ash on a Young Man's Sleeve*, 1954

RETURN TO CARDIFF

'Hometown'; well, most admit an affection for a city:
grey, tangled streets I cycled on to school, my first cigarette
in the back lane, and, fool, my first botched love affair.
First everything. Faded torments; self-indulgent pity.

The journey to Cardiff seemed less a return than a raid
on mislaid identities. Of course the whole locus smaller:
the mile-wide Taff now a stream, the castle not as in some black,
gothic dream, but a decent sprawl, a joker's toy façade.

Unfocused voices in the wind, associations, clues,
odds and ends, fringes caught, as when, after the doctor quit,
a door opened and I glimpsed the white, enormous face
of my grandfather, suddenly aghast with certain news.

Unable to define anything I can hardly speak,
and still I love the place for what I wanted it to be
as much as for what it unashamedly is
now for me, a city of strangers, alien and bleak.

Unable to communicate I'm easily betrayed,
uneasily diverted by mere sense reflections
like those anchored waterscapes that wander, alter, in the Taff,
hour by hour, as light slants down a different shade.

Illusory, too, that lost dark playground after rain,
the noise of trams, gunshots in what they once called Tiger Bay.
Only real this smell of ripe, damp earth when the sun comes out,
a mixture of pungencies, half exquisite and half plain.

No sooner than I'd arrived the other Cardiff had gone,
smoke in the memory, these but tinned resemblances,
where the boy I was not and the man I am not
met, hesitated, left double footsteps, then walked on.

From *Poems, Golders Green*, 1962

LAMENT OF HELEDD
(based on a fragment of a ninth century Welsh saga poem)

I

I had four brothers. A pike upholds the head
of noble Cynddylan. The corn is red.

I had four brothers. Cynon and Gwiawn
butchered in the straw, their swords not drawn.

I had four brothers. Vague, hesitant Gwyn
last to fall. Through his neck a javelin.

When will this brute night end? Where shall I go?
Morning's mortuary will be kitchen for the crow.

II

Cynddylan's Hall is dark tonight.
The stone stairs lead nowhere. No candle glows
behind the lower then the higher windows.

Cynddylan's Hall is dark tonight
and dark the smoke rising from its ruin.
Slain, slain, is Cynddylan and all our kin.

Cynddylan's Hall is dark tonight,
its great roof burnt down, I can see the stars.
Curse those Englishmen, their bloody wars.

Cynddylan's Hall is dark tonight.
No orison is wailed to harp or lute.
O ghost brothers, your sister's destitute.

Cynddylan's Hall is dark tonight,
its silence outrageous. I shall go mad.
I smell skeletons. O blood of my blood.

Cynddylan's hall is dark tonight.
Should I live on? I am no heroine.
O Cynddylan, Cynon, Gwiawn, and Gwyn.

From *Welsh Retrospective*, 1997

CASE HISTORY

'Most Welshmen are worthless,
an inferior breed, doctor.'
He did not know I was Welsh.
Then he praised the architects
of the German death-camps –
did not know I was a Jew.
He called liberals, 'White blacks',
and continued to invent curses.

When I palpated his liver
I felt the soft liver of Goering;
when I lifted my stethoscope
I heard the heartbeats of Himmler;
when I read his encephalograph
I thought, '*Sieg heil, mein Führer.*'

In the clinic's dispensary
red berry of black bryony,
cowbane, deadly nightshade, deathcap.
Yet I prescribed for him
as if he were my brother.

Later that night I must have slept
on my arm: momentarily
my right hand lost its cunning.

From *Ask the Bloody Horse,* 1986

CAR JOURNEYS
Down the M4

Me! dutiful son going back to South Wales, this time afraid
to hear my mother's news. Too often, now, her friends are
    disrobed
and my aunts and uncles, too, go into the hole, one by one.
The beautiful face of my mother is in its ninth decade.

Each visit she tells me the monotonous story of clocks.
'Oh dear,' I say, or 'how funny,' till I feel my hair turning grey
for I've heard that perishable one two hundred times before –
like the rugby 'amateurs' with golden sovereigns in their socks.

Then the Tawe ran fluent and trout-coloured over stones stonier,
more genuine; then Annabella, my mother's mother, spoke Welsh
with such an accent the vilage said, 'Tell the truth, fach,
you're no Jewess. They're from the Bible. You're from Patagonia!'

I'm driving down the M4 again under bridges that leap
over me then shrink in my side mirror. Ystalyfera is farther
than smoke and God further than all distance known. I whistle
no hymn, but an old Yiddish tune my mother knows. It won't keep.

From *Funland and Other Poems*, 1973

THE SILENCE OF TUDOR EVANS

Gwen Evans, singer and trainer of singers,
   who, in 1941, warbled
an encore (Trees) at Porthcawl Pavilion
   lay in bed, not half her weight and dying.
Her husband, Tudor, drew the noise of curtains.

Then, in the artificial dark, she whispered,
   'Please send for Professor Mandelbaum.'
She raised her head pleadingly from the pillow,
   her horror-movie eyes thyrotoxic.
'Who?' Tudor asked, remembering, remembering.

Not Mandelbaum, not that renowned professor
   whom Gwen had once met on holiday;
not that lithe ex-Wimbledon tennis player
   and author of *Mediastinal Tumours*;
not that swine Mandelbaum of 1941?

Mandelbaum doodled in his hotel bedroom.
   For years he had been in speechless sloth.

But now for Gwen and old times' sake he, first-class,
  alert, left echoing Paddington for
a darkened sickroom and two large searching eyes.

She sobbed when he gently took her hand in his.
  'But, my dear, why are you crying?'
'Because, Max, you're quite unrecognizable.'
  'I can't scold you for crying about that,'
said Mandelbaum and he, too, began to weep.

They wept together (and Tudor closed his eyes)
  Gwen, singer and trainer of singers,
because she was dying; and he, Mandelbaum,
  ex-physician and ex-tennis player,
because he had become so ugly and so old.

From *Selected Poems*, 1994

from A JEW IN THE MIRROR

I had but the vaguest conception of the difference between Christian and Jew. As a child, I knew there was something different in the way Christian and Jew worshipped. They prayed on their knees. We stood up. They took their hats off. We kept them on. It was all rather baffling. 'Who's Jesus Price, mama?' I asked. 'Not Price, son,' my mother said. Once again she explained to me that, as far as Jews were concerned, Jesus was not the son of God. 'A good man,' my mother insisted, as if she knew him personally, 'but not divine, not the son of God. Do you understand?' My mother knew many things. She could speak Welsh as well as English, Yiddish as well as Welsh. Some of the 'wise' sayings from Welsh and Yiddish she loosely translated into English. I know them still – but I am not quite sure, even now which proverbs are Welsh, which Yiddish:

If a man stares in the mirror too long, he will see the devil.
Love lasts as long as there are two people.
If the rich could hire the poor to die for them, what a living the
poor could make.
When you visit a restaurant take a seat next to the waiter.

My guess is that the first two philosophical' sayings are Welsh and the latter two, wry practical remarks, are from the Yiddish. At the school I attended before St Illtyd's, Marlborough Road Elementary School to be precise, a building that later, during the war, was to be destroyed by bombs, I became aware of a vague, minimal otherness. The class register, each morning, proved something. Thirty boys shared the names of Evans, Davies, Jones, Morgan, Thomas and Williams. Abse seemed a fancy name in that incestuous context. Besides, with another Jewish boy called Sidney Isaacs, during scripture classes, I was banished next door. While Evans-Davies-Jones-Morgan-Thomas-Williams bowed their heads over the New Testament, we, in our exile, discussed religiously the merits of the touring Australian cricket eleven. St Don Bradman and the Rev Ponsford. The googlies of Pope O'Reilly and that holy man, Grimmett. Anti-semitism hardly exhibited itself in the ambience of that elementary school in Roath so no pressures existed to make us feel basically different from our non-Jewish friends.

It just seemed quirky that we did not attend scripture classes with the the other boys. It was of no great moment that on Saturday mornings we were bundled off, tidy to a 't', Lifebuoy soap under our armpits, to Windsor Place synagogue instead of to church the following morning. I did not like the synagogue. I could not understand the Hebrew address to the one God which the elders there uttered so devoutly. Their chanting seemed so ineffably sad and, like God, inexplicable. The sermon, it is true, was delivered in English and sometimes the rabbi would refer to the outrages in Nazi Germany. 'We should be sad this November. For it is the anniversary of the Kristallnacht when Hitler's insane violence towards the Jews of Germany became official. On the ninth and tenth of November, ruthlessly, all the synagogues in Germany, in Austria, in Sudetenland, went up in flames. With Teutonic efficiency the Nazis burnt down shops owned by Jews and flats occupied by Jews. Imagine what it's like to wake up and to find the house on fire while maniacal mobs of uniformed men stand outside in the street shouting, with flaring torches in their hands. On that black night, some 30,000 Jews were dispatched to the concentration camps – a crowd that could fill the Arms Park when Cardiff play the Barbarians – and those Jews, those same Jews were dispatched to the concentration camps. Shouldn't this day be a day of mourning?'

The rabbi folded his arms and nodded his head up and down, up and down repetitively, silently, until he resumed. Some of you may have in your hearts vengeance, may have in your hearts wrath. Understandable... I say understandable. An eye for an eye, some of you may think. Yet... you should know that a primitive demand for retaliation is alien to our Jewish ethic. Our laws demand justice not blind retaliation. For the old law of an eye for an eye was not a law of retribution but of compensation. Apart from the commentary or the Talmud there is evidence for this in the holy scripture. The law of Moses meant that the equivalent value of an eye – not an eye itself – had to be paid for an eye. The equivalent value of a hand – not a hand itself – had to be paid for the loss of a hand. Do you follow? If a man lost an eye he should not have compensation worth two eyes or indeed something worth less than one eye. But he should have an eye for an eye, no more, no less. The primacy of justice not revenge is the notion Jews should be committed to. That is what our Mosaic law teaches us.'

I could not understand such academic argument. It was not too relevant to a young boy who, fortunately, was not exposed to anti-semitism, True, it was possible to hear, very occasionally, snide remarks about some Jewish villain who had made the headlines in the South Wales Echo. But men named Evans or Williams similarly figured in scandals, and of course, because of their numbers, more often. Besides, any doubts derived from having heard remarks about vagrant Jews so crooked that they had to be screwed into their graves were counteracted by my mother's insistence that I should be proud to be Jewish. 'Why?' I demanded, in a voice perpetully stranded on top doh. My mother would simplify for me our ancient traditions, pronounce on our heritage of high moral codes, and finally, defeated, resort to name-dropping. Spinoza and Disraeli were born Jews. And Yehudi Menuhin and Kid Berg are Jewish,' she said, proving something. I also learned from my parents about the more melancholy legacy of European anti-semitism, of pogroms and dispersion, of 'enemies on stilts'. I used to sing to the Smetana melody of the Hatikvah (the present Israeli National anthem):

Austria, Rumania,
And Russia too,
All com-bined
To persecute the Jew.

On the whole, though, if you were a schoolboy in South Wales, being Jewish had advantages. There were the usual holidays, Christmas and Easter and Whitsun, and there were the Jewish fasts and feasts also to keep or celebrate – which meant more days off from school. Again, one of the masters at elementary school, George Thomas – who was to become an MP and Secretary of State for Wales – unashamedly favoured the Jewish boys in his class. Possibly his pleasant bias had a complex aetiology. Or it may be that he showed us particular kindnesses merely in the hope that he alone, singlehanded, could compensate for certain disadvantages that we were sure to experience as we grew older, some time, somewhere else. Other gains derived as much from the idiosyncrasies of my parents as from the fact that we were Jewish. Thus, when I was about ten, I returned home one day from school with a form for my parents to sign. The form turned out to be a notice of intent that I, along with the other boys in the class would be given a scientific lecture by some visiting educational sex expert. My parents sighed, and signed. So, in due course, I listened to a ghastly pale flogged-out looking gentleman from the wrong side of Chepstow, humourlessly pontificating on the facts of life. One fact that I learned that afternoon worried me. 'In a year or two,' said the sex expert, 'you will experience nocturnal emissions. That is to say you will have wet dreams. Now let me explain.' I did not like the idea of having nocturnal emissions. I liked my dreams dry. And now, because soon I would break through some biological age barrier, they were going to become wet. It wasn't fair. For days I thought it over, and my mother sensing that I was anxious about something eventually asked me what I was worrying about. 'Wet dreams,' I confided, whispering. She looked at me, distressed.

'Oh, you are not to worry about that,' she said, hesitating.

'But it does worry me.'

'It won't happen,' said my mother suddenly, and I felt a sense of growing relief at her confidence. 'It just won't happen to you.'

'Why not?'

'Because you are a *Jewish* boy,' she said blandly.

And I believed her, so ceased worrying. Yes, I was fortunate to be a Jew.

True, it was irksome that certain evenings, instead of playing cricket or football in the back lane, I had to go to Cheder, that is to Hebrew classes. Here in the basement of the Windsor Place

Synagogue, I learned the aleph-beth, the Hebrew alphabet. Soon, I could articulate the correct Hebrew noises without, however, understanding what those noises meant. It seems to me now that such a discipline was quite absurd; yet the fact that one could utter prayers to God in a language which had no meaning did not seem to me, then, to be peculiar. Prayer, after all, was a ceremony and required a ceremonial language that should have no ordinary significance. If God was a mystery that could be understood by man then the language in which man addressed Him directly should perhaps be equally mysterious. Or so I reasoned. Yet learning the correct noises was a bore and all the youngsters in that shabby basement room with its maps of ancient Palestine on the wall yawned repeatedly. It was a relief when we were taught Old Testament stories in English. For the first time, in that small room, I heard Goliath's large forehead cruelly splintering as the small stone pierced it; I saw the ten mile long horizontal shadow cast across the desert of Shinar by the tower of Babel; I smelt the hot acrid breath of the lions panting in Daniel's face.

It wasn't until I was about eleven that I questioned whether I believed in God. Reading of the disasters abroad, aware of unemployment and the dole queues in the Welsh valleys, without having heard of Nietzsche, I wondered whether God was dead, or whether God had simply forgotten that he had created the world. I soon discovered that a Jew who doubts the existence of God, or who goes further to dismiss frankly all the relevance of the idea of God and all the mumbo-jumbo prayers, all the antediluvian rituals that are bound up with that idea, does not, as a result, cease to be a Jew. The Cohen who becomes Conway, the Levy who becomes Lee, it makes no odds – once a Jew always a Jew. It seemed being a Jew was not a matter of religion only or even race. It was a destiny. And judging from the newspaper reports and from the seemingly paranoid fears of Jewish adults it was a destiny that would become increasingly awesome and deplorable. 'Chosen People,' I heard my mother say bitterly. 'chosen to be persecuted.' Hitler, those days, was too much alive in the world, and one had to remain a Jew with dignity and with pride. All else was a pretence, a false name, a betrayal.

When I left Marlborough Road Primary School to study at St Illtyd's, my parents were anxious lest I should be indoctrinated by the Christian brothers. Apparently, the school had a small number of Protestant pupils but they had never had a Jewish lad before. 'You must tell them at the first opportunity that you are a Jew, son,' my mother insisted. So, the first morning at St Illtyd's I sat at a desk in Class 2B staring at the crucifix high above the blackboard and wondered when I could obey my mother's injunction. The muscular gym master, a Mr Welch, one of the few lay teachers, had breezed into the classroom. He appeared to be a fearsome man. Only later did I discover him to be all bark and no bite. That morning, though, he roared dragon fire. 'You mean to say that none of you have brought your gym shoes and gym shorts,' he bellowed. We all sat there, our eyes widening. If any boy comes in tomorrow without them I'LL FLAY THAT BOY ALIVE,' he shouted, louder than any Hell preacher. Then, 'ANY QUESTIONS?' The class sat there dumb. At last I stood up. 'YES, BOY?' he roared, thumping the desk with a huge fist. 'Please, sir,' I stammered, 'Please. sir? I am a Jewish boy.' Edgar Welch looked at me, baffled. After an interval of silence he said, foxed, 'What's that got to do with gym?'

Though I was the only Jewish boy in St Illtyd's I did not feel any great sense of alienation. I enjoyed playing cricket and rugby so my very normal interests allowed me to be totally integrated into that schoolboy world. Soon, too, I became used to observing the rest of the class crossing themselves before and after each lesson, and to hearing pathological stories related by one crazy brother about demoniacal agents. Indeed this particular Brother R. repetitively told us an admonitory tale about a student who could not cross himself because of being possessed by the devil. One day Brother R. disappeared from the school. I think he must have had a nervous breakdown.

Nor had my parents any need to fear my being converted. By the time I was fifteen I had read Llewellyn Powys's *The Pathetic Fallacy* and I had come to dislike Christianity as a theological proposition if only because it seemed to me to be death-rooted: the dead Jesus on the cross, the way the church itself was surrounded with littered graves. And then there was the church's deep anti-sexuality. I would like to think that I would feel the same antagonism even if I wasn't born a Jew. Though I liked a number of the Christian brothers who taught me, I felt that there was something unhealthy about celibate disciplinarians in long black skirts bringing down their canes far too often on to this or that boy's raw, shuddering hand. Frankly, I was repelled by the conjunction of the dry murmur of devout prayers and the buzzing cane that caused a boy's involuntary yelp, in the name of the Father, the Son and the Holy Ghost.

Not that I dared discuss Christianity, then, with any of my non-Jewish friends. Gentiles, such as Llewellyn Powys, could attack Christianity philosophically, but a Jew, I was led to believe, should not comment. Jews are powerless; Jews should be quiet; Jews should do nothing to offend. Was not that the code of the ghetto and the lesson of centuries of pogroms? It is a code and lesson that takes a long time to unlearn.

But at fifteen, absurdly juvenile, I merely wanted Judaism to be a better religion than Christianity – rather as I wanted Cardiff City to be a better football team than Swansea Town. Not that I ever went, by then, to synagogue or said Hebrew prayers. I really believed in religious anarchy, where everybody could have their own God and where worship was only expressed in terms of action, in terms of doing. Leo had said, 'Well, Judaism is essentially a practical religion, it does believe in action; it is a religion which, after all, defined the Ten Commandments. Perhaps the main ethic of Christianity is 'Love thy neighbour as you would yourself.' an impossibly idealistic aspiration, whereas the main ethic of Judaism is probably – 'Do unto others as you would have done unto yourself.'' I liked Leo's analysis. I wanted it to be true. I wanted Christianity to be an inferior theology. I was not glowingly proud of the history of the Jews in the Diaspora through the ages. I felt the harassment of a relatively threadbare cultural heritage – the absence of beautiful cathedrals, the absence of magnificent paintings, the absence of great sculpture: little music and only a limited secular literary tradition. Two thousand and more years ago seemed too long a time to go back to our cultural glory. Still, guilt-ridden Christianity with its doctrinal sense of sin, the gloomed history of the Church that had waxed on suffering, had its own spite and lack of charm.

By 1941 abstract theology had become an irrelevance in my young life. I had become interested in writing poetry and any religious formulations I had defined for myself had pertinence for me only insofar as they could help concretely in the making of poems. The language I spoke was English and it was the only language I knew. Here was my commitment: Solomon Molke and St Joan ceased to be Jew and Christian. Deluded, schizoid, they had more in common with each other than with their sane co-religionists. I was a Jew but that hardly seemed to matter very much. I did not wake up in the morning screaming, 'I am a five feet eight and a half inches

Welsh Jew.' Simply I had resolved to start with the visible and to be startled by the visible. I was in the sixth form in school. I was going to study medicine. I needed to write poems. I was interested in girls, and in football, and in talking politics, and in the green ordinary world where God only existed because He was absent.

★

I do not know why so many German-Jewish refugees were attracted to Swiss Cottage. One could hear their guttural cries all down the Finchley Road between the Odeon and John Barnes – on the pavements, in the shops. Like Mrs Schiff and Mrs Blumenfeld they lived in one room with a sputtering gas fire, heavy furniture, frayed carpets, patterned fading wallpaper, and a photograph on the mantelpiece of someone forever smiling who had years before vanished. Many were old and sat out half the black-out hours in one of the Swiss Cottage cafes, The Cosmo, The Dorice, The Glass House or The Swiss, where they would argue about politics and literature in English and abuse each other in German.

One night, not long after I had moved to 38 Aberdare Gardens, coming home fairly late from town, as the bus jerked to a halt and an insensate conductress shouted out good-humouredly, 'Tel Aviv', I resolved to visit one of those cafes instead of going straight back to my digs. I sat in the Swiss Cottage corner cafe over my cup of coffee alone, hearing the thick accents all around me. It must have been almost midnight when a burly man entered, shouting, 'Germans, Germans.' Uneasily the cafe became conspicuous with silence. Towering over a middle-aged couple, the burly man swayed and shouted, 'Where do you come from?' They did not reply. Eventually, from the other side of the cafe a pleasant voice asked, 'Why don't you ask me where I come from?' Pappy, the Cypriot owner of the cafe, pretended nothing was happening and the waitresses looked away. The burly man ponderously turned round, puzzled. Hesitatingly, he asked, his voice a threat, ' Well ...where *do* you come from?'

'Ireland,' came the surprising reply.

I was the only one who laughed and unfortunately, as a result, I attracted the burly man's attention. He deliberately thrust his face, magnified, into mine. He breathed out beer and I breathed beer in. 'And where do you come from? Germany, I suppose?' he yelled as if

I were the other side of the room, not a mere six boozy inches away. I had to keep my voice level, not to betray the anxiety that I felt: 'I come from South Wales,' I said politely. To my surprise, everybody in the cafe laughed and the burly man benignly smiled at them all as if he had made a great joke.

'I thought you were all bleeding German Jews,' he said, nodding apologetically. And quite soon he quit the cafe.

Afterwards a bespectacled man with a narrow face – his name I learnt was Peter Berg – began talking to me.

'So, you're Velsh,' he said.

I felt constrained to say that I was a Welsh Jew. He did not seem to know, until that moment, Welsh Jews existed. This information, of course, did not embarrass him. On the contrary, I became suddenly, an exotic. I was introduced all round: 'He's a Velsh Jew.' I joined Peter Berg at his table and smiled at a fair-haired girl called Anna. From that evening my social life changed. I, too, became a habitue of the Swiss Cottage cafe. So, while during the day I dissected a part of a body at King's, at night I argued with Peter or Bondy or Hans or Kurt in the cafes – and usually late I went home alone but sometimes with Anna. And from time to time I wrote to Cardiff letters which began, Dear Parents, All is well here. Thank you for the Welsh cakes...'

From *A Poet in the Family*, 1974

JUDITH MARO (b. 1927)

Judith Maro might be said to have swum against the tide of Jewish settlement in relation to Wales. She was born and brought up in Jerusalem, where, as a young woman, she fought in the Haganah insurrection against British rule. In 1947, she married Jonah Jones, a soldier with the British forces upholding the Mandate, whose account of the affair was given in the chapter on 'The Promised Land' earlier in this book. They left Israel and settled in Wales in 1949, where Maro immersed herself in the culture of her adopted land, learning Welsh and using it as the language of her literary work, comprising autobiography, a novel about the establishment of Israel, *Y Porth nid â'n Anghof*, (translated into English as *The Remembered Gate*), and political and cultural essays. Much of her literary output has dealt with her Israeli experiences and with the deep identification she has found between her homeland and her adopted country. Her work is an interesting instance of how the Welsh identification with Palestine shown in the opening chapter, has been reciprocated. The first extract here is taken from her 1972 account of the Haganah campaign, *Atgofion Haganah*, 'Haganah Memories'; this is followed by two extracts from her 1974 book devoted to the relationship between Wales and Israel, *Hen Wlad Newydd*, 'New Old Land'.[6]

from HAGANAH MEMORIES

The Wandering Jew

From the summit of Scopus Hill
I bow down to you, Jerusalem,
And from the top of the hill, I greet you –
'Peace be to you'.

Century after long century
I dreamt about you,
And longed intensely to see
The dust of your ruins.
Jerusalem, O! Jerusalem, hear,
And lift up your face
Upon your son's adversity.
Jerusalem, O! Jerusalem,
A second time I shall build you,
A second time I shall build you
Upon your old foundations.

This old lament from the seventeenth century is a picture of the longing of the Jews, the bitter longing of generation after generation of them, their pain intense and ceaseless because of their divorce from Zion and Jerusalem. This divorce was a wound, just like a physical pain. But there is also the passion of hope in the old lament. There is no possibility of understanding Israel without understanding that pain and longing.

This lament also belongs to the essence of my story. Another thing, I am writing about a HOME. There are many books to be had on Israel; journalistic reports, guidebooks for tourists, and books written by tourists or pilgrims who have visited the land. But I do not intend to add to those; nothing of the kind is in my mind. To me, Israel is a HOME, the only home I ever had, perhaps. I have lived in Wales for many years now, for more than half my life, to tell the truth. And it is true that Wales is very dear in my sight; the welcoming and warm-hearted affectionate land which accepted me with open arms. Despite all this, even if I live to a good old age (which may God forbid) I will still feel that I was a visitor here – a visitor who got a heartfelt welcome, it's true, but only a visitor all the same. 'My heart is in the eastern land, and I am in the furthest west.' So sang Yehuda Halevi, one of our greatest poets. The thing is inevitable. Indeed, it's almost a biological thing.

To an exile, whether son or daughter, the land of his fathers is the most glorious place in the whole round world. And I am no exception. And who could deny that I am such a one? Although there is a warm place in my heart, as I said, for Wales, I can never forget the old land of my own fathers. How could I? How could anyone? 'If I forget thee, Jerusalem...' so sang the old Hebrew exiles by the rivers of Babylon.

The mountains of North Wales remind me, almost every day, of Carmel and the land of Galilee. The rocky hills, rising and falling, and covered by a thin heat haze when the sun is gentle. It's true, of course, that quite rarely is the sun gentle in Israel, as it is also true that it does not shine as often or as strongly in Wales as it does in Israel. But that does not impair at all the appeal of the Biblical names that are to be found here, in Wales, on villages and chapels. As I travel here and there though the country, on many a summer's day, I often imagine I am back among the views of my childhood – back in Israel. Was it by experiences like this, I wonder, that the poet was inspired to write the lament I quoted above?

Translation from *Atgofion Haganah*, 1972

LIVING IN WALES

As a child in Israel, I hadn't the slightest idea that I would one day come to Wales, where the wind blows endlessly from the Atlantic, bending the trees inwards as though seeking shelter from the pitiless storms. When I was young, I loved to venture into the Arab souk, and I knew everything about kebabs, shashliks, hummous, falafels and susumyeh, as I knew about a host of other things. The souk was declared taboo by my mother, who feared, with good reason, fever and dysentry, which was so common in the Palestine of my childhood. But I took no notice, and I never missed an opportunity to sample the nourishing and tasty Arab food, whether in Haifa, Jerusalem, Jaffa Saphad, Tiberius or Hebron! I had never heard about pancakes, lobscouse or bara brith...Through marrying Jonah Jones and coming to live in Wales, I discovered a whole new culinary world... Our marriage was secret. It could not be otherwise in the last bitter days of the British Mandate, when the climate was deteriorating rapidly. We succeeded in persuading the Local Commissioner (a Welshman incidentally) to marry us without the army's official permission; otherwise, Jonah would have been transferred from the country immediately. Although he was on attachment to the Education Corps, he wore the red beret of the Parachute Regiment, and this made things worse. We gave the name Calanoit (a red anemone) to the brave young men from Britain who were sent especially in order to prevent us from bringing in 'illegal' immigrants and to prevent us from preparing for the day of our fast-approaching independence. In such circumstances, it was best to take care. But for those who were present, it was a happy occasion. Jonah had promised that we would head for Wales, to make our homes and to live there, once he was discharged from the army. I liked the idea.

★

The journey was on a thundery summer's day, and was long and tiring, with the carriage full and smoky. The train went quickly (according to the standards of the East at least) through the industrial areas of Northern England, from Durham to Wales. Time after time I looked out. Where were the leafy trees, the green glades and the flowing streams that I had read so much about in English poems? Where were the cattle, the sheep, the horses? Perhaps it all lay behind the endless factories and mills, the depressing terraces that stretched alongside the railway? I had been in England for more than a week and I feared that the 'green and pleasant land' was nothing more than a dream belonging to the past. But, without my knowing, I was seeing the worst part of the country.

Chester. A name I remembered from school lessons, from a Henry James novel, *The Ambassadors*... A depressing, colourless station, more smoke (these were still the days of steamtrains). Then, without warning, the landscape changed. I knew at once that I was arriving at a completely new and exciting home. Wales! As though to greet us, the sun broke through the clouds and scattered them. I opened the window and let the sun stream into the carriage.

We were travelling along the north Wales coast. I felt as if I had been revived by magic. I gazed at the whitewashed cowsheds, bright in the sunshine, and at the grey buildings with black slate roofs and granite walls around them; and big, square chapels. A perfect scene, rural mainly, apart from the ugly collections of caravans here and there. The 'blight' of tourism had just begun, it was clear. It looked almost like the mediterranean; it was so wonderfully smooth and green and tranquil. Not only in the landscape were things changing. The people who came into the stations were different too. So was the language in which they greeted one another. everything was strange. The signs we saw briefly as we passed: llad...llan..mawr...I asked myself almost in fright what did I know about Wales, apart from the name of a mountain, Cadair Idris? Very little, I knew; the Welsh were famous for singing, they played a mad game (rugby) that was said to be almost their national entertainment, they were very religious and puritanical, and they almost all bore the excellent name Jones. I had joined their ranks! I had a strange feeling, almost as if I had taken someone else's aspect, not my own...

Only once had I heard the Welsh language, some months after the Second World War had come to an end. I had returned to school in order to study English literature under the patronage of the army's Education Corps (part of the school on Mount Carmel had been taken over by the army for the purpose). One day, some noisy major came up to me suddenly and asked me why I was speaking in some 'unintelligible language'. When I answered that I was speaking my mother-tongue, Hebrew, he turned to his friend and began a lively conversation in a language which was foreign even to my cosmopolitan ears. The officer was Huw Wheldon. The language – Welsh.

We stayed for a week in Cwm Pennant, and the rain fell almost without a break. That, too, was new to me, and was welcome after the long dryness of the summer in the Near East. Cwm Pennant was lush and beautiful, and incredibly peaceful. After the constant tension and the recent fighting in my own land, so strange was the feeling of peace! I cannot relive it however hard I try. But I hear still, hour after hour, the echoing call of the silly cuckoo, a call I came to appreciate in time as a herald of summer and joy!

At that time, Cwm Pennant was a place untouched and unspoilt. Our nearest neighbours, the Hughes family, needed very little English. Welsh was their daily language, and I felt at once a degree of affinity between Wales and Israel. The two names, Golan and Bethel, were to be seen in the bottom of the valley, and this was something I came to notice time after time – the echoes between my own land and the one to which I had come to live. More came to light on our early journeys: Nasareth, Nebo, Cesarea, Soar, Hebron, Rehoboth, Salem. I was home – almost.

It was deeper than that. Since early childhood I had known Great Britain through its unfavourable image. Under the Mandate we were forced to bow the knee to British law. In our minds we linked the word 'British' with snobbishness and the oppression of foreigners – as the saying has it: 'wogs begin at Calais'. We knew about a huge structure stretching back, in the distance, to somewhere called Whitehall. That disappeared in a moment. As the late Mably Owen said to me: 'You can't be a snob in Welsh'; even at that time, I knew the Welsh language was a great leveller. Before long I learned that Jack Jones did not own his sheep farm, but that when the boss came from the coast, the conversation was on the same level and was 'equal'. I understood that characteristic too. I quote Robert Henriques: 'The Sabra is aggressively tough, he is also aggressively equal.' Perhaps the Welshman is less aggressive, as he hails from gentler hills. There lies much of his charm; there also lie many of his problems and the modern difficulties about his identity.

Very soon, the pattern of hospitality had been set by Maggie Hughes, my first friend in Wales, a pattern I had come to expect in this friendly country: a cup of tea, the smalltalk, and most of all, the fact that I did not have to speak cautiously as I had been accustomed to do with the British in Palestine.

There is a great deal said at the moment that Welsh is slowly dying. Perhaps that is true, perhaps it is not. I don't know if there's an answer to that question. However, I can clearly remember coming across many monoglot Welsh speakers (to all intents and purposes) not only in Cwm Pennant, but later on in Treflys where we lived for two years near the little village, and later in Pentrefelin too. This was a completely new experience for me; in the multilingual society of Israel, Hebrew was completely essential in order to communicate effectively. I realised before long that Welsh was completely different to any family of languages of which I had experience. Nothing I had heard before could help me with the syntax, the vocabulary or the pronunciation – more than anything the pronunciation hinders all attempts to speak Welsh! Despite this stumbling block (and I have regretted it ever since) I feel that I have been accepted in a way the English could never hope to be. Part of the reason for this, at least, is the connection that almost every Welshman has with the Bible and the Land of the Bible. I felt that the people, the hills, the moors, the place-names, and the Biblical background of the whole country offered a hand of friendship that England could somehow never offer...

While we were in our remote cottage in Cwm Pennant, we held long discussions about our home-to-be, Bron-y-Foel, a Thirteenth Century building originally. At one time it was the ancestral home of Hywel Bwyall, a man famed for his bravery at the Battle of Poitiers.

It was not an easy time, with the Cold War at its height, and building materials and other things strictly rationed. The annual rent was £12, including rates (it seems incredible today – why the long discussion about only £12!). We had some trouble restoring the old farmhouse halfway up Moel y Gest, but if we were to have a home we would have to do a lot of repair work. (The sick growth of the holiday homes had just started in rural Wales and we lost 'a most desirable residence' by the side of the road, by less than twelve hours. It was sold instead to a rich businessman from Leicester...). No-one had lived in the house for twenty-five years, and cattle had been grazing in the 'parlour'. Details such as doors and windows had been stolen as fuel by the local people during the hard years of the war. So we had to start entirely from the beginning.

We succeeded somehow. We were young. We succeeded so much, to tell the truth, that our oldest son, Dafydd, never had a single cold during his early years in Bron y Foel, despite the damp and the storms. And we had a number of illustrious visitors. One of the first who came to greet me was Wil Sam, the dramatist, who gave me a hare that had been poached, beseeching us not to let Mr Speke (the Wern keeper) see it. He spoke Welsh to me on that, as on every other occasion.

Kyffin Williams, the artist, came next, arriving on a particularly wet day when the fog was so thick that it was impossible to see further than the garden. We had 'met' Hywel's ghost once or twice and I thought Kyffin was a real ghost. That, too, was a new thing to me. Until then I had been sceptical about ghosts. But now, having come to Wales, and living with old legends and old heroes around me all the time, I had to change my ideas – or my *prejudices*. It was all very well being dry and rational in Israel, where most of the houses were comparatively new; but here in Wales, things were quite different. There were ghosts roaming the windswept landscape, whether I acknowledged their validity or not. For the first time in my life, Wales gave me a realisation of equality. I saw very quickly that I was not an all-knowing clever woman as I had always thought. Perhaps I also started to realise the value of humility too.

Later, we moved to Pentrefelin, where the children attended the Primary School and learned Welsh – and learned it, I should explain, not as a second language, but side by side with English. They played in Welsh, argued in Welsh, swore in Welsh, from a very young age. Is it possible to ask for a greater proof that Welsh was a living language then?

In Pentrefelin I found myself in a situation I could not but wonder at. I was not only welcomed by the local people because of my 'pretty eyes', but also because I was at hand to help them in their dealings with the Authorities, whether with their member of Parliament (no-one thought it would be possible to write to him in Welsh!), with the Council when someone desperately needed a Council house, with the Tax Department and even with the Police! I would write letters for them, fill in forms, and comfort them when they felt they were getting unfair treatment; I even gave them advice!

My accent reassured them; they didn't feel self-conscious about the standard of their English. We were partners in inadequacy, as it were! There's no doubt they would have hesitated to trust an Englishwoman. They felt comfortable with me, for I too had not been raised through the medium of English. When I remember those days, I realise that it is I who am grateful for having been accepted so readily despite my lack of Welsh, and for having been able to take part in the life of the village. The Pentrefelin years were very happy. These early memories came back to me the other evening when I went with my children to see Wil Sam and his family in their home near Llanystumdwy. The place reminded me of an untidy old monastery on Mount Carmel, near my home. Although the monastery had been modernised as a hotel under the care of the Blue Nuns, I still have a feeling of the place as it was in the days of my childhood. I'm bitten by the memories of the old monastery in many ways: Wil Sam's cottage with its outbuildings, the gentle sounds of the birds singing and nesting, the whisper of the leaves, and more than anything, the scent of new-mown hay mixed with rust. Wil Sam's dark and dusty sheds contain many strange things: pieces of old bicycles, wheels, axles, lanterns – some going back to the twenties and earlier – and behind the house stands a huge boiler bearing the name of its manu-facturer from the last century. The garden is wild with a stone bed here and there, some apple trees, a dog barking in its kennel, a tent pitched in the middle of the lawn for no apparent reason...

Wil Sam showed me his prized possession, an ancient motorbike from the First World War period. That sealed the occasion! It was a 'twin' to another of the same kind that I had the pleasure of riding upon with Ezer Weizman, my friend from nursery school; a film of that occasion was shown on television in Israel recently!

That night in the garden, I felt that my memories had come full circle. Does this mean I have completely settled in 'this strange Celtic fringe of Europe' (as I referred to Wales once in my diary) by now? Perhaps.

Translation from *Hen Wlad Newydd*, 1974

THE SACRED NAMES OF WALES

I have just returned to Wales after two months in Israel. I first landed in Israel at my birth, and there I stayed, with brief journeys abroad (including a period of foreign service with the ATS in the last period of the second world war) from time to time, even after my marriage. Now, after my pleasant holidays in Israel the 'return home', my return to my adopted country, reminds me very vividly of my early days in Wales.

It was with my husband that I first saw Wales, and I was struck straightaway by the astonishing beauty of it all. We were fortunate – we were able to rent a cottage near the upper end of Cwm Pennant. After the harsh heat of the Middle East, I was almost stupefied by the freshness around me, the entrancing changes of colour of the verdure, and even the rich moisture. For it rained, of course! But the rain was a blessing. Very little of it did we see in the spring and summer...

I was a complete foreigner. Even as a much-travelled child I had never visited these islands before. And suddenly I was here, in the peaceful shelter of the mountain sanctuaries that are best appreciated in Wales. Everywhere there was Heddwch, peace. Three thousand miles away my own country was still in the grip of a desperate war. Very little news reached me about my parents and my friends at home. The ceasefire between ourselves and our Arab neighbours was still some months away.

It was completely unreal to be shut in my mountains, shut away from the world and protected, as it were, from its harshest winds, in complete tranquillity. Yet I was still unsettled by it all somehow. I cannot stress too much the importance of peace to one who was raised on tension, conflict and constant danger...

... I cannot write about Wales without mentioning the Welsh language. From my earliest days in Wales I realised the pride the people felt in their language, and I was inspired by their diligent efforts to preserve it, to revive it and to extend its use in the face of overwhelming harmful influences such as the cinema, radio, commercialism, and that wretched opinion that it was a 'dead language' that was 'not of any use in business'... 'an obstacle to the young'... and so on. I remembered how the Jeremiahs had been proved wrong in Israel about the potential of Hebrew to get to grips with the needs of today's technology.

The problem of new words had arisen in Israel, and had been solved, and I knew the two languages had much in common: Hebrew and Welsh are an indispensible part of the peoples' spirit. Just as we spoke Hebrew in the nursery class and in the games of our child-hood, so Welsh was spoken by my children, and in Welsh they played in the local primary school. I only have to listen to their lively chatter (in Welsh) over a game of ludo to realise that the Welsh language can never die. You cannot force children to discuss their fleeting thoughts at playtime (in an unhindered way, as it were) in a dead language. I am proud of my children's success in Welsh, although I am somewhat disheartened by my own poor attempts to learn it...

Most of all (and I never tire of saying this) I was struck by the close and strange relationship between the landscape and placenames of Wales and Israel. They are both small countries, no bigger than the palm of your hand. Just as it is impossible not to know people from Dan to Beersheba in Israel, so in Wales I find that our 'acquaintance' stretches broadly and easily between Caernarfon and Cardiff. In addition, especially in north Wales, the landscape is rocky, and there are times in a dry summer when I suddenly feel I am back home. The hills of Meirionnydd, particularly, have a way of undulating that reminds one of parts of Israel. They are largely bare, a rocky desert, stretching down to the coast like Carmel or Galilee. Sometimes, on a fine sunny day, Cardigan Bay will be as blue as Akko (Acre) Bay. The grand expanse from Barmouth to Pwllheli reminds me of part of the coast south of my native town, Haifa.

Looking down towards the Mediterranean from the summit of Mount Carmel in Israel, one can see Atlit, the old castle of the Crusaders, rising from a rocky headland. It is typical of many a ruin in Israel, and there is an echo of it in Wales in the Edwardian ruins of Conwy, Harlech and Cricieth. However, there is no castle in Israel fully as grand and appealling as Caernarfon Castle.

Cedron is the name of the river that runs past our house. Early in our married life I showed Jonah the little lake of the original Cedron, which flows (in the rainy season only, and not always then!) under the walls of Jerusalem, through the Garden of Gethsemane. Up the path from our present home stands a chapel called Tabor: back in Israel, my parents live on the summit of Mount Carmel. Whenever I look across the broad valley of Esdraelon towards the hills of Nazareth, there in the distance is Mount Tabor, alone, with the outline of the monastery on its summit only just visible to the naked eye. The nearest comparison to Tabor in Wales would be Moel y Gest near Cricieth, which arises in similar isolation in the crook of Cardigan Bay – and which could invite a hermit of like mind to dwell upon its windy peak. The monastery of Tabor, it hardly needs to be said, commemorates the Transfiguration of Christ. It is this longing to bring the living tradition of the Bible to the environment of Wales that, without fail, touches my heart.

In Israel, the Old Testament is not only the book of the Lord, but the source of all the ancient history and even the geography of our land. In what other country but Wales would you find these names reproduced as part of the place itself, as signposts, the chapels in the villages, and often even house names – everything striking the chord of memory? Where else in the world could I reach Carmel, Nazareth, Tabor, Cesarea, Hebron, Rehoboth, Moriah, Seion, Bethel and Talpiot in a day's journey? Places corresponding to all these exist and have their precious Biblical derivation in Israel. I left them behind me – only to rediscover them being affectionately commemorated by a people as devout as my people were at one time. Is there anything that could touch more deeply an Israeli in a sudden exile?

I also find a deep and affectionate knowledge of the Book of Books. The names are not accidents. It is not only the obvious that is commemorated. Take Peniel, in Blaenau Ffestiniog and in other places, as an example. Now, Peniel (or P'niel in Hebrew) is not at all prominent, and I do not know of anywhere of that name in Israel now. The name recalls an incident rather than a place. Everyone knows the story of Jacob's ladder; some even know of his wrestling with the angel through the night; but few know the result, which is Jacob's complete submission when he realises that the Lord himself was his opponent. 'So Jacob called the place Peniel, which is the face of God. I saw the Lord face to face and lived, he said'. The exceptional incidence of the submission of a proud Patriarch before the face of God is worth commemorating, and I know I could rely on the Welsh to remember it.

Of course, the incident in Peniel denoted the changing of Jacob's name; from then on he was called Israel. Jacob refused to let his opponent go until he had first blessed him; and so the angel of the Lord said to him 'Your name is not Jacob, you shall be called Israel, one who is successful with God. If you are successful with God, how much more will be your success with men!' Then he blessed him.

My first visit to Tremadog is still very fresh in my memory. Although it had been built around a central square, it reminded me greatly of the little northern village of Rosh-Pinah in Upper Galilee, not far from the Syrian border. Now, unlike Tremadog, Rosh-Pinah stretches along a narrow winding street; but the colour and design of the houses, their sheltering under the high mountain, and the atmosphere of general relaxation and old-fashioned slowness of pace in the two villages was almost exactly the same. Rosh-Pinah is beside the slopes of the ancient mountain of Hermon in one of the few places in Israel which escapes the oppressive heat of the summer months. There I used to be taken on my summer holidays. It was so strange to breathe such familiar air in the distant village of Tremadog, so many hundreds of miles away!

As I see the absence of hurry which characterises so many village shops in Wales, along with their friendly atmosphere and their readiness to please, I am reminded of the hundreds of similar shops which are scattered through the villages and small towns throughout Israel, even today. Whenever I go into a Post Office to buy tea or butter, aspirin or tomatoes or stamps – like in Israel they sell almost everything – I find myself on the verge of speaking in Hebrew, they are so similar.

They are both old countries, Wales and Israel, and rich in folklore and history (though not so rich in geography!). Neither has forgotten its past, which is recalled with pride in the two nations' National Anthems. Hen Wlad fy Nhadau is a prayer for the old land to live on, the land of poets and minstrels, to live on among the harsh rocks for which its warriors once fought... 'Gwlad, gwlad, pleidiol wyf i'm gwlad.' The Hatikva (Hope), with its tune so yearning and passionate, this also sings of the longing and the hope for renewal. Od lo avda tikvatenoo, hatikva shnot alpaim...('Our hope is not lost, the hope of two thousand years').

This recollection of a distant past and the hope of its restoration is common to the two nations, the two lands. The Welsh sing Bydded i'r heniaith barhau, and the Israelis answer: Let us return to the old land. So different are the themes in so many other anthems!

The same spirit flourishes in the Welsh-medium schools. On the walls of these schools are displayed pictures of O.M. Edwards and his son Sir Ifan ab Owen Edwards, the two men who did more than probably any others to restore the Welsh language in this century. In Israel too, it is men of vision like Herzl, Ben-Yehuda (the first to make modern Hebrew a living language) and Bialik the poet, rather than politicians and soldiers, who honour the walls of schools.

Wales, like Israel, is experiencing the strange collision between the old and new directly in its language. In the sight of Christ's ministry in Galilee, can be seen huge water conservation, irrigation and hydroelectric schemes. Here in Wales, the argument continues, and although I do not dare take sides, I hope, that, whatever may be decided, the new will take its place in the old Biblical environment with the same efficiency and smoothness which it has, to a large extent, in Israel.

There, the old and new have to live together in a reasonable concord. The waters of the Jordan are no less sacred because they satisfy the need for irrigating new settlements. As in the old times, they are an indispensible part of the lives of the agricultural communities. On the other hand, there are some things which grieve me deeply, here and in Israel – but I am glad that the debate is continuing in the two countries, and is likely to continue for a long time to come. It would be a pity if Biblical places and names were to be buried for ever under a new 'Lord' without any appeal.

So, I hope the old tradition will persist in spite of, and alongside, the new, in these two small nations.

Translation from *Hen Wlad Newydd*, 1974

STEVIE KRAYER (b. 1947)

Born in London as the grandchild of Jewish immigrants from Eastern Europe, and brought up in a household in which Yiddish was spoken, Stevie Krayer pursued a career as a university administrator. Moving to west Wales with her Welsh husband in the early 1990s, she has since devoted herself increasingly to writing, publishing a collection of poems with the University of Salzburg under the title *Voices from a Burning Boat*. Although she does not practise the Jewish faith and has chosen to be a Quaker, Krayer has retained a strong interest in Jewish matters, and, as in the case of the poem quoted here, has combined this with a sensitivity to her adopted country.

HASIDIM ON HOLIDAY

I
Silky black they were, the beards,
to match the nap
of their homburg hats, the shine
of their watered waistcoats.
They were suddenly leaning white
shirtsleeves on the five-barred gate:
a row of waxy astonished faces
gazing at Aled's sheep.

The ewes had stopped grazing,
had lifted black faces to watch theirs, as if
in these monochrome townsmen
bewildered by green, they saw
the patriarchs of old
who could slaughter a ram
at the wag of an angel's finger.

II
It is sunset along the lane to Cilcennin,
and on the low parapet above the river
under the shade of beeches sit
two long-bearded elders, quietly talking.
Their faces are turned to each other;
their gestures cast for meanings.
We are not noticed, they're unaware
of tarmac, heat, the weight of gaberdine.

In many ghettos, shtetls, exiles, ages,
old men have sat like this, needing no more
than a low seat and a patch of shade,
absorbed in a discourse that's been going on
more than a thousand years. Wherever they are,
they always know how to find
the freedom of a scholar.

From *Voices from a Burning Boat*, 1997

NOTES

1. For a more extensive survey of Welsh subject matter in the work of Bernice Rubens, see Rosalind Elbolgen Harris, 'A Million Miles from Odessa' in *New Welsh Review* No 38, Vol X/II, Autumn 1997, 62.
2. An account of Lily Tobias's life and work can be found in *CAJEX*, Volume 8, No. 2, June 1958, 50. Also, see 'Hurrah for the Freedom of Nations', by Jasmine Donahaye in *Planet* 147, June/July 2001, 28, for an extended study of Lily Tobias's Zionist and Welsh context.
3. London, C.W. Daniel.
4. 'Glasshouses', *The Zionists*, 46.
5. For much of the biographical information here I am indebted to J. Gwyn Griffiths and to an article by the couple's son Robat Gruffydd (founder of the Lolfa publishing house) in *Golwg*, April 23, 1998.
6. Judith Maro is particularly perceptive about the extensive use of Biblical names in Welsh villages and chapels. Reading her essay 'The Sacred Names of Wales', collected here, I am reminded of how true it is that many Welsh communities are, or were, characterised by Biblical nomenclature. Thinking of my own home village, Coedpoeth, a former mining community near Wrexham, my primary school was called Bryn Tabor, and one could walk through Salem Road to the High Street where the butcher was Abel Moss, the greengrocer Isaac Llewellyn and the newsagent Jonah Lloyd. Nearby was the chapel whose Sunday school I attended – Bethel. All those Biblical names – pronounced the Welsh way, incidentally – were evidence of that identification of which Judith Maro speaks.

DIASPORA

This final chapter is essentially a miscellany, bringing together a range of material, mainly poetry, dealing with Welsh encounters with Jews in Wales and elsewhere, both in reality and in the imagination. The subject matter of these items does not come naturally under any of the specific issues tackled in the other chapters of this book. But then, not all human experiences are neatly classifiable, and rather than exclude some valuable contributions simply for the sake of tidiness, I have compiled this last chapter as a collection of varied pieces showing Welsh writers engaging, in one way or another, with the Jews.

WIL IFAN (1882-1968)

William Evans, known as Wil Ifan, was from Carmarthenshire. Although he was a Welsh speaker and a highly productive author in Welsh, he was a minister with the English branch of the Independent Nonconformist denomination. He was a prolific lyric poet and essayist in both languages. We have already encountered a quote from his work in the introduction to the chapter on 'The Promised Land', a chapter in which the work of his son, Elwyn Evans, is given a prominent position. The following poem shows Wil Ifan meeting a little Jewish child.

ON MEETING A CURLY-HEADED HEBREW CHILD
(R.M.)

My fingers I dipped in her hair,
    Every finger-tip listening
For the tales that were there ...

Of a well and a damsel's surprise,
    And the heart of Isaac thirsting
Before two deep eyes...

Of seven added patient to seven,
    Glad for he knew the road ended
In a white-bosomed heaven...

Of Him, Whose hand dreaming sweet,
    Caressed the head that tumbled
Its silk on his feet...

From *Short Poems*, 1943

RHYDWEN WILLIAMS (1916-1998)

Born in the Rhondda and identified with the Valleys for much of his life, Rhydwen Williams had a career which spanned the ordained Baptist ministry and work in television and as an actor. A prolific poet and novelist, one of his most influential works was the sequence of poems 'Ffynhonnau', 'Springs', which won him the National Eisteddfod crown in 1964 and which gave an optimistic picture of the contemporary Valleys. In the poem quoted here, we have Williams's own English translation of a poem depicting a Jewish glazier of the Rhondda valley of his childhood.

THE JEW

'Abraham!...Abraham! we called
as he came down our street,
the air savage with voices,
scorn and chuckles of children.

His flesh was gnarled like the bark of a tree,
the Jewish nose and jaw,
stains of his tack down the hairy apron,
an untidy patriarchal beaver.

His eyes wept in the wind
as he bent under his burden –
a wooden frame with its load of glass,
repairer of windows, bringer of light.

He had the semblance of a man carrying his cross
toward Moel Cadwgan, his feet heavy
as he made his way through the throng,
wiping his brow with his sleeve.
We looked at him there,

a sight as gleaming as the glass
spiked with suffering,
haloed like the head on the Cross...

As one day, we found him,
arms and feet spread wide apart,
bleeding and nailed to the wood,
and we pointed, 'Look, look, the man!'

From *Rhondda Poems, 1987*

ALEXANDER CORDELL (1914-1997)

Details of Alexander Cordell's life and work were given in the opening chapter.
The following extracts from his historical novel *This Sweet and Bitter Earth*, set
in the south Wales Valleys shortly before the First World War, depict Heinie
Goldberg, a Jew working in the mines. The first scene shows the narrator accompanying Heinie to work, then discussing a riot during a strike, and then depicting
an accident in the mine.

from THIS SWEET AND BITTER EARTH

Four abreast, the Ely colliers, my gang, came marching along De
Winton, their numbers swelling as others joined the column.

Doors were coming open like magic all round the square; files of
men ran out of Church Street, Pandy Terrace and Cwrt to shouted
good-byes.

'Bore da' chwi!' saluted Heinie Goldberg, my stall mate, and
Mattie Kelly, an inch higher than Heinie's five foot, waved greeting
beside him.

I took my place between them.

'Don't waste a lot of time, do ye, bach? I thought you was keeping
Mrs. Best happy?'

'*Cythril!* Do you get around?' cried Mattie, his little cherubic face
cocked up.

I ignored them, enveloped in the din of tramping boots and
banter, and marched on, grinning.

'Barmaid at the Pandy, ain't she?' asked a third. 'Ach!, I'd rather
have five minutes with her than the Chinese Strangler.'

'She even kissed him good-bye!'

I made a mental note to see it didn't happen again.

You had to take it; if you didn't they'd give you a hell of a day.

'But how do you handle a piece like that?'

'He handles it, if I know him,' said Heinie Goldberg.

'Reckon you'd be best down the Scotch,' growled Ben Block, all seventeen stones of him thumping along in front of me. 'Being nearer, ye could keep an eye on her.'

'It'd need my missus to get me down the Scotch,' said Mattie Kelly. 'I wouldn't take a stall down there if they paid me a fortune, eh, Heinie?'

Heinie shrugged, 'Mabon do think well of it, though.'

'O, aye?' shouted another, turning in the ranks. 'He wants to work it. Mabon himself's turning out to be a fraud, never mind coal owners.'

All I hear around these parts is talk of this chap Mabon,' I said, happy at the change of subject.

This was the leader of the big Miners' Federation that was fighting to get better working conditions and pay for colliers. His true name was William Abraham, but he was better-known by his Bardic title of Mabon. Member of Parliament for the Rhondda, he was the biggest thing that had happened to Welsh coal for a century, according to Heinie.

'Don't talk balls, Jew boy,' said Mattie Kelly', now. 'Mabon's like the rest of 'em – they start out all right but end in the pockets of the bosses.'

'Aye,' said a man nearby, and his face was that of a hawk, coal-grimed still, despite the bath; his eyes, black-laced, shone fiercely from his scarred cheeks. 'Big in the stomach now, and that is all. Time was that Mabon was all for the colliers; now he's in bed in the south of France with a coalowner either side.'

'I wish I was,' said Mattie, 'especially with a couple of their daughters, instead of going down the blutty Ely.'

'You don't treat folks fair,' said Heinie, bitterly. 'When you negotiate, you've got to hunt a bit with the hare as well as the hounds, stands to reason.'

I chanced a look at Heinie as we marched on towards the Ely. Fact was, I'd seen little enough of him, save for his little bald head popping up and down as we worked the stall in the light of the lamps. He looked to me more like an outsize gnome than a collier, with his little bits of cauliflowered ears attached to his skull, and his nose was as flat as a Japanese wrestler's, the Rhondda being a spawning ground for the Noble Art.

Gone was Heinie's first flush of youth, but he could fill a tram faster than any man on the five foot Bute seam, the new face causing all the trouble. Nigh forty years old, was Heinie, with the criss-cross tell-tales of hewing and fighting white above his cheeks. In his time he had held the great Shoni Engineer to a ten round draw at Scarrott's, but that was when he was young. When he was old he had taken on a lad called The Tylorstown Terror, a shin-bone wisp of a boy called Wilde: and the lad had laid one on Heinie's chin within seconds, knocking his eyes as crossed as Alfie Tit's in the Tonypandy Co-op. Down the stalls you had to watch him, too, since he'd eat out of other people's tins: once he had a wife, a slim-boned girl who died: Heinie hadn't eaten properly since, said Mattie.

'What was her name?' I asked early on, turning to face him under the eighteen inch roof.

'Leave me what I got of her,' said Heinie.

★

'I claim a public enquiry,' said Hardie, in Parliament.

'On what grounds?' asked Winston Churchill.

'On the grounds of the charges against the police,' said Hardie. 'Charges of having ill-used women and other unoffending persons, not during a baton charge against a mob but under circumstances in which revenge could be the only motive.'

'But, be fair,' said Heinie, when he came to again. 'Nobody can say we're unoffending persons – after all, we're Welsh.'

'Are ye?' asked Mattie, 'I thought you was with Moses when the sea divided off Porthcawl.'

'I'm Welsh,' interjected Dai Parcel, smiling through split lips. 'And right now I feel a bit anti-English.'

John Haley said, 'Count ourselves lucky – so far we've had it easy. If Lindsay keeps pestering Churchill, he'll send in the military.'

★

Owen was dead when they brought him out. I crawled in, with Gwilym and Dai Parcel following.

'Just the one, is it?' called the overman.

'No,' I shouted back, 'there's another in here.'

He was lying where the fall had thrown him, heaped in a corner with his chin on his chest. I knew him instantly, and held the lamp higher.

'Jesus,' whispered Dai, 'it's poor little Heinie.'

Instantly, I was beside Heinie, but I knew it was too late; I straightened him out, and pulled the boulders off his legs: not a heart-beat, not a sigh. And there wasn't a mark on him.

'*Duw,* I remember!' whispered Dai, now kneeling beside me. 'He came down an hour after we started shift. He came looking for that wallet.'

He came looking for this,' I said, and took from Heinie's cold hand the photograph of his wife.

'His missus?' asked Dai.

'Who's this one, then?' asked the overman, crawling in.

He peered from me to Heinie.

I couldn't see him for tears.

★

Possibly, it was sheer habit that took me back to the Square. And then I recalled Heinie saying how he used to wander around the streets of a Sunday evening, listening outside the chapels and churches to the services in English and Welsh. Great choirs were here, as he said: the soaring tenors and mud-caked basses, their tonsils liquid with Allsops, all joining in massive shouts of praise. Sometimes Heinie used to sing at the face, I remembered – aye, Jew-boy, he used to say, but a Welsh Jew-boy, with songs in my belly.

Especially, he used to love the breathy, adenoidal singingof the children.

Where is he now, I wondered – he who faced the might of the great Shoni Engineer?

From *This Sweet and Bitter Earth.* 1977

RICHARD BURTON (1925-1984)

Richard Burton was born Richard Jenkins into a mining family in Pontrhydyfen in the Afan valley in south Wales. His talent for acting was honed by the local schoolmaster, Philip Burton, whose protege he became and whose surname he adopted. Richard Burton's outstanding dramatic talent, allied with his thrilling voice and his compelling personal charisma, secured him early success in the theatre before he concentrated his later career in film. Although his film career was of variable quality, with his filmography containing as many flops as classics, he became one of Hollywood's legendary figures, not least through his two tempestuous marriages to Elizabeth Taylor and through his self-destructive drinking exploits. He died at the age of 58. This Welsh speaker and proud Welshman had a strong intellectual bent, and although his ambitions to be a writer were frustrated by the demands of his career and lifestyle and by his own uncertainty as to his likely success in the field of literature, he relentlessly devoured books on all subjects and admired writers probably above all other people. His own publications – a few articles and the rather Dylan Thomas-esque but nonetheless engaging *Christmas Story* – showed that he had the raw material of a writer even if he lacked the application. His most sustained writing enterprises were his own extensive diaries. The author Melvyn Bragg was given full access to the diaries for his 1988 biography of Burton, *Rich*. The extract here is from 1972, when the Burtons were at the height of their fame. However, although he was feted by the American elite, Burton never forgot what it meant to be part of a minority, and this passage shows his ready identification with the Jews. His claim to Jewish ancestry is merely an expedient of the moment and is only intended to discomfit his prejudiced hosts, but it is nonetheless gratifying to note that, for Burton, to claim Jewish heritage, even if falsely, is a matter of pride.

from RICH

(Jan. 28) Last night I had an unique experience – for me that is: I went to have dinner with the Ws in the swankest country club in the area or the richest, or both. However, the uniqueness was that I discovered towards the end of the dinner that the club was restricted to Gentiles only. NO JEWS ALLOWED. Mary Frances told me so. She said that they, the club, had told them, the Jews, that there are just too many of you and before long you'll be running the place so why don't you form a club of your own. I was flabbergasted. I should have immediately announced this to the rest of the family and we would have undoubtedly swept out *en masse*. However I thought of Sarah and that the only reason why we were dining with the Ws was to get her out as easily and unrancorously as possible, but I simply couldn't sit there and say nothing. She promptly gave me an opportunity to salvage my conscience as she said with twinkling glee, 'And do you know, Richard, they ran into financial difficulties and had to appeal to us Gentiles for help. What about that!' I swooped. 'How strange to hear that,' I said. 'Our lot doesn't usually get into that kind of difficulty.' She took the blow with an air of not knowing quite whether I was making a little British joke or not. I now laid it on. 'Elizabeth, as you obviously don't know, is a convert to Judaism and our daughter Liza is of course a Jewess and my grandfather was a Jew.' She was helpless. She said 'Yes' but it had several additional vowels in it, impossible to write down but it was something like 'Yeaaeahowes'.

To re-iterate here the platitudinous idiocies of their conversation would be tedious. E. and I and Howard and Mara had gone there knowing what to expect but so exactly did they react to any given suggestion that they were little different from Pavlovian dogs. One rang the bell of this idea and they tolled the precisely expected answer. To the very anticipated word. We all agreed afterwards that they were so brain-washed that nothing, no argument, no appeal to intelligence, could possibly change them. For instance, and only one example will I give, W. said that the thing that had made this country great was that it was a melting pot for all the peoples of the world. Yawn. Yawn. But they had just said that Jews were not allowed in their club! There was therefore absolutely no point in asking about the blacks.

We reduced ourselves to hysteria in the course of the post mortem in our suite but under it all we were sick at heart.

From Melvyn Bragg, *Rich: The Life of Richard Burton*, 1988

JOHN TRIPP (1927-1986)

John Tripp was a productive and versatile poet in the English language. He was brought up in the Whitchurch area of Cardiff, and in the poem quoted here he uses a Cardiff setting. John Tripp was a determined advocate of Welsh identity, and I cannot help but think that there is a very Welsh instinct at work in this poem about a visit by the British Prime Minister Benjamin Disraeli – who was of Jewish descent – to Llandaff. Am I wrong in thinking that it is the particular sensibility of a fellow member of a minority that leads Tripp to describe Disraeli admiringly as 'the bright Jew' before he gets round to the fact that he was a world statesman? It is the same instinct that leads to Welsh people thinking of David Lloyd George as a Welshman first and a statesman second.

DISRAELI AT LLANDAFF

Under the window his small chipped head
is carved in stone. My overnight bag
replaces his portmanteau in the brown room.
An ostler freshened the horse
before a brougham whisked him in a loop
to the ruffed Widow Lewis at Greenmeadow.

The shoppers in the village street
do not mark the odd carving.
From here the bright Jew paid suit
to his Welsh lady, sharp and chockful
of charm over drumsticks and lemon tea.
The great house buzzed with importance.

That famous beak and black goatee
are left in split stone. This room
enclosed the bane of Peel
and Gladstone, hob-nobber with Khedive
and Empress, the wit who trimmed
through bloat of dull transaction.

Below, tucked in their own hour,
the shoppers pass the mouldered carving.

From *Selected Poems* 1989

JAN MORRIS (b. 1926)

Born of Anglo-Welsh ancestry in Somerset, Jan Morris came to identify increasingly with Wales, for whose cultural distinctiveness she has
become a persuasive advocate. As James Morris, before her change
of sexual identity, she wrote a far-ranging and evocative history of the
British Empire, the *Pax Britannica* trilogy, as well as earning a reputation as a world-class travel writer, a genre in which she excels. The
following extract is taken from her evocation, in typically colourful
style, of New York in 1945, *Manhattan '45*.

Diaspora

from MANHATTAN '45

In many streets, Yiddish signs were at least as common as English, and everything in sight was pungently Jewish. The people themselves looked extremely Jewish, whether they be old Russian couples, in long coats, walking silently hand in hand along the sidewalk as though they had never left Kiev, or absolutely New York housewives out for business, purses at the ready, shiny black shopping bags over their arms, faces set in a formidable resolve not to buy anything at more than a knock-down price. Shop after shop in Essex Street was full of Jewish religious objects: bar mitzvah sets, tallisim, yarmulkes, Torah mantles, mezuzahs. Elsewhere all was Jewish food, bagels and lox, fresh-grated horseradish, fruit-flavored cheeses, onion rolls, pickles on big outdoor stands. There were famous knish shops like Yonah Schimmel's, which had been putting potatoes into pastry crusts since 1910, and bakeries like Gertel's, fragrant with challahs, corn ryes, pumpernickels and chocolate icings, and candy stores like Julius the Candy King, in the Essex Street market, which fulfiled for the abstemious some of the functions of a saloon. There were hosts of movie houses, the Ruby, the Windsor, the Palestine, the Florence – Lower East Siders had loved the movies from the start – and plenty of bookshops, and well-known restaurants like the Garden Cafeteria, where the Yiddish press people liked to go, or Ratner's, famous for its cheese blintzes, or the Lupowitz where Rumanian gypsies played the violin. On Rivington Street was the venerable Schapiro's Winery, the only winery in Manhattan, where in premises marvellously musty wines pressed from upstate Concord grapes were put into bottles under scrupulous kosher supervision – rich sweet wines most of them, made famous beyond the bounds of the ghetto by Schapiro's advertising slogan 'Wines You Can Almost Cut With a Knife.'[1]

Most of Hester Street has since been demolished, but the nearby Orchard Street market still offers, on Sunday afternoons, much the same vital scenes.

Many of these establishments still thrive. Julius the Candy King is on the same market stand, Unit Stand 100, that it has occupied since 1900, and Schapiro's, still a family concern, now also offers kosher wines from France, and kosher sangria.

Up the now shabby and colorless Second Avenue, between East Houston and 14th Street, was the area they used to call the Jewish

Rialto, in its time an astonishing forcing-house of talent. Here one could still see the facades, if nothing more, of the theatres that once represented a climax of Yiddish culture: the Orpheum, the Public Theatre, the Yiddish Arts, home of the most famous of all Yiddish repertory companies, the Grand, where the almost supernally hand-some Jacob B. Adler had filled every seat at the turn of the century. One or two limply survived as live theatres, the rest had been turned into shops or movie houses, and among them there still precariously functioned the Cafe Royal, on the corner of 12th Street. This was a place of nostalgic pilgrimage for many Jews because it had been in the twenties and thirties a resort of Parisian allure, a meeting-place for artists and writers of all kinds, where sightseers came to stare at the great men sitting over their coffees, and ideas had been thrown about from table to table all day long for a couple of generations.

There survived, too, some of the institutions founded long before to help ease the Jews into American life – the settlement houses which had provided every assimilative tool from literary class to shower-bath, the famous Yiddish newspaper, the *Jewish Daily Forward* (Forverts in Yiddish), Which had been since 1897 at once the mouth-piece and the guardian of the immigrants. Lordly in its eleven-story tower, a skyscraper by the standards of the neighbourhood, in 1945 the Forward was still producing each morning, if in rather smaller press-runs than it used to, its inimitable mixture of material: stern. sometimes hectoring editorials, news columns enlivened by dispatches from correspondents in Paris, London, Palestine, and above all a celebrated advice feature. 'Bintel Brief' ('Bundle of Letters'), which was halfway between an agony column and a social advisory service. Here are two characteristic 'Bintel Brief' inquiries of the period. addressed as was the custom to the Worthy Editor, with the answers they received:

> A woman signing herself 'The Worried Mother' reports that her younger son, aged nine, has become a vegetarian. Her doctor has told her to have patience, but 'there is no end to it – he refuses to eat anything that was once alive. Worthy Editor, advise me what to do. I'm afraid my son will grow up to be sickly.' Answer 'The mother is advised to find out where her son got the idea to be a vegetarian, and then, with the help of a specialist, she might be able to bring him to eating meat and fish. A good doctor would know how to treat her 9-year-old vegetarian.' Your reader H.Z. says that her 8-year-old orphaned nephew is being looked after by

a Gentile family. and they are reluctant to give him up. 'They are fine people, but I don't want my brother's child to remain with the Gentiles. Help me to save this Jewish child from getting estranged.' Answer 'Knock on many doors. Write letters to special offices. H.Z. is given hope that somehow she will be able to get the child away from the Gentile family.'

But Worried Mother and H.Z. were like voices calling from long before. As the East Side Jews dispersed across the city, and lost something of their intense communal loyalty, so by 1945 they were looking back to the years before the war with a detectable nostalgia, balancing what they had gained with what they had irretrievably forfeited. In America these were, in many ways, golden times for Jewry. The horror of Nazi Germany had put anti-Semitism to shame: if there were private clubs or social neighborhoods still reluctant to accept Jews, publicly hardly anybody now would have the bad taste to be openly anti-Semitic. Jewish jokes were out of favor, and even in literature characters with Jewish names were sometimes found, when reprints were called for, to have been unexpectedly Gentilized. On this continent, at least, it seemed for the moment that God had answered the prayer of the Yiddish poet Kadia Molodowsky –

O God of Mercy
For the time being
Choose another people

– and was allowing the Jews to become human beings more or less like anyone else.[2]

But inevitably this meant a relaxation of the burning hope and eagerness which had been, only a generation before, the chief characteristics of the Lower East Side. The once powerfully Jewish trade unions were far less Jewish now. The once militantly Jewish Communist cells had mostly been dissolved. Yiddish itself was gradually being abandoned – fewer and fewer writers thought it worth their while to use it, and the readership of the Forward grew older every year. Yet it was all quite fresh in the memory in 1945. If you were not old enough actually to remember the great immigrations, you were certainly old enough to have heard, probably all too often, your parents' memories of them, and very likely to have suffered their overwhelming ambition to get you yourself up in the world, out of the ghetto, beyond the call of pogrom and sweatshop alike.

Many of the heroes of that heroic age were still alive and honored.

They included writers like Sholem Asch, Shmuel Niger, I.B. Singer
or Abraham Cahan (whose long editorship of the Forward had made
him a prophet-like arbiter of manners and morals among the Lower
East Siders), besides world-famous stars of the theatre and the
concert hall such as Jan Peerce (ne Jacob Perelmuth), Richard Tucker
(ne Reuben Ticker) or Sophie Tucker (nee Sophia Abuza)[3]. The early
lyrics of Irving Berlin (ne Isidore Baline) had included 'Yiddishe
Eyes' ('Oy, oy, oy, those Yiddishe eyes'); the comedian George Burns
had begun as a member of a Lower East Side children's combo called
the Pee Wee Quartette; Eddie Cantor had spent half his childhood, he
said, sneaking free seats in the theatres of the Rialto, waiting till the
crowds came out at intermission time, finding himself an empty seat
when they returned.

All these celebrities, and many, many more, were fondly remembered on the Lower East Side, and perhaps the recollection of them,
if it gave pride to the neighborhood, also gave it a kind of sadness.
Never again, people felt, would their society burn as brightly as that,
or throw such glittering particles into the world. But there was a far
greater sadness, too, hanging over those shabby fateful streets in the
summer of 1945. Happy in general though the denouement of the
Jewish immigration had been, its people were grief-stricken now, by
the knowledge of the European Holocaust, whose dreadful images
were only revealing themselves in that summer of 1945. History had
expunged for ever the Jewish communities of eastern Europe whose
synagogues, charitable societies and even ghettos had, at so far a
remove, implanted their traditions in New York. Thousands of
Manhattan Jews had lost relatives in Europe, and even those who had
not, whose families had managed to transfer themselves complete to
the New World, had lost something almost as precious: their past.

Ghosts of many kinds, then, ghosts blithe enough, ghosts
poignant, ghosts utterly tragic, haunted those few streets of the
Lower East Side, between Mulberry and Delancey, and over to
Second Avenue.

From *Manhattan '45*. 1987

ELWYN EVANS (b. 1912)

The chapter on 'The Promised Land' showed Elwyn Evans's engagement with the issue of Palestine both before and after the establishment of the state of Israel. The following poems are on a less political theme and give appreciative pictures of Jewish womanhood. They are reminiscent of the romantic Orientalism of Byron's poem 'She walks in beauty, like the night'.

THE JEWESS

Behold the fair Jewess:
Her full breasts seem to tell
That she expects the gentle maid
To become a mother in Israel.

Translation from *Amser a Lle*, 1975

A JEWESS

Behold my friend the Jewess fair:
soft lips, small dimple, raven hair,
the green eyes hiding fire there.

And as the palm trees softly blow
in a secret grove when the wind is low,
her hasteless quiet movements go.

But through the windless angry ways
of Jerusalem town she idly strays
where her fathers walked in other days.

Her fine-drawn brows the colour of night,
as finest silk are to the sight:
her eyes upon my own alight.

All wisdom of an ancient race,
if I could just its scripture trace,
is writ in her half-smiling face.

Fairer than this girl there was none,
who ever held, her breast upon,
at night the great king Solomon.

And if her gleaming strong bare arms
in Salem were to soothe my harms
then more than Solomon's heaven, her charms.

Translation from Eds. Gwynn ap Gwilym, Alan Llwyd,
Blodeugerdd o Farddoniaeth Gymraeg yr Ugeinfed Ganrif, 1987

GWYN THOMAS (b. 1936)

As a lecturer and later a professor of Welsh in the University of Wales, the poet, scholar and critic Gwyn Thomas, from Tanygrisiau in north west Wales, was well-placed to make the comments he offers in the following poem. In it, he depicts a Jewish academic who has found professional security in Wales after fleeing the Holocaust, but whose understandable horror of nationalism leads him to resist the innocuous requests for greater status for a disadvantaged minority language in his adopted country. Rather than simply condemning the academic for misplaced intolerance, Gwyn Thomas seeks to show that there are reasons why he feels the way he does.

A REFUGEE

Professor Bruno Heidegger, refugee,
With his feet at a quarter to three,
Working now on a lexicon
And busy with the A.U.T.
But sometimes wires will tighten in his brain
And the eagle-emblem coalesces within,
Footsteps make the world the thirties' again
And fear wraps tight around his skin.

Herr Heidegger, the learned doctor,
Is an authority on the influences on Proust,
He sucks a pipe, drives a motor,
Allows himself a break at the end of August.
But from the night, to basely scour the brain-stem

Come the screams clicking through his skull,
He will be a Jew in flight, as he was then.

The Professor rises to address
The college Senate now and then
To scorn the Welsh language and to suggest
That nationalists are dangerous men.
He grasps his nightmare and his fears
Telling himself, 'In myself I will kill the infection,
This time I will be one of the vast majority,
And be safe in the day of persecution.'

Professor Bruno Heidegger,
refugee.

Translation from Y Pethau Diwethaf a Phethau Eraill, 1975

TIM SAUNDERS (b. 1952)

This is the second poem in this anthology by Tim Saunders, whose details can be found in the section on 'Conflict and *Shoah*'. In this poem he displays concern with the cultural heritage of the Jews, particularly within the linguistic and historical mosaic of the middle east.

BIRDS

*'Four languages it would pay the world to use: Greek to sing, Latin to
wage war, Syrian to elegise and Hebrew to speak every day,'*
– Rabbi Ionatan Beit Ibrin.

Four languages are acceptable in all,
Syrian, the curlew's call,
the Greek of the unchaste nightingale,
the Latin fairground parrots wail,
And at night
A pretty vulture might
Warble her gentle Hebrew.
Four birds which roam

Away over the dust and stone,
Up out of the wilderness
Like spots of blackness,
And the vulture small
Can make her call
On the branches of the sweet vine groves.

Four creatures which cease to sing
When dawn tears their wings,
Unless the lightning, flash by flash,
Turns their lineage to ash,
And the vulture shyly
Contemplates inwardly
While grazing on the grapes.

Four who are to give away
Their cosy nests that they might play
Their carols on measures still unbroken,
Each a potential lover's token
And the vulture mild
To almost every child
Carries his cheerful message.

Translation from *Teithiau*, 1977

MIKE JENKINS (b. 1953)

Mike Jenkins has made the territory of the modern south Wales valleys, where he worked as a schoolteacher, very much his own domain in his frequently demotic and always passionate work imbued with his fiery Welsh republicanism. However, as well as being one of Wales's leading radical literary voices, he is also capable of more reflective work, as in this fine poem in which he encounters an elderly Jewish woman in south Wales.

MEETING MRS BERNSTEIN

Mrs Bernstein, the dogs sniff suspiciously
in your plotted neighbourhood,
while you open your door and your life
to strangers, trying to sell us your house

when we came for a piano:
sprightly body nudging a doddering mind.

You introduce us to your husband
who, impassively from the sideboard,
remains your dear boy.
With your father, the town's last rabbi,
your pride is framed. In a small drawer
is tucked away your profession.

'Here they all are!' you say.
On a table's planet
the seas and cities defined
in pictures of your family.
Confident fathers and dark-skinned
daughters explained by qualifications.

Incongruous amongst a trilled dresser
and desk where you drum out the past
are Harvard and Yale pennants:
two sails beckoning your sight
beyond the whispering walls.

Mrs Bernstein, we listen to your playing:
Rachmaninov's chords bluster to America
where your anger declares itself;

during Chopin's night you commune
with your restless dead.

Down the garden steps you grip my hand
with a ring of bone. We cannot buy
this instrument of emotions
only your fingers know.

From *Invisible Times*, 1986

RAYMOND GARLICK (b. 1926)

Although English by birth, Raymond Garlick learned the language of the country to which his family moved when he was a schoolboy, and he subsequently became an important English-language poet, editor and critic in Wales. The two poems given here arise out of a period in the 1960s which he spent in the International School in the Netherlands, where he had a number of Jewish students.

ROLL CALL

Monday the twelfth of November
seventy-three, and I remember
today like faces of one thought
three young people whom I once taught
in that mirage of time, it seems,
when days were hurtless, and their themes
mere essay titles: not today's
imperatives, death and the praise
of sacrifice.

At least, thank God,
no blood's been shed here – except the odd
policeman's fistful, in a cell
where no eye sees, no tongue can tell.
But in those sun-glazed rocks and sands
the blood dries brown on the world's hands,
and Cardiff and Caersalem both
give deep-dug ground for grief's sharp growth.

Was it for this, in Holland, Wales,
we pared away the layered veils
of meaning, seeking to see plain
the green text in the poet's brain?
It was. You trained yourself to read.
Editing life's untidy screed
later, in Hebrew, Welsh, your eyes
probed the syntax of sacrifice,
with variant readings for all three –
a life; a husband; liberty.

The brief day dies. I light my lights
for Amnon, fallen on the heights
of Golan and, in desert Wales,
for Terwyn thrown back to the gaols.
For Noemi – my grief, my dear,
the night that falls on a dark year.

From *Planet*, March 1976

SHALOM

Amnon, Gideon, Shimon,
where are you now?
Practising precision?
I taught you how.

Joel Giora, David,
what are you at?
Taking the line's full sweep?
I taught you that.

Daniel, Ilan, Elisha
what is your task?
Interrogation?
I taught you to ask.

Rachel, Nourith, Yael,
what do you do?
Reject the sentimental?
I taught that too.

O children of Israel,
my pupils once
in a Dutch oasis,
genius and dunce,

what have I taught you,
what will grow next
from those tranquil mornings
at work on a text?

But I send my greeting;
for what I heard
grow through those lines
was this green word.

From A Sense of Time, 1972

MIHANGEL MORGAN (b. 1955)

Aberdare-born Mihangel Morgan is one of the newer generation of experimental Welsh prose writers, whose novels defy many normal literary conventions. He is also a poet, and the following poem, 'The Wandering Jew', is informed by a degree of bitterness which Morgan feels towards organised religion, and by a sympathetic identification with marginalised minorities.

THE WANDERING JEW

'Vade Jesu citius, vade, quid moraris? et Jesus severo vultu et oculo respiciens eum, dixit: 'Ego vado, Expectabis donec veniam.'
– Matthew Paris

'Move
A little more quickly
If you please' –
And those are my own words
Bringing me back again
Two thousand years after they escaped from my mouth,
When he paused
By the window of my shoe shop
With the heavy cross on his back.
Well,
Move
Is the word;
That's all I have done for centuries
And every place
Is cold and comfortless
And there is something or other wrong with every lodging,
Some fault in every room,
Some problem with every house,

300

And I have to move
A little faster all the time.
That is my fate
And my punishment
For thoughtless words
(I hadn't meant to be so disrespectful).
But there are advantages.
Who would think
That I am two thousand years old?
I can still walk strongly
And have learned to rest and sleep while walking, like a horse
       or camel
I have seen many lands
And have lived through enough disasters and wars and plagues
So that I don't fear anything any more.
Yes, there are advantages
In being accursed.
Needless to say, I can't put down roots,
(And after all there are disadvantages
To roots).
But I go back
To my old home every two centuries –
No-one knows me.
But this inability to settle
Is truly a punishment,
And I haven't got used
To the ceaseless moving-house
And I don't have a home in the world.
He takes His time
Doesn't He?

And in my occasional prayers I ask –
'Move
A little more quickly
If you please'.

Translation from *Beth yw Rhif Ffôn Duw?*, 1991

NOTES

1. On one occasion she playfully adapted the Jewish concept of the 'righteous gentile' to refer to those English people who sympathise with, and help promote, Welsh aspirations, calling them the 'righteous English'.
2. (Jan Morris's note) The prayer is translated by Irving Howe in his *World of Our Fathers* (1976), an incomparable account of Jewish immigration to which I am indebted for much of this section.
3. (Jan Morris's note) And *morte*, 1966. 'The Last of the Red Hot Mommas.'

PUBLISHER'S ACKNOWLEDGEMENTS

Every attempt has been made to contact the copyright holders of the work. Acknowledgements are due to the following for permission to reprint work in this collection.

Dannie Abse: all works by permission of Peters Fraser and Dunlop Ltd; **Alexander Cordell:** by perission of David O'Leary; **Tony Curtis:** by permission of Seren; **J. Eirian Davies:** by permission of Gwasg Gee; **Donald Evans:** by permission of the author; **Gwynfor Evans:** by permission of the author; **Raymond Garlick:** by permission of Gomer Press; **Geraint Goodwin:** by permission of the Estate of Geraint Goodwin; **Josef Herman:** by permission of Mrs Nini Herman; **Wil Ifans:** by permission of Gwasg Gee; **Mike Jenkins:** by permission of Seren; **Bobi Jones:** by permission of the author; **David James Jones (Gwenallt):** by permission of Gomer Press; **Dewi Stephen Jones:** by permission of the author; **Jonah Jones:** by permission of Seren; **Stevie Krayer:** by permission of the author; **T.E. Lawrence:** by permission of the Trustees of the Seven Pillars of Wisdom Trust; **Saunders Lewis:** by permisison of the Estate of Saunders Lewis; **Judith Maro:** by permission of the author; **Roland Mathias:** by permission of the author; **Mihangel Morgan:** by permission of the author; **Paul Morrison:** by permission of the author; **Bernice Rubens:** by permission of Penguin Books Ltd; **W.G. Sebald:** by permission of the author; **Gwyn Thomas:** by permission of the author; **Harri Webb:** by permission of the Estate of Harri Webb; **Rhydwen Williams:** by permission of Gwasg Dinefwr.

NOTE ON THE EDITOR

Grahame Davies was born in Coedporth near Wrexham. A journalist for several years in the south Wales valleys, he currently oversees the on-line news service in the Welsh language for BBC Wales. He is the author of *Adennill Tir,* which won the Harri Webb Memorial Prize for poetry, *Cadwyni Rhyddid,* and a work of criticism, *Sefyll yn y Bwlch.*